MARLON
BRANDO

MARLON
BRANDO

THE ONLY CONTENDER

• • •

GARY CAREY

ST. MARTIN'S PRESS | NEW YORK

Editor: Toni Lopopolo
Assistant Editor: Andrew Charron

Design by Victoria Hartman

Library of Congress Cataloging in Publication Data

Carey, Gary.
Marlon Brando : the only contender.

1. Brando, Marlon. 2. Actors—United States—Biography.
I. Title.
PN2287.B683C32 1985   791.43'028'0924 [B]   85-1693
ISBN 0-312-51543-X

First Edition

10 9 8 7 6 5 4 3 2 1

This book is a revised and updated version of *Brando!* originally
published in 1972 by Pocket Books.
Film stills courtesy of the Museum of Modern Art Stills Archive.

Contents

MARLON
BRANDO

· 1 ·
TALL TALES AND HOME TRUTHS

Back in the heyday of Hollywood, studios manufactured biographies to fit their stars. Not so with Brando. He had his own fantasy factory. Sometimes he altered the facts to color an outwardly unexceptional, though frequently troubled, childhood; other times he did it to hoodwink the prying eyes of interviewers. Though the tall tales usually were related with mock-serious self-amusement, reporters often missed the glint in Marlon's eyes, and printed them with straight-faced, verbatim authority. Some of them still circulate as gospel, and hopelessly confuse the record of the actor's personal life, a subject he now places off limits to all "navel-pickers" (his name for exposé-minded columnists).

The earliest patsies of Brando's vivid imagination were the press agents for his Broadway shows. Following the information he supplied, they prepared some of the most outrageous biographical sketches ever concocted. Here is one account of Marlon's life as it appeared in a 1946 *Playbill:*

> Born in Bangkok, Siam, the son of an etymologist now affiliated with the Field Museum in Chicago, Mr. Brando passed his early years in Calcutta, Indochina, the Mongolian Desert and Ceylon. His formal education began in Switzerland and ended in Minnesota, where he found the rigid restriction of military school too confining. After a period in which he

saw himself as a potential tympanic maestro, he came to New York and studied acting.

A variant version of this profile was written for each new stage appearance: twice Marlon decided he was born in Calcutta, where his father was engaged in zoological research. On another occasion, the elder Brando was a geologist and the place of birth was Rangoon. Once Marlon admitted he had touched American soil before his first birthday, but this detail was quickly deleted as being too close to the truth.

Until he was famous, Marlon never visited Switzerland, India, or any of the other exotic places that have fascinated him in his adult life. He was born in Omaha, Nebraska, on April 3, 1924, the third child of Marlon and Dorothy Brando. Both parents came from old American prairie stock, originally French on the father's side. (The family name was once spelled "Brandeau.") Marlon Senior was a solid, conventional citizen with conservative tastes, a solemn temperament, and a sound business head. At least, that's one view of him. Others remember him as hot-tempered and aggressively masculine—"a man's man." He was a manufacturer of chemical feed products and insecticides, and made a good living from the trade. The Brandos weren't rich, but they were "comfortable," even during the worst Depression years.

Dorothy Pennebaker Brando ("Dodie" to friends) was a lovely, lyrical woman with blond, banged hair and a reputation for her "liberal mind and advanced ideas." She had a natural inclination for the arts: She wrote, painted, sculpted, and acted, the latter being her true forte. She was one of the mainstays of the highly respected Omaha Community Playhouse, a semiprofessional theater group which served as a training ground for many important actors, including Henry Fonda and Dorothy McGuire. (Mrs. Brando played with Fonda, one of her protégés, in the Playhouse's 1927 production of Eugene O'Neill's Beyond the Horizon.) "Dodie loved the theater," says one of her old chums. "She was happiest when doing something in or connected with it."

Another acquaintance described Dodie Brando as "a heavenly, lost, girlish creature who always longed for a more brightly footlighted world than her surroundings provided." As this description suggests, Marlon's mother also had a dark, troubled side to her nature. Her husband was a martinet and a womanizer, whose crass behavior drove her into periodic alcoholic binges. Marlon learned about this problem when he was in his early teens. Returning from school one day, he found the house empty and the phone ringing. At the other end of the wire, a gruff voice said, "Look, we've got a drunk woman down here in the bar. Come and get her."

Marlon never blamed his mother for these episodes. He realized she struggled valiantly with her addiction, and though there were always to be relapses, there were also long stretches when she was totally sober. And always she tried to perform her maternal duties. Marlon adored her: "She was everything to me."

Prior to Marlon's arrival, the Brando household included two daughters, Jocelyn ("Jody") and Frances ("Fran"). Both girls bore a strong resemblance to their mother, as did Marlon, after he passed that age when all babies look like small Winston Churchills. Mrs. Brando raised her nursery brood in what used to be called the "progressive method" of upbringing: she stressed self-expression and underplayed discipline. Jody and Fran had been exemplary pupils, but Marlon (or "Bud," as he was nicknamed to distinguish him from his father) might have benefited from more traditional guidance. A tow-headed cherub of a child, fat-bellied, pink, and angelic-looking, baby Bud was actually a holy terror with a lusty disdain for proper behavior.

Never a partisan of his wife's newfangled ideas of child-rearing, Marlon Senior escalated his opposition when Bud showed precocious symptoms of rebelliousness. Dodie persevered and prevailed, as she usually did when it came to family matters. But her victories were never easily won. She and Marlon Senior often argued bitterly, and the shouts and tension clouded the family atmosphere for days at a time.

The children were, of course, well aware of their parents' battles, and as he grew older, Marlon came to side with his mother. But he also tried to emulate and please his father—apparently with little success. "Nothing I ever did interested or satisfied him," Brando once said.

"Mrs. Brando made it almost impossible for Marlon to develop a sense of security about being a man," said Maurice Zolotow, one early Brando biographer. "All his life, he oscillated between the polar attractions of his parents and has had a difficult time finding out what he himself is."

Zolotow goes on to point out that all three children, born with artistic inclinations, naturally gravitated to their mother. She was the center of their existence. They worshiped her and vied continually for her attention. Young Marlon was so intensely wrapped up in this pattern of sibling rivalry that competition became his sole mechanism for dealing with the outside world. Everyone he met was forced into some kind of contest: "Who Can Tell the Biggest Lie?" "Who Can Hold His Breath the Longest?" "Who Can Eat the Fastest?" "Who Can Walk the Closest to the Quicksand Pool?"

There was one contest Bud won hands down: "Whose Family Relocated the Most Frequently?" Shortly after the boy's sixth birthday, Mr. Brando's business kept the family on the move, first from Nebraska to Evanston, Illinois, then, California, Minnesota, and finally Illinois once again. The frequent relocations coincided with Marlon's early school years and perhaps contributed to his distaste for formal education. No sooner had he acclimated himself than it was time to travel on, time to make new friends, to please new teachers, to learn old lessons in new ways. Brando was a poor, inattentive student, smug and rebellious, and the bane of teachers, even though they recognized his intelligence. He spent more time scuffling than studying, said late TV comic Wally Cox, a fellow pupil at Marlon's elementary school. Most recess periods ended with Marlon fighting some kid who made fun of his fancy-nancy name. (It usually came out as "Marlo" or "Marlyn Brandon.") Brando's belligerence made him a familiar face in the principal's office; later he boasted, with no more than forty percent truth, that he had been expelled from every school he attended.

In 1936, when Bud was twelve, the Brandos settled in Libertyville, Illinois, a prosperous town on Lake Michigan, about ten miles south of Waukegan and forty miles northwest of Chicago. Libertyville then had a population of about two thousand and offered the prospective resident a wide choice of spacious, unglamorous homes with sprawling lawns, some separated by vacant lots overgrown with wild flowers and brambles. The Brandos moved into a three-story house of nine rooms, unprepossessing in appearance, but constructed to accommodate comfortably the needs of a large family with catholic interests. Marlon Senior had a hankering to be a gentleman farmer and he equipped the ample grounds around the house with a wide assortment of livestock. There were geese and hens and rabbits, a Great Dane, a horse, twenty-eight cats, and a cow which refused to be milked by any hands other than Bud's.

To this menagerie, Marlon added wounded snakes and birds which he nursed tenderly and efficiently. He was very softhearted about animals. Once, when a chicken died, Mrs. Brando buried it; Marlon dug it up; Mrs. Brando reburied it; Marlon removed it again. And on went the macabre routine until Marlon was persuaded to let dead chickens lie.

Whatever may have gone on behind closed doors, the Brando household presented a harmonious front to the outside world. "Their house was always a place where the dignity and privacy of the individual—children and grown-ups alike—were respected," remembers a neighbor. But every Eden has its serpent and Bud Brando was Libertyville's. More aggressive as each year passed, he pestered his fellow students, aggravated his parents and their friends, and overtaxed even the most patient teachers.

Invited to a birthday party, Marlon disrupted the scheduled entertainment by setting a lighted match to the sleeve of his woolen sweater. While the guests hollered with terror, he stood giggling until the flame went out. By painstaking experimentation, he had discovered a blend of wool which, once set afire, would blaze menacingly for a moment and then harmlessly extinguish itself.

As childhood photographs commemorate, Bud was an incorrigible exhibitionist. A seaside snapshot catches him astraddle a friend's shoulders, arms above his head in a crazy parody of a Ziegfeld showgirl. In another picture, he is tap-dancing while Fran and Jody sit in the background, oblivious to the camera. A third has him thumbing his nose at Fran while coed Jody smiles tolerantly at little brother's antics.

Adult gatherings also suffered from Marlon's continual bid for center-stage attention. When he was still quite young, he would shinny up the mantelpiece, pose like Columbus scanning the horizon for the Indies, then clutch his heart, shriek, and crumple corpselike to the floor. At a later age, he interrupted adult conversations to deliver lengthy, unorthodox views on any subject—fascism, FDR, the WPA, a new O'Neill drama—with a glib authority that belied his total ignorance of what he was discussing. When he wasn't talking, he was playing the drums. In a first flush of enthusiasm for Gene Krupa, he bought a set of trap drums and jived on them twenty-four hours a day. As soon as guests were comfortably seated in the Brando living room, Bud entered and gave them an impromptu concert that drowned out all attempts at conversation.

His school record remained substandard. "Brando was rather irresponsible," reports H. E. Underbrink, principal of Libertyville Township High School. "He wasn't interested in anything in particular. His record was poor. He rarely took part in any extracurricular activities because practically every afternoon he was in our three-fifteen disciplinary period."

Marlon was the school smartaleck. Whenever a teacher shouted, "Order, please!" Brando answered back, "Make mine a beer!" Once he raised his hand in class and asked if he could be excused to get his glasses. The teacher granted permission, unaware that the glasses were at a distance of four miles from the school.

But the show-off was only one side of Marlon. Anna Johnson, a Libertyville English instructor, remembers Brando as a dreamy, remote child: "I'd ask him a question and he wouldn't even hear me call his name. He'd be staring out the window, lost in thought."

When his spirits were low, he revealed himself as a withdrawn, introverted boy, intensely shy, and sensitive to slights, real or imagined. His sister Jocelyn reports that he so desperately wanted honesty that "when somebody was blatantly dishonest, Marlon was so disappointed he couldn't talk, he couldn't cope with it, he was too emotional."

In addition to this hypersensitivity, Marlon was also plagued by a serious inferiority complex, the result of his ungainly appearance. The cherubic baby had grown into an awkward adolescent, with poor eyesight, bad teeth, and a tendency toward overweight. Naturally enough, he hated the thick glasses and dental braces he was forced to wear, and removed them whenever his parents weren't looking. But his schoolmates still jeered at him, and he became acutely self-conscious, especially around girls. About his first dates, his grandmother once laughed, saying, "Marlon always picked out the cross-eyed girls."

As a teenager, he voluntarily embarked on a physical fitness program. Mrs. Brando derided the notion of her son becoming tomorrow's Charles Atlas, but Mr. Brando was delighted as he watched Marlon hefting dumbbells and fifty-pound weights. This tentative rapport between father and son was strengthened when Marlon began to participate in high school athletics. A strong, fast runner, he was the star attraction of both football and track teams, until the day he limped off the gridiron with a fractured leg and kneecap. The accident left him with a trick knee which barred him from future athletic contests and later earned him a 4-F rating with the selective service system.

Shortly after leaving the playing field, Marlon also exited the halls of Libertyville High. In his junior year, he was expelled for smoking in the gymnasium, or so went the official explanation for his expulsion. Unofficially, it was reported that the principal might have used any excuse to rid himself of a persistently troublesome student. In the family conferences that followed, Mrs. Brando proposed that Bud finish his education at an experimental school where problematic but gifted children were guided toward constructive creativity. Marlon Senior, however, decided his son was already adept at self-expression; what he needed was an old-fashioned dose of discipline, the kind dished out at military academies. And this time Mr. Brando prevailed. Early in 1942, Marlon was enrolled at Shattuck Military Academy in Faribault, Minnesota.

Cadet Brando cut a handsome figure in his well-tailored serge uniform. At age seventeen, he had reached his full adult height of five feet, ten inches (like many movie stars, he is considerably shorter than his screen image suggests); his hair had darkened, and the baby flab had disappeared. His face had elongated, a change that accented his delicate, finely chiseled nose and full, sensual mouth. But, while his appearance had improved, his behavior was as crude as before; Shattuck alumni remember Marlon as an inveterate prankster.

Marlon hated everything about "the military asylum," as he dubbed Shattuck—the hair shirt uniforms, the rigorous regimen, the kowtowing to an oligarchic authority. Most of all, he hated the chapel bell which chimed every fifteen minutes. It became a symbol of the plodding, ritual precision which regulated the cadets' lives. Late one night, Marlon decided the bell had tolled once too often; he sneaked out of his dormitory, climbed the bell tower, pried loose the clapper, and buried it. He got away scot-free, but his one-man rebellion was in vain: the next day the chimes were replaced by buglers who announced the quarter hour with an off-key fanfare. "Those buglers were worse than the chimes," said Marlon.

Brando spent most of his time at Shattuck in the infirmary. It was easy to feign illness and easier still to prolong the symptoms. Whenever a nurse's back was turned, Marlon rubbed the thermometer against the bed sheets until friction forced the mercury well above 98.6 degrees.

Marlon blasted his way out of Shattuck—literally so. Years before do-it-yourself demolition was fashionable with teenage revolutionaries, he constructed a bomb of two-inch fire-crackers and placed it against the bedroom door of a Simon Legree teacher. Then he drizzled a trail of hair tonic from the bomb to his room and put a match to it. He presumed the fire would burn away the fluid; instead, it scorched the wooden floor and left a telltale trail to his room. Another version of this incident—or perhaps it was another prank—has Brando writing a four-letter expletive in hair tonic and burning it into the Shattuck floor.

Before the smoke lifted, Brando was on his way back to Libertyville, where another family congress was called to discuss his future. What did he intend to do with his life? his parents asked. Marlon astounded them by announcing his decision to enter the ministry. This was no joke, though his choice of vocation sprang less from spiritual commitment than from compassion for his fellow man. Since childhood, Marlon had shown an adult concern for society's displaced persons. In the worst years of the Depression, he often appeared at the kitchen door with a tramp for his mother to feed, and once he brought home a woman he found lying sick and hungry in a vacant lot. He pleaded with his mother to shelter her, but Mrs. Brando adamantly refused. Marlon then raged until his browbeaten parents staked the derelict to a hotel room where she recuperated in style.

The Brandos discouraged Marlon's clerical ambitions, since they believed him to be too introverted to be successful in a profession which demanded a gift for both public speaking and public relations. (Some years later Mr. Brando told Marlon's agent that he and his wife had already sensed that their son was fated to be an actor.)

Marlon's second career choice was music. He organized a five-piece combo, "Brando and His Kegliners," which disbanded when there was no rush on bookings. Then he loafed around the family home until his father demanded that he find some kind of responsible work. He took a blue-collar job with the Tile Drainage and Construction Corporation, a company which laid irrigation ditches. He hated it. "The job wasn't very interesting," Marlon recalls. "It was dull and dirty, but I stuck to it for six weeks."

Afterward, he drifted around Libertyville, striking everyone as a feckless youth bound for failure. In desperation, Mr. Brando ordered his son to join him in the insecticide business, but Marlon wasn't ready to be badgered into his father's trade. Instead, he decided to follow his mother and sisters to New York, where he might—no definite commitment—study acting.

After graduating from Lake Forest College, Jody went East to enroll at the American Academy of Dramatic Arts, and in 1942 she made her professional debut in a short-lived Broadway production, *The First Crocus*. A year later, Fran joined her sister in New York as a member of the Art Students League. The girls were frequently visited by their mother, a vicarious participant in their artistic progress.

Marlon's decision to study acting has been interpreted as just another round in his battle for his mother's undivided attention. And he himself once gave a startlingly Oedipal interpretation of this episode. He told an interviewer, "I thought that if she [Mrs. Brando] loved me enough, trusted me enough, I thought, then we can be together in New York. We'll live together and I'll take care of her."

Whatever the immediate psychological motivation for his trip East, Marlon had shown a penchant for acting which first appeared in early childhood. His sisters remember cowboy-and-Indian games in which six-year-old Marlon "died" so realistically "you got goose flesh watching him." Jody, Fran, and Bud often entertained parents and friends with plays they staged, and all three children hung around Mrs. Brando's community theater groups. (At age twelve, Bud appeared with his mother in one production.) During his high school athletic career Marlon's interest in the stage waned, but at Shattuck he was in two school productions, playing a "Who goes there?" watchman in one, and, in the other, a sword-carrying supernumerary.

One summer, when he was still in his mid-teens, Marlon and his mother visited relatives living in the Los Angeles area. While on the Coast, Dodie looked up her old protégé, Henry Fonda, who was then working in Hollywood. Marlon was impressed by Fonda, and decided he'd be an actor when he grew up. Of course, it was no more than a childhood fantasy, and Brando quickly forgot his Fonda-inspired ambitions.

Marlon has always insisted he drifted into acting because there was nothing else for him to do. And he's always maintained that acting has brought him little personal satisfaction. Throughout his career, he has been haunted by the suspicion that there is something more worthwhile he could have done with his life. But the fates and his own talent were against him.

Mr. Brando agreed to stake his son to a six-month exploratory period in New York, with the understanding that if he hadn't found his professional footing by then, he would return to Libertyville and the insecticide business. And so, in the summer of 1943, Bud Brando boarded a train for New York where, in less than two years, he emerged from the faceless crowds as Marlon Brando, one of Broadway's most promising new actors.

·2·

LOOK, MA, I'M ACTING!

During his first weeks in New York, Marlon camped out on the couch in Fran's living room. After a few days of sightseeing and family reunion, he confronted the problem of finding an acting teacher. The city was teeming with them, and they all had different theories and methods, ranging from crank avant-garde to nineteenth-century *démodé*.

The most fabled charlatan was Frances Robinson-Duff, a snowy-haired patrician, as broad as her hyphenated name, who taught in a townhouse presided over by a French butler. In her Louis XVI studio, she sat on a red velvet throne chair, while her students—who at one time or another included Helen Hayes, Katharine Hepburn, and Clark Gable—went through their exercises. She taught the Delsarte system, in which acting was divided into mental, emotional, and physical categories, with charts under each heading. There was a multitude of charts, including one for fingers and another for eyeballs. "Watch your eyelids, darling," Miss Robinson-Duff admonished. "They aren't in the sorrow position."

To help him avoid the quacks, Marlon asked Jody's advice. (She was then understudying a very healthy Dorothy McGuire in *Claudia*.) She recommended Erwin Piscator's Dramatic Workshop at the New School for Social Research. Piscator, a German producer who had emigrated to America in 1930, was noted for his experimental stagecraft and social commitment. When his first New York production was dismissed by the critics as "drama with a pointer," the cranky

12

Piscator abandoned the vulgar Broadway arena for left-wing groves of academe.

As director of the Dramatic Workshop, Piscator did little teaching; that chore he relegated to a staff of professional theater people who shared his view of drama as social force, and disparaged the commercialism of the Broadway stage. The workshop attracted large numbers of students who were dissatisfied with the superficial training teaspooned out at traditional stage academies. Maureen Stapleton went there in 1943, after wasting five hundred dollars on Miss Robinson-Duff, and at one time or another the enrollment included Shelley Winters, Rod Steiger, Ben Gazzara, Tony Curtis, Anne Jackson, Anthony Franciosa, Walter Matthau, and Elaine Stritch.

When Marlon entered the Dramatic Workshop in the early fall of 1943, he was assigned Stella Adler as a teacher. Miss Adler, then in her early forties, was a tall, willowy blonde, with a brittle glamour and a regal flamboyancy, the birthright of her theatrical heritage. She was the daughter of Jacob Adler, one of the great stars and personalities of the American Yiddish theater.

She had joined her father's troupe in 1906, when she was four years old. For the next twenty-five years, she acted continuously for both Yiddish- and English-speaking companies, playing over a hundred leading roles between 1927 and 1931. Then she made several Broadway appearances with the Group Theater, a cooperative, socially oriented producing unit of the 1930s, whose other members included Clifford Odets, John Garfield, Luther Adler (Stella's brother), Harold Clurman (her husband), Franchot Tone, and Elia Kazan. In the late thirties, she migrated to Hollywood where she was done in by films with skittish titles like *Love on Toast*. Returning to New York, she directed a few respectfully reviewed Broadway flops and then joined the Piscator faculty at the New School.

Miss Adler immediately recognized Brando's talent—"This puppy thing," she told friends, "will be the best young actor on the American stage"—nurtured it, fought to see it appreciated. But she is extremely modest in taking credit for the development of her star pupil: "I taught Marlon nothing. I opened up possibilities of thinking, feeling, experiencing, and as I opened those doors, he walked right through."

At the Dramatic Workshop, Marlon became a diligent pupil for the first time in his life. He rarely cut up, and never to the point where his stunts hindered class progress. Once, during a rehearsal of Ibsen's *Ghosts* in which he was playing Oswald, the tragic, degenerate hero, everything was going wrong. Tempers were tense enough to snap at any moment. Then Brando swept in, his face disfigured by a ruby red, W. C. Fields—sized putty nose. "Everyone was in hysterics for five minutes," Miss Adler recalls. "He relieved the tension and made the rest of the rehearsal easier for us all."

That bulbous nose was the first sign of the ham actor lurking in Brando. He loved to experiment with makeup, false whiskers, wigs, foreign accents, phony dialects. But there was little opportunity to fool with the surface accoutrements of acting in Miss Adler's class. There the emphasis was on "inner truth," both the actor's and the character's, with an attempt at interweaving as neatly as possible those two interior worlds.

Stella Adler was a disciple of Constantin Stanislavsky, the Russian director and theater theoretician who founded the famous Moscow Art Theater. Stanislavsky searched for a more "truthful" style of performance; he rejected "outward acting which does not come from inner experiences but simply from the eye and ear, acting which is simply a photograph of the painting and the sound they have before them."

To aid the actor to "feel" what he expresses, Stanislavsky evolved many techniques, including certain modes of improvisation, "the emotional recall," and what was known as "the method of physical actions." (It was the latter technique which Miss Adler stressed, while Lee Strasberg, the other principal instructor at the Piscator Workshop, favored the emotional or affective recall.) The Stanislavsky actor concentrated on the subtext of the play—the thoughts and problems behind the dialogue and the plot. His primary task was to illuminate the playwright's creative purpose. In this way, the actor becomes more than a mere technician; he shares, wrote Stanislavsky, "the inspiration of the true artist."

In Stella Adler's class, Brando was taught that acting was more than a bag of technical tricks; it was more than mimesis, more than moving with grace and enunciating properly. It was a creative process in which the actor used every fiber of himself—his experiences, knowledge, observations—to create a form for the playwright's ideas.

To widen his experience and knowledge, Brando took courses at the New School in French, fine arts, and philosophy; he studied dance, fencing, and yoga—at which he became so expert that he could rotate his stomach muscles around his navel. He scrutinized both friends and strangers, and stored away his impressions for future reference.

"Actors have to observe," he once said. "They have to know how much spit a person's got in his mouth, and where the weight of his elbow is. I could sit all day in the Optimo Cigar Store telephone booth on Forty-second Street and watch the people go by."

"If he is talking to you," said Stella Adler, "he will absorb everything about you—your smile, the way you talk, the way your teeth grow. If he must learn to ride a horse for a role, he will watch that horse like no one else has ever watched a horse, and when he does the scene he will be both horse and rider."

During his first years in New York, Marlon lived a gypsy's existence—he was forever on the move. Sometimes he rented furnished rooms, sometimes he shared apartments with a roommate; either way, the arrangement was temporary. He moved from West Side to East Side to Greenwich Village, from one drab apartment to the next cold-water flat. The furniture was always minimal and the housekeeping almost nonexistent. Actress Shelley Winters met Brando in this period and recalls the time he decided to do a little interior decorating. He painted one wall of his living room and then grew bored with the task. "But for one solid year," Miss Winters remembers, "the canvas, the buckets of paint, and the brushes lay in the middle of the floor. Everybody just stepped over them."

Marlon's closest friend and onetime roommate was the late Wally Cox, the jug-eared, chicken-necked comic later to become famous as TV's Mr. Peepers. The two first met in elementary school, but later fell out of touch until Marlon arrived in New York where Cox was working as a silversmith, turning out cufflinks and other items of men's jewelry for New York's better boutiques. It wasn't until 1948 that Cox turned entertainer, and then only at the insistence of Brando and other theater people who enjoyed the witty, milquetoastish monologues he ad-libbed at private parties.

Brando once described Cox as "an old, fragile, beautifully embroidered Chinese ceremonial robe with a few Three-in-One Oil spots on it," but he has never discussed his friend on a less fanciful level.

About Brando, Cox said, "Marlon is a creative philosopher, a very deep thinker. He's a liberating force for his friends."

Then he clammed up. And anybody privy to inside information about their friendship isn't talking. To be Marlon's friend entails a vow of silence; if the muzzle comes off, then there is one less intimate in the Brando circle. Therefore, those who do speak usually demand the shield of anonymity, and often they aren't the friendliest witnesses.

One of these anonymous ex-friends describes Marlon's New York buddies as a bunch of "strays, idolizers, characters who were dependent on him one way or another, nobody he'd have to compete with. Some of this stemmed from his insecurities, his inferiority feelings."

It was the same syndrome when it came to girls. Though no longer cross-eyed, they were usually from the stenographer or waitress line of work. "Nice enough girls," his friend says, "but nothing that was going to start a stampede."

That, at least, is the legend. In fact, Marlon frequently dated Ellen Adler, Stella's daughter. One of Ellen's fellow classmates at Bard College remembers Marlon very well.

"Of course, at that time he wasn't famous—he hadn't done anything on the stage—but we all knew he was Ellen's 'actor boyfriend,' and he was something of a character. He was always hanging around the school co-op, wearing blue jeans and a T-shirt, or a black turtleneck sweater. In those days, that mode of dress really made him stand out. And he was very handsome in a sullen, unapproachable way. I never forgot him. A few years later, I went to a play and there he was. I elbowed my companion and said, 'My God, it's Ellen Adler's old boyfriend!'"

At this time, Brando was something of a brooder, or so says one of his old-time chums. "He seemed to have a built-in hideaway room and was always rushing off to worry over himself and gloat, too, like a miser over gold."

During these fits of melancholia, Marlon was unresponsive and withdrawn. Actor Martin Wolfson, who knew and worked with Jocelyn, met Brando several times, but was never able to strike up a friendship.

"I didn't know how to talk to him; I tried, but he just wouldn't communicate." Asked if he thought Marlon was "disturbed," Wolfson exclaimed, "Oh, brother! Was he ever!"

Once the somnambulistic moods passed, Brando soared into a childish exhilaration—"a wild kind of fun thing," as someone described it. Then, the phonograph blared while Marlon clobbered out a syncopated accompaniment on his new bongo drums. On a wall of his flat, he tacked a crudely crayoned sign, *You Ain't Livin' If You Don't Know It,* and his way of knowing he was "livin'" was through noise and adolescent high jinks. When he was living above a jazz joint on Fifty-second Street, he and his cronies used to climb to the roof, fill paper bags with water, and drop them on the departing clientele. Or they opened a window and threw ignited matches down on unsuspecting passersby.

These guerrilla theatrics were about the only form of entertainment Marlon could afford. Though he still received a small stipend from his father, it didn't stretch far in the war-inflated New York market. Brando learned to economize, particularly in the areas of clothes and food. His impoverished wardrobe included blue jeans, T-shirts, and sneakers, with an occasional purloined sweater added for variety. He had a passion for peanut butter, and subsisted on it, cough drops, bouillon cubes, and fresh fruit.

Marlon also economized by walking around without any money in his pockets. If he wanted a cup of coffee, he mooched a nickel, saying he "forgot" to take change out of his dresser drawer. He made a sly and insistent game out of mooching, and one of his rules was to borrow only from business people, never from his friends.

Sometimes when he was flat broke and there was no one to touch for a loan, Brando did odd-job work, including stints as a night watchman and elevator boy at Best's department store. After four days of announcing "Fourth floor, Lingerie," "Fifth floor, Foundation Garments" to Best's customers, he quit. None of his jobs lasted longer than the period needed to entitle him to an unemployment check.

Compared to most struggling actors, Brando spent little time standing in line at his local unemployment office. If his rise to fame was not of the Hollywood "overnight" variety, it was nonetheless rapid and free of self-doubt. When questioned about his early success, Brando answered, "I took it as a matter of course. I never consciously thought of failing or not failing. Those were my fervent years and I had other fish to fry."

Carlo Fiore, a student at the Dramatic Workshop, says Brando's classmates were quick to praise him as "the best actor we have down here," and it was not long until the theater community at large shared this intramural enthusiasm.

In the spring of 1944, Piscator produced a series of lecture-demonstrations, "The March of Drama," which gave his students an opportunity to perform demanding roles in rarely seen plays. Brando was cast in the first presentation.

He made his New York debut on May 24, 1944, in Gerhardt Hauptmann's *Hannele's Way to Heaven*, a "dream play" in which a young girl, dying from parental maltreatment, hallucinates about her reception in the hereafter. Brando played Jesus Christ, a role which required him to chant lines like "come close, sweet children turtle doves," while a seraphic chorus plinked on golden lyres.

It hardly sounds like a promising role for Brando (or any other actor, for that matter), but he performed it well enough to be singled out for praise by George Freedley, the knowledgeable and respected critic of *The Morning Telegraph*. Freedley wrote, "Easily the best acting of the evening was contributed by Marlon Brando. . . . He has authority, smoothness, careful diction and an easy command of the stage to commend him." Freedley returned to the Dramatic Workshop to see Brando in two later productions, *Doctor Sganarelle*, a Molière pastiche, and an abridged version of Shakespeare's *Twelfth Night*. Though Marlon did not have a prominent part in either production, the critic again gave his performances several lines of thoughtful analysis. His point was clear: Marlon Brando was an actor worth watching.

The summer of '44, the Dramatic Workshop students organized a nonprofit summer theater in Sayville, New York, a shady, one-street town on Long Island. Their playhouse was a remodeled country club with living quarters, kitchen, and bar, which had been donated to Piscator by a wealthy admirer. The students planned to work, live, and eat together on a cooperative basis: each contributed one hundred dollars to cover the initial operating expenses and pooled ration coupons to buy enough canned tomatoes, tomato juice, and tomato paste to brew a three-month supply of watery spaghetti sauce. The troupe arrived in Sayville in late June and began cleaning up the theater for its July first opening.

On their first day in Sayville, the actors were told to stake out their own living quarters anywhere on the premises, and Brando chose the loft of a barn, inviting Carlo Fiore to find a mattress and join him "in the upper berth." The two overgrown adolescents became fast friends and occasional rivals for the same girl, though usually they were content to share their conquests: Bud's romance on one evening became Carlo's for the next night. Just about the only girl Marlon couldn't catch called herself Blossom Plum—the first of those exotically named beauties who were to play so important a part in Brando's private life. In appearance, Miss Plum was not quite as lush as her name suggests, but she was lovely, spirited, and flirtatious. She was not, however, foolish enough to get caught up in Brando and Fiore's summer barn version of *Design for Living.*

Blossom played Viola in the Piscator company's opening production, *Twelfth Night*, this time played in its entirety. Brando was cast as Viola's twin brother Sebastian, a small role demanding little except good looks and proper diction. As in the past, Piscator took very little interest in the production, delegating all the preparatory work to his wife, Maria Ley, a retired prima ballerina with virtually no directorial experience. On opening night, the company was still unprepared and the première was a fiasco.

Dodie Brando had come East for the occasion, and the next morning she chewed her son out in front of Carlo Fiore. He wasn't allowed to use lack of direction as an excuse—he was terrible: no concentration, no sense of what his character was about, no respect for what he was doing. "Either make up your mind about whether you're serious about acting or give it up right now," she said. And then she returned to Libertyville and Marlon Senior.

Chastened, Marlon Junior got down to work with Piscator, who suddenly appeared to see if he could undo his wife's mischief. A small, wiry man with a terrible temper and a thick German accent, he swiftly inaugurated a reign of discipline and terror that resulted in passable performances of *Twelfth Night* by the end of its two-week run.

The end of the run, however, was also the end of Brando's engagement with the Sayville players. He was discovered one afternoon in bed with one of the youngest actresses, and while both insisted nothing naughty had gone on—they had simply collapsed after an exhausting rehearsal—Piscator dismissed Brando and sent the teenaged girl back to her family. He explained that he was indifferent to how they chose to amuse themselves, but such behavior, if leaked to the press or the Sayville citizens, might reflect poorly on his management of the company.

This dismissal was no setback for Brando's career. Because of Piscator's reputation, many theater people had come out to Sayville to observe his apprentices, and one of them, a leading actors' agent, took an immediate interest in Marlon. A wiry, hypertense bachelor, Maynard Morris had few interests outside the theater; he was really happy only when sputtering over the telephone, wheeling and dealing to get his clients the best possible deal. He was a noted agent, well-respected throughout the profession for the record number of actors he scouted out and promoted to stardom. But of all his "discoveries" he was proudest of Brando and, in the last years of his life (he died in 1964), he often spoke of his first meetings with Marlon.

They were not easy conversations. Morris often stuttered when he was excited, and Brando became tongue-tied outside his small circle of close friends. It was impossible for him to sell himself to anyone who might help him, not because of any scruples, but because of his intense shyness. He answered all Morris's questions with the same noncommittal grunts. The agent wasn't put off by Marlon's backwardness; in fact, he found it a refreshing change from the hard-sell tactics used by most young actors. He promised to do whatever he could for Marlon.

Brando's lack of opportunism impressed some people as lack of ambition, and later a legend formed that as a young man he was indifferent to his career. Apparently, it's not true. "Don't you believe it for a minute," hooted one of Morris's assistants. "He was always hanging around the office. You couldn't miss him. He was there every day, sitting in the anteroom, always wearing blue jeans and a T-shirt, just waiting for Maynard to see him."

Morris sent Brando around to the major film companies, most of which were then looking for new faces, since the draft had depleted Hollywood's stock of virile leading men. For one studio, Marlon made a screen test and flunked it. He was told he had no future in the movies because his nose "dribbled down his face like soft ice cream."

When Morris exhausted his film contacts, he began looking for a stage role for Brando. He thought there might be a part for Marlon in Richard Rodgers and Oscar Hammerstein's forthcoming production of John Van Druten's *I Remember Mama*. As it happened, Stella Adler had read the play, and she too felt it was right for Marlon. She gave him a copy of the script to read and study for a possible audition. Marlon took it over to Fran's apartment where Mrs. Brando, once again visiting New York, read it aloud to her three children. "We thought it was a terrible play," Marlon recalled, "and we all fell asleep while Dodie read it."

The next day, Marlon told Miss Adler the play was so awful he didn't want to appear in it. She replied that it was sure to be an enormous success and insisted he go to the audition Morris had arranged with Rodgers and Hammerstein.

The meeting went badly. "I was so scared," Brando said, "I was just one jump ahead of a blood clot." Rodgers and Hammerstein turned thumbs down after hearing Marlon gulp and gurgle his way through a few pages of the script. Playwright Van Druten, however, was intrigued; he sensed the raw talent behind the badly garbled line readings. Much to everyone's astonishment, he insisted Marlon have the part.

I Remember Mama is a family comedy about a group of Norwegian immigrants living in 1910 San Francisco. Marlon's role was Nels, the oldest son of a family in which the daughters have all the good lines. It was a nondescript role and Marlon wasn't entirely wrong about the play—it's charming, but very slight. However, when it opened at the Music Box Theater in October, 1944, Van Druten's skillful blend of humor and heartbreak enchanted the critics. As Stella Adler predicted, it was a smash hit.

Though overlooked by reviewers, Brando's performance electrified theater people. Morton Gottlieb, a young theater buff later to become a well-known Broadway producer, remembers that "there was a rustle of theater programs as soon as Brando walked on stage; people were leafing through the pages trying to find his name." Director Robert Lewis said he couldn't believe Marlon was an actor: "He was so real I thought he was a boy they had hired to walk on stage and be himself." Edith Van Cleve, an actors' representative then working for the MCA agency, "tingled with excitement" as she watched Marlon. "He had very little to say, but he concentrated on what he was doing," she recalled. "And when he did say something, he seemed to come from another country compared to the rest of the cast. He was so *natural*."

After the performance, she hurried backstage to offer her congratulations and professional services.

At the time she entered Marlon's life, Edith Van Cleve was a tallish, handsome, champagne blonde in her mid-forties. Formerly an actress (and a good one), she had only recently turned agent, but already had a formidable reputation. Beneath her quiet air of refinement, she was a shrewd, tough-minded businesswoman. When she wanted something, she went after it tooth and manicured nail, as she did in the mid-1950s when she tried to steal Tammy Grimes from another lady agent. In a state of blustering apoplexy, the other agent called Miss Van Cleve and, couching her message in the gentlest language she could muster, she said, "Now, listen, Edie dear, *I want you to lay off!*"

In his grunting, monosyllabic way, Brando tried to get across the same message. Did he have an agent? Miss Van Cleve asked. No, and didn't want one, he answered. (This was true; he never signed a contract with Maynard Morris.) Miss Van Cleve resisted the temptation to high-pressure. Instead, she said that if he ever needed an agent, please contact her.

Weeks passed before she heard from him. Then, on a snowy day that kept most people off the streets, an MCA receptionist buzzed her to say that a Marlon Brando was there. "Ever since then, I've called those awful, blizzardy days Brando Weather," she said. "Nobody but Marlon or Eskimos would go out in that kind of weather unless they had to."

Brando hinted that he wanted an agent, but there were still ifs and buts bothering him. "Trust me," Miss Van Cleve pleaded. It was an instinctive response, but the right one. "I sensed that there could be no big-agent double-talk, no lying, no insincerity," she recalled. "It all had to be straight-shooting or I'd lose him."

In Miss Van Cleve, Brando found much more than a professional mentor; like Stella Adler, she was to be friend and, to some degree, mother-surrogate.

"Marlon thinks he owes me a good deal," she once said, "but really, I'm indebted to him. I never had a more gratifying client."

She was being far too modest. Without her, Marlon would still have become a star—but her support, comfort, and expert guidance made his ascent all the smoother.

·3·
MORE BROADWAY NOTICES

The long-run success of *I Remember Mama* barely rippled the surface of Brando's life. He continued to study with Miss Adler, went through the same moody ups and downs, and still hung out with his old friends. Blossom Plum and Carlo Fiore often dropped by for breakfast at his new apartment—a top-floor walk-up on West End Avenue. These morning coffee klatsches were the scenes of some of Brando's more spectacular feats of skylarking. One cold, heavily foggy morning, he pushed back his chair, rose from the kitchen table, and ambled out an open window into the blanketing mists. Blossom screeched and Carlo dashed to the window where he found Brando dangling precariously from the sill. Marlon smiled up at Carlo and said, "Don't mind me, I'm just out here relaxing."

There were many dark moments in the West End apartment. Mrs. Brando had moved in with her son, but things didn't work out the way Marlon planned. "I tried so hard," he said, "but my love wasn't enough. She couldn't care enough." During her visit, she began to drink on the sly. "She was there in a room holding on to me and I let her fall . . . I couldn't take anymore—watching her break apart in front of me, like a piece of porcelain . . . I was indifferent. Since then, I've been indifferent."

But he wasn't indifferent—only a few chosen people were told about Dodie's problem. One was Carlo Fiore, who didn't need to be told because he discovered Mrs. Brando hiding a gin bottle in the bedroom. Another was Edith Van Cleve, who learned about the family secret in a roundabout way.

"Once he broke an appointment, and I was furious," she remembered. "But he explained that his mother drank and he had been out looking for her in bars. Of course, I didn't doubt him—I had no reason to do so. Then, a few days later, Mrs. Brando called and asked if we could have lunch. I couldn't say no, but really, I was very nervous. I thought, what am I going to do with this lush? So I couldn't have been more surprised when this intelligent, well-groomed, perfectly poised woman arrived. When we went to lunch, the first thing I asked was whether she'd like a cocktail. She said, 'Oh, no!' And I never remember seeing her take a drink—ever.

"Later I learned Marlon hadn't made the whole thing up," Miss Van Cleve continued. "I should have realized that at once, as there was something in his mother's voice as she refused that drink that made me wonder. . . ."

Often Dodie came to New York to visit her children when she and her husband were going through a particularly rough patch. When enough time had elapsed, she would pack up and go home. This time her departure coincided with the first anniversary of the opening of *I Remember Mama*. Marlon was not in the happiest of moods for the birthday party held on the stage of the Music Box Theater. He arrived in an unpressed, oversized suit, and posed with the other actors as Mady Christians ("Mama") sliced a huge, icing-covered cake. In the photographs, the cast looks like one big happy family, but after a year's strait-jacketing in the same limited roles, several were ready to leave home. Marlon couldn't wait to move on to bigger and better-paid things.

He was then making seventy-five dollars a week, which wasn't enough, he told Edith Van Cleve, to support himself and the woman (Miss Van Cleve couldn't remember her name) who was soon to be his wife.

"Oh, Marlon," Edie exclaimed, "are you serious? Or is this another of your whims?"

Brando didn't answer, he just smiled. "Whenever he

couldn't think of anything to say, he smiled," Miss Van Cleve said dryly. "Consequently, he smiled quite a lot."

She couldn't get him a raise, but she did send him out for auditions. "He was *terrible*," she recalled. "At each and every one, he was *awful*. He just couldn't read. At first, I thought it might be an eye problem, so I insisted he get glasses. He got them, but God knows where, probably at a five-and-dime or at Walgreen's, but they didn't help. Sometimes he'd open his mouth and nothing would come out, or if it did, it would be in a rush, a terrible jumble of mumbled words. Later, he'd laugh at how bad he was; he'd dash in my office and hoot, 'I just gave the *worst* reading!' But at first, it was very painful for him, and half the time he wouldn't go to the readings I'd arrange for him."

Marlon did show up to audition for *O Mistress Mine*, a drawing-room comedy by Terence Rattigan, which starred Alfred Lunt and Lynn Fontanne, the darlings of the international theater world. He came on stage wearing sloppy clothes, unshaven, and scowling. He glowered at the Lunts, who were sitting in the theater auditorium.

"You may begin now," Lunt said.

Marlon looked at the script for a moment, and then threw it in the air. "I can't do it," he muttered, and then started to leave.

Lunt stopped him. "All we really want is an idea of your voice. Recite anything."

"Hickory dickory dock, the mouse went up the clock," snarled Brando, before marching out of the theater.

That is Marlon's version of the interview. Alfred Lunt remembered it differently. He said that a neatly dressed Brando appeared at the theater and walked across the stage a few times. Miss Fontanne explained that he looked too old for the part, and thanked him for coming. Marlon in turn thanked her and left. "I've heard the hickory dickory dock story many times," Lunt said, "but I must tell you in all honesty that he was not in the least rude to us."

Lunt suggested that Marlon altered the facts to fit his image as a social primitive. And certainly Brando was not above making himself unattractive to win a little publicity. "To get attention, I'd walk across Times Square on a tightrope," he was once quoted as saying.

Marlon was quick to learn the newsworthiness of a colorful, cranky personality and quick to play up any personality quirk that caught the public fancy—he may have even invented a few. In creating his image, Brando discarded as unmarketable many of his more sympathetic traits—his shyness, his gentleness, his awkwardness. A tongue-tied actor dismissed by the Lunts wasn't going to make Earl Wilson's column, but a pariah who hickory-dickoried dear Alfred and darling Lynn, that was news.

Marlon's audition technique did not improve. The MCA executives were so concerned by his poor showing that they asked Edie Van Cleve to stop sending him out. "He's got to go," she snapped. "He's got to learn. And don't ask me how, but I know it will all work out the way it should. Somehow."

It worked out with a little help from one of Marlon's friends—namely, Stella Adler. Harold Clurman, her former husband, and Elia Kazan were producing Maxwell Anderson's *Truckline Café*, a roadhouse tragedy about two waitresses who stray while their husbands are serving overseas. The producers were having casting problems—none of the stars they approached was interested in the Anderson drama. Stella begged and cajoled until Clurman and Kazan agreed to audition Marlon for one of the two cuckolded GIs. It was a meaty role: the husband murders his unfaithful wife, throws her body in the Pacific, and then publicly confesses his crime.

After Brando's audition, Kazan rushed from the theater, doubled up with laughter. "That was the worst reading I've ever heard in my life," he told a friend, "but still, I'm going to give him the part. He's got real talent."

When Miss Van Cleve heard about the offer, she was upset. She told Marlon she had read the play and thought it was very poor. Brando didn't disagree, but argued that he could turn his part into an important showcase. "What salary do you want?" she asked.

"Well, they orginally wanted Burgess Meredith for the

part," Brando said. "And they probably would have paid him at least five hundred dollars, so I think that's what I should get."

Edie gasped. "Marlon, I'm sure they know you're making seventy-five dollars a week, so I doubt very much if they'll be willing to jump you to five hundred." Marlon insisted, and so Miss Van Cleve started her negotiations at that figure.

"I thought Kazan would have a heart attack when I said five hundred dollars," she recalled. "He was thinking in terms of a hundred twenty-five. But after a lot of bickering, I got Marlon two seventy-five a week."

During the first rehearsals, Brando did nothing to justify this exalted salary. He mumbled and slouched and refused to interplay with the other actors. Clurman decided desperate measures were needed to free Brando from his introspective trance.

Dismissing the rest of the company, he asked Marlon to read an important speech while he listened from the auditorium. Brando spoke his opening lines indistinctly.

"Louder!" shouted Clurman. Brando raised his voice. "Now scream," the director ordered. Brando screamed. "Now scream while you climb the rope at the back of the stage." Brando climbed and screamed. "Now roll on the floor and scream." Brando rolled and screamed. Clurman bounded on stage and began to kick Marlon, who was by this time almost hysterical. The director then called back the other actors and proceeded with the rehearsal. Brando didn't mumble anymore—at least not during this production.

When *Truckline Café* opened in February 1946, the critics joined hands in a dance of death: "The worst play I have seen since I have been in the reviewing business" (New York *Daily News*); "Downright unbearable" (New York *Sun*); "Hollow and preposterous" (*The New Yorker*); "The most old-fashioned piece of stage stuff I ever saw" (*Cue*). Kazan and Clurman took large advertisements in the papers to denounce the incompetence of daily criticism, and this rebuttal turned the play into a *cause célèbre* of the theater world. But the controversy didn't help box office sales: *Truckline Café* closed after thirteen performances.

Once again, Brando was overlooked by the critics; only the *Cue* reviewer called attention to his "honey of a performance." This is a strangely mellifluous description for a piece of acting that left many spectators puzzled and uncomfortable. For instance, Pauline Kael, the film critic of *The New Yorker*, recently described her initial disagreeable impression of Brando in *Truckline Café* this way: "Arriving late at a performance, and seated in the center of the second row, I looked up and saw what I thought was an actor having a seizure on stage. Embarrassed for him, I lowered my eyes, and it wasn't until the young man who'd brought me grabbed my arm and said, 'Watch this guy!' that I realized he was *acting*."

Theater people were galvanized by Brando's performance; they realized that here was an actor with the divine spark, an actor with a great and original, if still inchoate, talent. Immediately they envisioned him in the great roles of the theatrical repertory.

Margaret Webster, a British actress and director noted for her Shakespeare productions, thought Brando would make a noble Hamlet for the repertory company she was opening in the forthcoming season. She approached Edith Van Cleve, who enthusiastically agreed that only repertory could offer Marlon the heroic assignments his talent demanded. Brando was dubious about the project, but he agreed to discuss it with Miss Webster.

When he arrived at her West Twelfth Street apartment, he dived into the nearest chair, propped his feet on a coffee table, and, without a word, began to devour a centerpiece display of grapes. While he spewed fruit seeds into the air, Miss Webster outlined her plan to make him America's finest classical actor since John Barrymore. "He didn't say a word," she recalled, "though I think he may have grunted once or twice."

Trying to draw him out, she asked if there were any roles he dreamed of playing. Brando muttered that he was thinking of doing a Chekhov play in Provincetown. "I'm not at all sure he was serious," Miss Webster said, "but I acted as if he were.

I asked if he couldn't play Chekhov in the summer and still join my company in the fall."

Brando didn't answer. He got up and walked into the kitchen where he fell into animated conversation with Miss Webster's French-Canadian cook and absolutely bedazzled her with his earnest interest in her recipes. When he left, he promised the woman he'd be back to see her soon, but made no promises to Miss Webster about *Hamlet.*

And he did return a few weeks later, carrying a small, carefully wrapped tin of imported pâté. "He gave it to me, though I knew it was for my cook," Miss Webster said. "He chatted with her for a good while, and said a few words to me. But there was nothing about the repertory company. Then I received a polite note of refusal. I don't remember what excuse he gave. He was evasive. I think he just didn't want to be tied down."

Miss Webster meant to imply that Brando wanted a quicker and easier success than could be won in a repertory theater. And while that may be true, it is also possible that he had enough common sense to realize that he was far too inexperienced to attempt *Hamlet.* At this point, he was technically a very unsteady actor.

During the run of *Truckline Café*, as he came off stage, he'd often turn to co-actor Karl Malden and say, "Gee, I was great tonight!" or "Christ, I was lousy, I wonder why?"

"Don't you know?" Malden asked in surprise.

"No," Marlon shrugged. "It's like I get on a one-way railway track and can't get off."

Brando was relying entirely on intuition and his own emotional flow to build a character. But he didn't know how to trigger the emotion if it didn't come naturally, or how to restrain it if it came too quickly, or how to reach the same emotional peaks night after night. Consequently, at one performance, his playing would be pitched too high; at the next, it was too low.

This problem was to plague Brando in his next Broadway appearance, or so it seems from the widely divergent estimates of his performance. He went directly from *Truckline*

Café into rehearsals for a revival of G. B. Shaw's *Candida*, starring Katharine Cornell, "the First Lady of Broadway." Brando played Marchbanks, a budding poet who is in love with the title heroine, the smug wife of an English pastor. Miss Cornell had been playing Candida off and on since 1924 and her former Marchbankses included a teenaged Orson Welles and the young Burgess Meredith. It was an indication of Brando's growing importance that Miss Cornell chose him to uphold this distinguished lineage.

Candida was put on after only three weeks' rehearsal. This tight schedule was no handicap for Cornell or the other cast members, many of them already familiar with their roles, but Brando was still stumbling over his part when the production opened in early April 1946. Because of the audience acclaim he won in *Truckline Café*, the critics now gave considerable attention to Brando, and found him wanting. In one way or another, they all echoed the opinion of George Jean Nathan, New York's most sardonic critic: "Marlon Brando's young poet's weakness becomes almost wholly a matter of weak acting . . . [he must learn] that sensitiveness lies in more than a pale makeup and an occasionally quivering hand."

Later, when he had worked his way into the part, Brando won some word-of-mouth praise, but his performance was always controversial. One seasoned theatergoer remembers him as "impassioned and volatile, a very impressive and strong Marchbanks," while another says, "He sounded like a cab driver and moved like a third baseman, but he had some affecting moments."

Throughout this period Marlon kept up his nomadic existence. Some friends say he continually moved to elude young ladies who banged on his door for a night of romance; whenever he got tired of his current harem, he moved without leaving a forwarding address.

At one time, Marlon lived in an apartment building that adjoined Leon and Eddie's, a former New York nightclub, which featured a bevy of show girls and a sliding roof which could be pulled back to allow the customers to "dine under the stars" in clement weather. On his way home from the theater, Marlon always stopped by to gaze at the club's billboard of lightly clothed damsels.

The doorman took a dislike to Brando. He thought the disreputable-looking actor discouraged passersby from entering the club. The doorman asked his friend, the block policeman, to chase Brando from the entrance. A scuffle ensued in which Marlon was slapped across the rear with a billy club.

In a rage, Brando walked to First Avenue where there was then a row of slaughterhouses, scooped up a bucket of cow manure, and returned to his apartment building. He climbed to his roof, and from there jumped onto the top of the nightclub. The roof was rolled back and Marlon looked down on the unsuspecting diners. He raised the bucket, emptied its contents, and screamed, "Beware the flying horse!"

Brando spent the summer of 1946 touring with Katharine Cornell's company, playing Marchbanks in *Candida* and the Messenger in a modern dress adaptation of *Antigone*. The latter role he played a few times in New York prior to the tour, and at one performance he was seen by Laurence Olivier, who immediately became a Brando fan. "Marlon had a very small part—no more than one speech, really," the English actor recalls, "but he was electrifying. It was obvious that he was a star in the making."

Katharine Cornell loved the road and prided herself on keeping her company in tip-top shape, even when playing the shallowest backwaters of the theatrical circuit. Marlon didn't understand this tradition, and frequently he just walked through his roles.

Miss Cornell asked her husband to take Brando aside and lecture him on the responsibilities of an actor to his audience. The results were immediate. "On opening night in Chicago, Marlon out-acted Miss Cornell," said a member of the *Candida* production team.

In the fall he returned to Broadway in Ben Hecht's *A Flag Is Born*, a dramatic spectacle which chronicled the plight of stateless Jews. With music, dance, and swirling prayer shawls, it swept through Jewish history from Solomon's court to "a graveyard somewhere in present-day Europe," and propagandized a Zionist Palestine.

"Marlon didn't ask my advice on this," Edith Van Cleve recalled. "He just told me he was going to do it; it wasn't much of a play, which I'm sure he knew, but it was for a cause he believed in."

Brando enjoyed his stint in *A Flag Is Born*, since it gave him the opportunity to work with Paul Muni, "that great, fine and sensitive actor," Marlon called him. Muni was all of those things, but, like most actors from the Yiddish Theater tradition, he was also a consummate ham, and it was this side of Muni that Brando really relished. He particularly admired his co-star's histrionic death scene. "When he died," Brando said, "it was like the birth of an elephant!"

After Muni had gasped his final breath, Marlon held the stage alone. Facing dead front, he eulogized his dead compatriot, and never failed to spellbind the audience. Dressed in a black turtleneck sweater and rope-belted trousers, he was breathtakingly handsome—a figure of charismatic, mythic beauty.

Lying prone on the stage floor, Muni kept a close, competitive eye on Marlon during this scene. Late in the run, he came down with a cold and, fearful of theater drafts, he asked Brando to cover him with a flag before beginning his eulogy. Marlon obliged and then launched into his speech. Halfway through, he heard a persistent rustling and, looking over his shoulder, he saw Muni stealthily tugging the flag away from his eyes, so that he could watch Brando's effect on the audience.

Marlon kept a straight face that night, but on other occasions he almost lost his stage composure. Once, as Muni was riding the crest of Ben Hecht's rhetoric, he reached for a crescendo and out plopped his dentures. Brando and the cast were completely nonplussed, but not Muni. He casually scooped up the false teeth, turned his back to the audience for a second, and then continued as if nothing untoward had occurred.

While playing in *A Flag Is Born*, Brando received his first film offer. Elia Kazan was about to start production on *Gentleman's Agreement* and had chosen John Garfield for one of the leading roles, but Garfield couldn't decide whether he wanted the assignment or not. Remembering *Truckline Café,* Kazan felt Brando would be a good substitute, and he approached Marlon about the film. Brando said he couldn't quit *A Flag Is Born.* "I couldn't do it," he explained. "The Jews are persecuted and they need help."

Hearing about this, Ben Hecht sent Brando a telegram:

DEAR MARLON. THE JEWS HAVE BEEN PERSECUTED FOR 3000 YEARS. THEY LIKE IT. TAKE THE JOB.

Eventually Garfield accepted the role in *Gentleman's Agreement* and Marlon went on playing *A Flag Is Born* for a while longer. Then, early in December 1946, he left the cast a few weeks before its scheduled closing. Miss Van Cleve had found him a plum assignment. He was to play Tallulah Bankhead's leading man in Jean Cocteau's *The Eagle Has Two Heads.* It was his biggest opportunity to date and it was disaster from the outset.

·4·

TROUBLE WITH TALLULAH

Someone should have known better. Bankhead and Brando—
it's a combination to set off fireworks in the imagination.
And the fireworks were not long in blazing on and off stage.
Temperamental, theatrical, erratically talented Tallulah de-
plored the new breed of actors with their constant analysis,
their subtexts and emotional recalls. She thought the
Stanislavsky technique was fake and impractical. "Any actor
who loses himself in a part is a stupid ass," she said. Asked
about her own acting technique, she answered that she leaned
toward "the French tradition," and then airily changed the
subject. Actually, Tallulah belonged to no acting tradition—
she built her performances on instinct and nerve—but what
she probably meant was that while strutting as Sadie
Thompson or capering through a Noel Coward farce, she
might also be counting the house or figuring her income
taxes.

"When I'm playing a very emotional scene," she once
boasted, "I might be thinking about the steak I'm going to
have after the show."

When Tallulah approved Marlon as her leading man, she
had never seen him act. But he came highly recommended by
Edith Van Cleve, Bankhead's intimate friend for over twenty
years. And John S. Wilson, the director of *The Eagle Has Two
Heads*, was a fervent admirer of Brando, though the two men
had nothing in common.

Jack Wilson was one of those sleek sophisticates whose

photograph keeps popping up in high-priced, cosmopolitan biographies—there he is again and again with Noel and Cole, all three beautifully bronzed by the Lido sun. Born to money, Wilson was also blessed with wit, intelligence, and a dazzling handsomeness. After graduating from Yale, he played at being a stockbroker, and then entered the theater by walking into Noel Coward's dressing room. For many years thereafter, he was Coward's constant companion, business manager, producer, and director.

Wilson first saw Marlon at the *O Mistress Mine* audition (he produced the play for the Lunts) and later sent him the script of *Present Laughter*, a second-drawer Noel Coward comedy. Marlon returned the script with this note: "I have read it. Don't you know there are thousands of people starving in Europe?"

That retort should have told Wilson that he and Brando didn't speak the same kind of stage language, but no, he insisted that only Marlon could play Cocteau's hero. And Tallulah, badgered by Edie and Wilson, said yes, she'd take Marlon.

A fourth member of this unholy alliance was the play itself. Cocteau wrote it for his good friend Jean Marais, who asked, "Write me a play in which I say nothing in the first act, talk all the second, and die dramatically in the third." Cocteau's answer to this challenge was a Ruritanian fantasy about an Austrian queen obsessed with the premonition of imminent assassination. ("My dream is to become a tragedy," she explains.) When Stanislas, her assassin, appears, she delivers a thirty-minute monologue and then, exhausted, she takes him to her bed. In the second act, Stanislas does most of the talking. (He says, "We are the dream of one who sleeps so profoundly that he is not even aware that he is dreaming us," an aphorism to trip the tongue of any actor.) Finally, after another loquacious act, Stanislas shoots the queen and drains a fatal quaff.

While cluttered with empty-headed pretensions, the Cocteau drama has its fustian charms when acted by two players of the grand manner. Tallulah could be very imperious in a swanky sort of way, but that wasn't what was needed, and neither she nor Brando had the vocal technique to deal with the intricate monologues. Her Southern contralto hammered away at Cocteau's delicate conceits and left them a rubbish heap of mystifying words.

During the first rehearsals of *Eagle*, relations between Brando and Bankhead were fairly cordial, or so claimed Edith Van Cleve. "Marlon liked Tallulah, respected her, understood her problems, but she wasn't the kind of person he could talk to. Tallulah recognized his talent and tried to be friendly. Several times she invited him to her apartment and tried to draw him out. But she never really understood him. She couldn't understand why he was so aloof, why he wouldn't join the rest of the company for a drink after rehearsals."

(Brando has never been much of a drinker. In his youth, when overweight was not yet a severe problem, he drank beer or red wine. Today he takes an occasional vodka, and nurses it in a teacup, apparently because he doesn't want anyone to know he tipples.)

Instead of boozing with Tallulah, Marlon hung out with Cherokee Thornton, a black actor cast as the queen's major-domo. Between acting engagements, Thornton played drums for the Pearl Primus dance troupe, and it was the bongo that brought him and Marlon together. Tallulah, whose ear for music inclined toward Dixieland and "I'll Be Seeing You," couldn't fathom this rapport; she couldn't comprehend why Brando preferred the company of a bit player when he could be frolicking with a star.

Tallulah was also puzzled, but fascinated, by Marlon's addiction to physical fitness. With rehearsals cutting into his gym time, Brando spent every spare minute doing sit-ups and other calisthenics in the theater alley. Tallulah marveled at the bulging muscles and he-man exertion. "He's terribly talented, but rather strange," she told a reporter who asked about Marlon. "Whenever the director needs him for a scene, he's out back doing those ridiculous pick-me-ups!"

That was the last laugh of the production. Bankhead's sense of humor trickled away as day after day Brando muttered his way through rehearsals, and gave her no indication of the final performance she would be playing against. Already tense and uneasy in the role, she didn't need the added irritation of a disrespectful leading man. After one rehearsal, she rampaged off stage and, pointing in Brando's direction, snapped, "He's driving me nuts!"

If director Jack Wilson had been a steadier helmsman, this tempest might have been avoided. On the few occasions when Tallulah did create a character instead of flaunting her public image, it was because a director browbeat her into subservience. But Wilson handled her with velvet gloves. "The main thing with Tallulah is to keep her happy," he once said.

Nor did Wilson give Marlon much direction, though Bankhead pleaded with him to do something about her co-star's trancelike readings. Wilson was certain Marlon knew what he was doing, and reassured Tallulah that on opening night her Stanislas would give a performance that would have everyone cheering. Tallulah wasn't convinced, but to her credit, she didn't pull rank and insist Brando be fired.

"Marlon was very unhappy," Edith Van Cleve recalled. "He liked Wilson personally, but he was accustomed to Kazan and Clurman and the other Stanislavsky people, and of course that wasn't Jack's way of working. Marlon wanted to leave the production and I said that wasn't possible. He had a run-of-the-play contract which could be broken only by mutual consent. Wilson gave no indication that he was unhappy with Marlon."

And so Brando was still in the cast when *Eagle* began its try-out engagements in Wilmington, Delaware. On the opening night, the play plodded along on course until Marlon entered and Bankhead began her first-act monologue. Brando was directed to be as inconspicuous as possible during this scene, but on this occasion he put on an unparalleled display of upstagemanship. As Tallulah slunk about the stage, drawling the Cocteau conundrums, Marlon preened, scratched, picked his nose, fiddled with his fly, leered at the audience, dusted the furniture, ogled a stagehand.

The worst was still to come. Tallulah's greatest moment

arrived toward the end of the third act when the queen is shot as she stands at the top of a staircase. Bankhead then plunged downward, head first, in one pure, unbroken line. It was a perilous *coup de théâtre*, one that might give pause to an experienced stuntman, and Tallulah counted on it to bring her a standing ovation.

That night she carried it off with aplomb. There were gasps of admiration from out front, which unexpectedly changed to titters, then guffaws.

After the queen's death, Stanislas is supposed to drink his poison and die, straight off. Marlon wasn't so death-prone. He swallowed the lethal dosage and then began to stagger around the stage, gasping, clutching his throat, desperately searching for a final resting place. By the time the curtain fell, the audience was in hysterics, and for all they remembered of Tallulah's heroic tumble, she might have hopscotched down the steps.

Bankhead bolted off stage, hellbent for Brando's blood. "Get rid of him! Immediately!" she ordered. And so that night a search party returned to New York to find a Stanislas who would die on cue.

This version of the Bankhead-Brando fiasco comes from press agent Richard Maney, Tallulah's close friend and ghost biographer. Edith Van Cleve swore it wasn't true. "Nothing like that happened. Marlon kept calling from out of town, imploring me to get him out of the show, and I kept saying my hands were tied by his contract. Then, when the company was in Boston, Jack Wilson phoned to say that he knew Marlon was unhappy and that he was willing to let him go. There had been complaints that Marlon was too young to play Tallulah's lover." (Brando was then twenty-two, Bankhead forty-four; according to Cocteau's script, Stanislas is twenty-five, the queen thirty-one.)

Miss Van Cleve agreed to Marlon's dismissal, but reserved the right to recast the part. "There were a lot of young actors around Broadway who were very jealous of Marlon's fast rise; they had their tongues hanging out waiting to do him in. And I wasn't going to have them jumping on his bandwagon. If the official explanation for Marlon's dismissal was that he was too young for Tallulah, I was going to make sure he was replaced by someone older."

Twenty-eight-year-old Helmut Dantine inherited the role of Stanislas in Boston where the show was a complete shambles. Tallulah was toadying to her fans' tawdry expectations. She camped unabashedly and raced through her half-hour monologue in twenty-two minutes. In New York, she had it down to seventeen minutes flat.

Brando came to the Broadway opening, wearing jeans and sneakers, and sat in the first row. He left after the first act, evidently content that he hadn't made a mistake in quitting the show. He hadn't. The production was drubbed by the critics and denounced by Cocteau as "a vulgarization" of his play. It closed after twenty-nine performances.

Being replaced in a play during rehearsals or previews always smirches an actor's reputation, even when the replacement is "by mutual agreement." There's always the suspicion of incompetence or temperament, and so there was when Brando was released from *The Eagle Has Two Heads*. True or false, stories about Marlon's maverick misconduct circulated along Broadway, as did reports of a misbegotten performance.

This notoriety diminished Brando's slim chances of finding a new assignment that season. He quit *Eagle* in February 1947 and returned to New York to find casting for spring productions almost set. The producers who had lead roles open were reluctant to hire an actor who was reputed to be a troublemaker. Edith Van Cleve did a yeoman's job trying to scotch the rumors, but to no avail. For the next several months, Brando's only regular engagement was at his unemployment office.

During this hiatus, Edie suggested that Brando consider the movies. She did so gingerly, since Marlon had made it clear at their first meeting that he wanted no part of Hollywood—"a cultural boneyard" he called it. Now he told Edie he might be interested in making *a* movie (no long-term contracts) if he liked the script (no giddy comedies, no glitzy romances, no

Westerns, no De Mille spectacles). If he went to Hollywood, he was going to appear in a picture with a purpose, something on the order of Kazan's *Gentleman's Agreement.*

Edie sighed and said she'd do what she could with such terms, but she didn't hold high hopes. At this time, movie studios were still signing actors to seven-year contracts with options and serfdom clauses. Only stars with proven name value were offered one-picture deals, and Marlon wasn't in that class.

When MCA president Lew Wasserman heard of Brando's presumptuous demands, he called Miss Van Cleve on the carpet. "I told him I knew Marlon's terms were excessive and premature, but there was nothing we could do about it," she recalled. "I said that if we tried high-pressure tactics, we would assuredly lose him, which we couldn't afford, since some day he'd bring the agency millions. Fortunately, Wasserman allowed me to play it Marlon's way."

She sent out feelers to the film companies and the answer was the expected no thanks. And so she went back to reading Broadway scripts with an eye to finding Marlon a role. A fellow agent passed on to her a copy of Tennessee Williams's *A Streetcar Named Desire,* and immediately she realized Marlon could be brilliant in the role of Stanley Kowalski. Marlon read the play and enthusiastically agreed. He really wanted the part.

There was only one problem. The producer didn't want Brando.

·5·

A STREETCAR NAMED SUCCESS

Irene Mayer Selznick, producer of the Williams drama, had stars on her mind. If she had had her choice, theatergoers would have seen John Garfield and Margaret Sullavan in *A Streetcar Named Desire.*

Mrs. Selznick was used to thinking big. Though a neophyte in theater production, she was born and reared in the cream of show biz circles. The daughter of Louis B. Mayer and pre–Jennifer Jones wife of David O. Selznick, she was, a playwright friend wrote, "used to domination, risks, secret decisions; used to men, women, and money." (Marlon once said much the same thing in a simpler way: "Irene Selznick— there's one shrewd lady!")

Her first choice of director was Joshua Logan, but he was busy preparing *Mister Roberts* and *South Pacific.* Next on her list was Elia Kazan, a daring choice since there was little in his background to predict the mastery with which he would stage Williams's play. He entered the theater as an actor, reaching prominence in several Clifford Odets plays. (He looks like an Odetsian character: diminutive, bushy-haired, with a strong, sensual face.) He switched to directing in the late thirties, and while his credits included a number of solid Broadway hits, most of his work was slick, conventional fare: a historical drama, a couple of prosaic problem plays, a Mary Martin musical, a handful of comedies.

Kazan and Selznick agreed that John Garfield was their best

43

bet for Kowalski. He had the right qualities for the part: strong and sexy, he looked and sounded like a stevedore. Furthermore, he was eager to return to Broadway, and was favorably disposed to working with Kazan. The two had been friends since their days together as members of the Group Theater and had only recently finished working together on *Gentleman's Agreement.*

And, for one week in June 1947, it looked as if Garfield was definitely set for *Streetcar.* With great fanfare, Mrs. Selznick announced that Garfield had signed a contract; a few days later, she hedged about "unresolved complications"; and then, before the week was out, bemoaned her "grievous disappointment." For reasons she didn't specify, Garfield had withdrawn. According to Kazan, Garfield wouldn't sign a run-of-the-play contract as Mrs. Selznick wanted. Others say the actor thought Kowalski was overshadowed by Blanche Du Bois, the play's leading female character.

As soon as Edie Van Cleve heard that Garfield was out of the running, she phoned Kazan to suggest Marlon. She had done so once before, immediately after reading the play, and the answer had been a firm no. The reason: "Brando was ten years too young for the part." (Williams describes Kowalski as twenty-eight or thirty. Garfield, incidentally, was thirty-five.) The second time around, Kazan was receptive to the suggestion of Brando, but he was still wary, and with good reason. Kowalski is a long, difficult part, and demands an actor with a sure-footed technique and an electrifying personality. Kazan wondered if Marlon had the necessary experience. He asked Miss Van Cleve if Brando would audition.

She refused. "Since he had already worked with Marlon on *Truckline Café,* I thought he should decide without an audition," she recalled. "I told him that an audition would prove nothing except that Marlon was a lousy reader, and he already knew that."

By this time, the other major roles were cast. Jessica Tandy, a British actress with a flair for playing high-strung gentlewomen, had replaced Margaret Sullavan as Blanche; Kim

Hunter was penciled in as Stella, Stanley's wife; and Karl Malden was assigned the role of Mitch, Stanley's sidekick. With rehearsals to begin in a few weeks, there could be no further stalling on choosing a Kowalski and, with no better prospect in view, Kazan told Brando the part was his, provided he was approved by Tennessee Williams. The playwright was then secluded in Provincetown, Massachusetts, and planned to stay there until he finished polishing his play. Kazan urged Brando to visit the playwright on Cape Cod immediately.

Flat broke and unable (or unwilling) to borrow the train fare, Brando hitchhiked to his interview with Williams. "He got lost," Edie Van Cleve said with a laugh. "Marlon always got lost. He was forever riding past subway stations and bus stops. Maybe he was truly absentminded, maybe it was an unconscious trick to put off getting to where he didn't want to go."

When Brando arrived in Provincetown, it was several hours past his scheduled appointment. Williams's beach cottage looked deserted, but the Southern playwright was at home, and beside himself. A fuse had blown and a stopped-up pipe was trickling water onto the bathroom floor. Williams was too artistic to cope with such mechanical irregularities so Marlon volunteered to pitch in. He hadn't the foggiest notion of what he was doing, but after fumbling around for half the night, he got the lights on and the plumbing patched up.

In appreciation, Williams fixed Marlon some ham sandwiches and a glass of milk. Brando asked for more milk and polished off the whole quart. By this time, it was the wee hours of the morning, too late (sigh of relief from Marlon) for an extended audition. Williams listened to him struggle through a few pages of the script and then, acting mainly on intuition, he told Brando the part was his.

When Marlon left Cape Cod that night, he had bagged more than the role of Kowalski. In the hip pocket of his jeans was a twenty-dollar bill. Williams had proved to be a very easy "touch."

*　　*　　*

Rehearsals for *Streetcar* started on October 5, 1947, in the rehearsal hall on top of the New Amsterdam Theater. It was a musty, dismal place, not conducive to settling the butterflies actors get on the first day of a new job. Brando had a terrible seizure of the flutters when he went to work on *Streetcar*. "They should have got John Garfield for Stanley, not me," he kept muttering nervously. "Garfield was right for the part, not me."

Asked how he built up Marlon's confidence, Kazan looked very surprised. "I never knew he was nervous. I don't know why he should have been—everyone was thrilled with his performance from the very beginning. Of course, most actors get the jitters at the start. They think, what I am doing here? or, I'll never be able to play this role. If they don't, then usually they're not much good."

Kazan must have a short memory. Other cast members report that the first *Streetcar* rehearsals were very stormy. Karl Malden was once so frustrated by Marlon's perfunctory performance he slammed his fist into a brick wall.

Possibly Marlon doubted his ability to play Kowalski, a character he strongly disliked. "Kowalski was always right and never afraid," he once said. "He never wondered, he never doubted himself. His ego was very secure. And he had the kind of brutal aggressiveness I hate. I'm afraid of it. I detest the character."

But under Kazan's meticulous guidance, he was able to find within himself the lewd and gaudy colors of Stanley's personality. "Directing finally consists of turning psychology into behavior," Kazan once wrote, and, true to his theory, he put all of Williams's characters on the Freudian couch. According to his *Streetcar* notes, Kowalski is "the hedonist" who "sucks on a cigar all day because he can't suck on a teat"; who lives by "ball and jowl" and "conquers with his penis."

Kazan closes his dossier on Stanley with the notation, "In the case of Brando, the question of enjoyment is particularly important." Brando's past performances had been tense and introverted, a style ill-suited to that crass and vital extrovert, Kowalski. It could not have been easy for Marlon to liberate himself to the point where he luxuriated in Stanley's savagery, but he did it without a trace of strain.

"It was awful and it was sublime," said a New Haven theatergoer about Brando's first public appearance in *Streetcar*. "Only once in a generation do you see such a thing in the theater." When the play moved on to Boston, the Puritan fathers thought once in a generation was once too often. The local censors demanded a tempering of language and action, particularly the rape scene. In Philadelphia, there was further temporary expurgation. All during its tryout engagement the play was a storm center of controversy, being extravagantly praised and rebuked, sometimes in the same breath, by critics who admired the steel-like accuracy of Williams's writing, but disdained his salacious subject matter.

By the time it arrived in New York, *Streetcar* was easily the most talked-about play in seasons, and the sensational pre-opening publicity intimidated some members of the cast. "Even before rehearsals started, the newspapers began building up *Streetcar*," Kim Hunter (Stella) remembers. "Irene Selznick kept advising us not to get overconfident about it— just to treat it as a nice little play. After a while it got so much publicity that we had to work hard against overconfidence. Then we began to feel that even if it was the greatest play ever written, we couldn't live up to its reputation."

The play opened on December 3, 1947, to an impressive array of Mrs. Selznick's Hollywood and café-society friends, including Cary Grant and John Hay Whitney, both of whom had invested in the production. Perhaps there have been more glamorous première audiences, but rarely has a group of first-nighters been so keyed up with excitement. From the beginning of act one, when Brando bounded on stage shouting, "Hey, Stella! Hey, there, Stella, baby!" to the final line, "The game is five-card stud," the auditorium was a live wire of electricity. As the final curtain slowly fell, there were bravos, then curtain call after curtain call, and finally a standing ovation.

The opening of *Streetcar* stands as a landmark in the American theater. It immediately established Williams as a theater writer of the first rank and Brando as the most gifted actor of his generation. And the Kazan directorial style—described by critic Walter Kerr as a mixture of "animal vitality, an almost hysterical surface tension, and a markedly rhythmic pattern of eruption"—was to change the whole look of American theatrical production in the next decade.

By the final curtain call, it seemed as if *Streetcar* had lived up to its advance reputation, but first-night audiences are deceptively partisan, and no one was counting his rave reviews until they were printed. Therefore, the opening-night party thrown by Mrs. Selznick at the posh 21 Club started as a subdued and tentative celebration. Marlon arrived, neatly dressed in a suit and tie, with Mr. and Mrs. Brando, whom he treated with the utmost deference. Those present who knew Marlon's tales of a drunken mother and curmudgeonly father wondered at this model son and his gracious, eminently respectable parents. (Earlier that evening, they may have been surprised to open their *Playbill*s and read the first truthful Brando biography—no mention of Rangoon or Bangkok, no etymologists, geologists, or tympanists. Evidently Marlon's work in *Streetcar* gave him sufficient pride and self-assurance to place himself, not some flamboyant alter ego, on public display.)

Early in the morning the reviews dribbled in, and as one rave followed another, the party's mood rose euphorically. A few critics questioned whether the subject matter had to be quite so nasty, but the quibbling wasn't severe enough to tarnish a shining and total triumph. Brando was praised as "magnificent," "astonishingly authentic," "brutally convincing," "our theater's most remarkable young actor at his most memorable."

Two years earlier, when Brando failed to turn up for an audition, an aggravated Edith Van Cleve exclaimed, "Oh,

Marlon, I wish I knew what you wanted from your career; then I might be able to help you better!"

He thought for a minute and said, "I'd like to be important enough for my word to mean something."

On the night *Streetcar* opened, Marlon realized his goal—at least partially. He was now celebrated enough to be courted by syndicated columnists, though none of them wanted to discuss politics or world affairs or the starving people in Europe, as Brando wished. Instead they asked what he liked to eat (peanut butter, pomegranates); what he read (Spinoza); about his hobbies (drums, tom-toms, motorcycles); his favorite sports (boxing, swimming in the nude); his pet peeves (shoes, large parties, interviews); his love life (no response); and how he lived.

Despite his $550 salary, he lived as inelegantly as before. During part of the run of *Streetcar*, his home was a two-room attic flat in a dilapidated Murray Hill tenement. Its bedroom was just big enough to hold a small red upright piano and a brass bed where he ate his breakfast, a raw egg. ("It saves time," he explained to a reporter as he swallowed his morning meal.) The living room was virtually bare, except for a tom-tom, a recorder, and a stack of books, which included a prominently exhibited *Lady Chatterley's Lover*, then banned in America, and probably serving mainly as shock prop.

Later he moved uptown, taking an apartment across from the penthouse pad leased by his pal, Bob Condon, then an employee of an advertising agency. Marlon developed a passion for fresh orange juice, but he never got around to buying a squeezer; instead, he borrowed Condon's. At this time Brando was an early riser, and not wishing to awake Condon, he perfected an unusual method of entering his friend's apartment. He'd go through the fire door onto Condon's terrace and climb through the kitchen window. Then he'd carefully remove two oranges from a paper bag, slice them, squeeze them, drink their juice, tidy up, and depart as stealthily as he had arrived.

He spent many free hours with his sisters, both of whom were living in New York with their families. Jocelyn was the wife of actor Don Hanmer and mother of a son, David. (Motherhood didn't interfere with her career. In 1948, she played a small but prominent role in *Mister Roberts:* the only woman in the cast, she was Lieutenant Ann Girard, a Navy nurse much admired for the strawberry birthmark on her behind.) Fran was married to Richard Loving, a fellow painter, and they were parents of a daughter, Julia.

Marlon loved children, and was an attentive and reliable babysitter; his sisters (Fran particularly) were to repay this favor many times over when he had children of his own. The Brandos were always to be a tight-knit and loyal family, the more so as they grew older. After *Streetcar,* Marlon and his father became closer than ever, and all because the younger Brando couldn't manage money.

"I don't know what happens to it," he said. "I don't buy any clothes. I don't go to nightclubs. I don't drink. I eat in cafeterias. I haven't got a car. I've never paid more than sixty-five dollars a month rent."

He was giving the money away. Once a famous moocher, he was now the easiest touch on Broadway. Anyone who needed the price for anything, from a cup of coffee to a trip to Havana, could get it from Brando. On occasion, he'd give away his entire salary on payday, and then borrow to pay his own weekly bills.

To end this vicious circle, Marlon asked his father to act as his financial advisor.

"Pop," he said, "I can't handle this money situation. Will you give me a hand?"

Mr. Brando was happy to help his son. "All his life, Marlon never cared anything about money. It's never been important to him so I figured somebody had to help him and I agreed."

Each week Marlon sent home all but $150 of his salary for his father to invest. Even after Marlon was making a good deal more than $550 a week, this arrangement stood; for several years he received exactly $150 to pay his weekly expenses.

Marlon carried his Broadway success lightly. "It took me a

long time before I was aware that I was a big success," he said. "I was so absorbed in myself, my problems, I never looked around, never took account."

But once he realized he was a success—a sensation he likened to "sitting on a pile of candy"—he didn't let it go to his head. His old friends were still his best friends, and he stayed safe within their bohemian circles. He didn't hobnob with the Broadway first-name droppers, and was embarrassed by their quick compliments and fishbowl curiosity. He hated being told how great he was. Once, when a lady oozed praise for his performance, he waited patiently until she had finished her hymn, and then said, "You've got a run in your stocking."

After a performance, Jessica Tandy brought Hollywood columnist Sheilah Graham to Marlon's dressing room. As he well knew, his visitor prided herself on her youthful appearance. He stared at Miss Graham and then, turning to Jessica Tandy, he cooed, "Ah, Jessie, this must be your mother!"

Often Marlon went on playing Kowalski after the curtain had fallen. His real-life adaptation of Stanley's trash clothes and churlish behavior was to some extent motivated by his astute sense of publicity, but it went deeper than that. It was also a ploy to keep potentially inimical eyes from really seeing him. With old friends he was articulate and relaxed until a stranger entered the room; then out came the Kowalski slouch and mumble, the scratching and nose-picking.

The role also invaded his love life. According to one unsympathetic member of his circle, he would bring a "girl" to a party and ignore her for a couple of hours while he fooled around with his buddies, and then, when the poor "girl" was ready to leave in a snit, he would suddenly leap on her with ferocious familiarity. This predatory courtship may have been, explained another acquaintance, Marlon's way of establishing whether a "girl" was relating to him more in terms of his image than his real self, but still the method seems roundabout, if not perverse.

Friends worried that for Brando, Stanley was becoming more than just a part: it was his private Mr. Hyde. And Marlon himself was so plagued by his psychic ghosts that during the run of *Streetcar* he entered intensive analysis. Elia Kazan sent him to his psychiatrist, Dr. Bela Mittelman.

At first he was scared of taking this step and rationalized that psychiatric treatment might cure his neuroses only at the expense of his talent. "I was afraid it might destroy the impulses that made me a creative artist," he said. "A sensitive person receives fifty impressions where somebody else may only get seven." But he plunged in and stuck with it more or less steadily for the next ten years.

Brando was to play Stanley for a year and a half, a long time to be indentured to such a demanding role. After six months most actors feel like they're performing a play under water, and are hard put to stave off their stagnation. (Later, Brando cited the boredom of a long run as an explanation of why he abandoned his stage career.)

To keep the *Streetcar* actors on their toes, Mrs. Selznick and Kazan dropped by unannounced at the theater once a week, watched the show, and read the riot act if there was any relaxation of tension or concentration.

On one such occasion, Mrs. Selznick phoned Edith Van Cleve to report that Marlon was mumbling so much he was inaudible in the higher reaches of the theater. Miss Van Cleve attended the next performance. "He was perfectly audible that night," she recalled, "but I gave him a pep talk I knew he wouldn't ignore. I told him there were complaints that he couldn't be heard in the balcony. I said I knew that those were the people he really cared about, not the orchestra crowd, and that he owed it to them to speak up."

When she finished, Brando said, "Well, some of the lines are so bad I have to mumble them."

"Oh, Marlon!" Edie gasped. "You know as well as I that you're fortunate to have such brilliant dialogue."

Marlon didn't say anything. He just laughed. But there were no further complaints about his mumbling.

Brando made a valiant attempt to keep his performance fresh and emotionally supported for each new audience. A lesson he learned from Jacob Adler stood him in good stead.

"Old man Adler taught me something I've never forgotten," he said. "To hold back twenty percent of your energy and you're always being honest with an audience. Try and show them more than you have to give and they catch on right away."

To keep up his interest, Marlon often varied his approach to a scene from performance to performance. Kim Hunter has described the little shifts of emphasis he made in the famous scene in which Stanley ransacks Blanche's trunk. "Marlon never, never did that scene the same way twice during the entire run," Miss Hunter says. "He had a different sort of attitude toward each of the belongings every night; sometimes it would lead me into getting into quite a fight with him, and other times I'd be seeing him as a silly little boy." Whichever way he played it, she concludes, had the same "uncanny sense of truth. . . . He'd always yank me into his sense of reality."

Irene Selznick was less appreciative of the liberties Brando took with the text and Kazan's directorial plan, particularly when he began eliminatng or rephrasing lines and inventing new stage business. She called in Tennessee Williams, who checked out Brando's alterations for several nights. "He's brought a new dimension to the part," Williams decided. "Let him play it his way—it's better." (Some years later the playwright said, "No one has equaled Marlon Brando's performance of Stanley Kowalski. And no one should try to imitate it.")

The Broadway cognoscenti said Williams had given Marlon the right to "Carte Blanche," a reference to his on-stage shenanigans at the expense of Jessica Tandy. The actress did not approve of the American version of the Stanislavsky system, and, unlike Kim Hunter, she had difficulty in adjusting her performance to Brando's nightly shifts of emphasis. She thought his behavior was often unprofessional, as indeed it appears to have been on occasion. There are reports that late in *Streetcar's* run, when audiences were less sensitive and came to the play mainly because of its sensational reputation, Marlon pushed for laughs and indulged in on-stage mischief. At one performance, Miss Tandy was working hard establishing sympathy for Blanche and getting unwarranted snickers as her reward. Glancing at Brando, she saw he was nonchalantly puffing a cigarette through his nostrils.

He rigged up a punching bag in the theater boiler room, where he worked out when he wasn't required on stage. Some nights he was joined by stagehands and his understudy, Jack Palance, and sometimes the noise of their antics carried upward onto the stage, much to the annoyance of the other actors.

During one of these bouts, Palance missed the punching bag and landed a left jab square on Brando's nose. Marlon finished the performance in throbbing pain and then went to the nearest hospital, where he was told his nose was broken. After it was set, Marlon was put to bed.

The next morning he was feeling fit, but wasn't in any hurry to get back to *Streetcar.* When he heard that Irene Selznick was coming to call, he went to work with bandages, iodine, and mercurochrome. As she walked through the door, Mrs. Selznick took one look at Brando's Halloween face and moaned, "Oh, Marlon, you poor, *poor* boy!"

He insisted it was nothing, that he'd be back at work that night. She said no, they could manage without him for at least a week. Marlon said he wouldn't dream of being out of the show for that long. "I *forbid* you to come to the theater!" Mrs. Selznick proclaimed irrevocably.

"And so," Marlon laughed, "I stayed in the hospital and had a ball."

Brando's nose was not set properly. When it came out of the bandages, it was prominently humped and gave a whole different cast to his face. He looked tougher. Mrs. Selznick insisted he had been ruined; she pleaded that he have his nose rebroken and set properly. "Luckily for him, he didn't listen to me," she says. "I honestly think that broken nose made his fortune as far as the movies go. It gave him sex appeal. He was too beautiful before."

During the run of *Streetcar*, Brando had his first brush with television, a medium he abhorred. Mrs. Selznick, however, recognized the publicity value of TV, and booked Marlon to appear on the Faye Emerson show. At the time, Miss Emerson was the queen of the networks, a position she had won less for her gift of intelligent gab than for her décolletage.

Marlon shuffled into her show, sat down, and clammed up. Miss Emerson chattered brightly, but soon became nervous when she realized that Marlon was ogling her prominently displayed bosom. For fifteen minutes Brando's eyes never strayed from his hostess's cleavage, and by the end of the show Faye was on the verge of hysteria.

On his next TV outing, Marlon was accompanied by Wally Cox, then at the beginning of his show business career. Once again the moderator was a pretty and peppy lady, who smiled desperately while trying to initiate a conversation.

Suddenly Brando turned to Cox and said, "Wally, there's something on the bottom of your shoe."

"What is it?" Cox asked.

"I don't know," Marlon replied, "but it smells *awful*."

The hostess's face was frozen into a pained smile. Any minute she expected to hear the four-letter word that would undoubtedly result in the cancellation of her show.

Marlon got down on his hands and knees to inspect Cox's shoe. "Ah, gee, Wally, it's just chewing gum." And then he gave the hostess a big, cheery grin.

This would be Brando's last TV appearance for many years.

When his *Streetcar* contract expired in June 1949, Marlon decided not to renew it. The nightly ordeal of playing Stanley had become so strenuous he was suffering memory blackouts, a common affliction of actors in long-running shows. The first time he forgot his lines, he was amused. "I just stood there looking out at the audience with a grin on my face. I looked at the people and all over the house and it seemed terribly funny. There were fourteen hundred people waiting for me to say something and I didn't have the slightest notion of what it was supposed to be."

It was no longer funny when the blackouts recurred with alarming regularity. Marlon decided he needed a long vacation. He didn't have anything definite set for the fall season, and wasn't sure what he wanted to do. Maybe another play, or possibly, if he got the right deal, he might make a movie.

·6·
ONE OF *THE MEN*

There's a famous anecdote about Brando's first meeting with a big-time movie producer, which goes like this: Marlon decides in advance he doesn't like the mogul and, when they meet, he shakes hands with a fresh-laid egg concealed in his palm.

Perhaps it's true; more likely it's another hickory-dickory-dock story. In all the other tales of his dealings with the Hollywood bigwigs, it's Brando, not the producer, who emerges covered with egg.

The movie companies started courting Brando shortly after *Streetcar* opened. Miss Van Cleve told Marlon about the interest, and asked what to do. He repeated what he had said previously: He would be agreeable to making a movie if he approved of the subject matter. So Edie proceeded to set up appointments for him, and the results were nearly disastrous. "What a terrible time that was!" she remembered. "Almost as bad as his early stage auditions. He just couldn't talk to those Hollywood people."

One of the first appointments was with Hal B. Wallis, a veteran picture producer who decorated his home with Picassos and post-Impressionists, and the screens of the world with *Desert Fury, Sorry, Wrong Number, I Walk Alone,* and similar melodramas. During the hour or so they spent together, Wallis did all the talking, Marlon's contribution to the conversation being a big, brilliant grin. When Brando left,

Wallis called Miss Van Cleve and said, "Well, I couldn't tell anything about his voice, I'm afraid, but he has a dazzling smile. He might make the last of the great silent-screen stars."

Edie accompanied Marlon to his interview with David O. Selznick, who was producing few films in this period, but who kept a small group of actors under personal contract. Selznick liked to pace while he interviewed, and he lumbered about the living room of his Waldorf Towers apartment, vainly trying to snare a word from Brando. But Marlon sat there in comatose silence, nervously clutching a book of poetry.

When she got him outside, Edie asked, "Marlon, what am I going to do with you? Selznick was sincerely interested in what you think. Why couldn't you talk to him?"

"I couldn't think of anything to say," Marlon answered. "I wanted to ask him why, with all the millions of silver feet of film he's made, he's never shown any pictures of the starving people of the world."

"Well, why didn't you say that?" Edie snapped. "At least it might have started a conversation!"

Marlon looked abject for a moment and then laughed. He held up the book he was carrying and said, "I guess I should have read him a poem."

Brando's reputation for crude deportment gave pause to many Hollywood producers. One Warner Brothers executive who wanted Brando for *Rebel Without a Cause* spent days looking for a New York restaurant that would seat a T-shirt-and-blue-jeans-clad actor. And, naturally, on the night of the dinner, Brando arrived at the greasy spoon the producer had selected neatly dressed in a suit and tie. Over the meal, Marlon and the producer warmed to each other and, at Brando's suggestion, they went for a hansom ride in Central Park. (Marlon insisted on driving the horse.) When they parted at dawn, they had discussed the world's affairs, but not a word about the film. (It was shelved until 1955, when it was made as a vehicle for James Dean.)

Shortly after he left the cast of *Streetcar*, French director Claude Autant-Lara made Marlon an intriguing offer. He wanted Brando to look over the European locations for his forthcoming film version of Stendhal's *The Red and the Black*, with an eye to appearing in said film; in exchange he would pay all expenses plus $350 weekly salary. His only stipulation was that Marlon stay on the "job" for at least three weeks, during which time he could consider night and day the possibility of appearing in the Stendhal film.

Marlon wasn't keen on the film project, but he liked the idea of a free European vacation. And so, late in June 1949, Edie took him down to the pier, got him aboard the right luxury liner, checked to see that he had his passport, waved good-bye, and then waited several weeks for a postcard.

None arrived. When Edie learned that Maynard Morris, the casting agent who had "discovered" Brando in summer stock, was shortly to leave on a European vacation, she asked him to keep an eye out for Marlon. Maynard promised he would.

One night he was walking around the Montmartre district in Paris when he heard someone yell, "Hey, Maynard!" Morris looked around, but all he saw was a line of *clochards* (the Parisian equivalent of Bowery bums) sitting against a wall. One of them got up and strode toward him. "Maynard, don't you recognize me? It's Marlon!"

Brando had abandoned Autant-Lara and moved in with a commune of French actors who helped him fritter away his savings. Then he had lost his passport, and had ended up begging. But, he told Morris, he was having a wonderful time. Maynard gave him some money and wired Edith Van Cleve about Marlon's whereabouts.

She immediately went to MCA president Lew Wasserman with Brando's predicament. Wasserman is a tolerant and astute man, notably low-pressured for an agency executive, but he was weary of Marlon's finicky attitude toward Hollywood. He told Miss Van Cleve that he had just read a script which seemed ideally suited to both Brando's talent and purposefulness. It was *The Men*, the story of a paraplegic war veteran's painful adjustment to civilian life. It had been offered to Marlon prior to his European trip, but he had turned it down without waiting to see a script. Wasserman said that if Brando would reconsider appearing in the film after reading a synopsis sent to him air mail, special delivery, he would then be prepared to send him his passage home. He would even pull strings to get him a new passport without undue red tape. Otherwise, he could remain with the *clochards* on the Left Bank. Edie relayed the message to Marlon.

Within a few days, he was on his way back to the States.

Though Marlon accepted *The Men* without having read the script, he was safe in assuming it would be a worthwhile film. Stanley Kramer, its producer, was Hollywood's latest young Turk, much admired for his liberal ideas and courageous picture-making. He made A movies on B budgets by using young players and economical directors. His films were melodramas in format, but they had "redeeming social importance"— punches and uplift, that was the Kramer formula. Some of his productions tackled subject matter previously unexplored by the big studios. (*Home of the Brave*, for example, treated racial prejudice in the armed forces.) As a result, he accumulated scrapbooks full of critical raves for his "elevation of the motion picture business."

Fred Zinnemann, director of *The Men*, was another rebel within the Hollywood studio system. In 1948, he made his mark with *The Search*, a compassionate account of Europe's displaced persons. Working along the lines laid down by the Italian neorealists, he shot the film in actual locations and mixed amateur actors with professionals. He planned to use the same method in *The Men*, which was to be filmed in and around a Los Angeles hospital with real-life paraplegics in supporting roles.

Brando's Broadway friends shook their heads when they heard he was going to Hollywood; he'll never come back, they said. Nonsense, Marlon answered. "I may do a picture now and again, but mostly I intend to work on the stage."

He announced he had chosen *The Men* because of its "social usefulness," but when a cynical interviewer asked about his $40,000 Hollywood salary, Marlon said, "I don't have the character to turn down such big money."

Most probably the remark was a put-on, for Marlon obviously prided himself on having had the character to withstand the lure of movie money until he found an honorable acting mission. Still, there was a grain of truth in what he said. Brando was acutely conscious of the value of money, though he didn't like people to know it. (Miss Van Cleve said he would walk out of the room whenever salary negotiations began.) The increasing number of zeros on his paycheck seemed both to please and embarrass him; in his own eyes they cast a shadow of doubt over his integrity. And his struggles to live as he had before he was famous, his clinging to old values and old friends, his fanatical distaste for any display of show-biz sham, all this is knotted up in his efforts to retain a sense of integrity.

Before leaving for the Coast, he joked at the mere idea of his becoming a superstar phony. "If I ever invite you to the MGM commissary," he told friends, "you're to cut me dead."

When he got off the train at Los Angeles' Alhambra station, the only superstar he resembled was Henry Fonda in *The Grapes of Wrath*. True, he was wearing his Sunday best, but his blue woolen suit had a hole in the knees and a large tear in the seat of the pants. The rest of his wardrobe—three pairs of blue jeans, three white T-shirts, and a set of leather-soled socks—were distributed between two suitcases that looked like props for "The Beverly Hillbillies."

He was met at the train by Jay Kanter, an MCA representative, who was so brainwashed by stories of Marlon's dress peculiarities that he checked to see if his charge was wearing shoes, which he was. Kanter had been personally selected by Lew Wasserman to shepherd Brando during his Hollywood visit. "He's going to need someone to watch over him out there," Edie Van Cleve told Wasserman. "He needs a steadying hand."

"I know just the person," Wasserman answered. "Jay Kanter—one of my assistants. He's young, he'll get along with Marlon. And he's a good trouble-shooter. If Marlon leaves his overcoat under some girl's bed, Jay'll know how to retrieve it."

Judging from surface appearances, Jay Kanter was an unlikely candidate to win Marlon's confidence. Handsome, suave, well-dressed to the point of being a Beau Brummell, he was patently a young man going places at precocious speed. "Where angels fear to tread, that's where you'd find Jay," a former MCA employee said. But aggressiveness was only one side of his personality. He was also charming, vital, refined; people liked and trusted him. So did Marlon. They became fast friends, and Kanter was to play a major role in shaping the disastrous middle period of Brando's career.

Also on hand to welcome Marlon to California was his aunt, Mrs. Betty Lindermeyer, a resident of Eagle Rock, one of the myriad suburbs that make up the Los Angeles sprawl. Though happy to see her nephew, she was taken aback when he announced he'd stay with her until he found a place of his own. She explained that the bungalow she and husband Oliver occupied was already overcrowded, but Marlon told her not to fuss, he'd flop on the living room divan. And that's where a very disgruntled Oliver found his famous in-law when he returned from work that night.

Soon the household was on the friendliest terms, though Marlon was not Emily Post's ideal guest. He rarely got around to eating dinner before two A.M. and turned down Mrs. Lindermeyer's substantial breakfasts for his usual raw egg and orange juice. Mostly he just snacked on "barrels of peanut butter" and large numbers of pomegranates, which he pierced and then held to his mouth and sucked. (After he left, the Lindermeyers spent days scouring pomegranate stains from walls, ceilings, and upholstery.) His relatives were staggered by his table manners. "He doesn't bring the food to his face," one of them said. "He brings his face to the food."

Marlon had arrived in California several weeks before the

October shooting date of *The Men* to take part in the extensive rehearsals that were a well-publicized part of every Kramer production. But once in Hollywood, he learned rehearsals would be delayed until he was introduced to the movie press. He balked, but Kramer taught him to toe the line.

"You ordered Marlon—you never asked," the producer said. "His rebellion snapped in a minute if you said, Damn it, be there at three o'clock."

Brando got there, all right, but he didn't say much. According to an eyewitness, when he met Hedda Hopper, he grunted exactly twice. (Brando later referred to Hopper as "the one with hats" to distinguish her from Louella Parsons, "the fat one.")

As the days passed and there was no rehearsal call, just interviews, Brando wearied of lazing around the Lindermeyer living room. He called Kramer and said he wanted to move in with the paraplegic patients at the Birmingham Veterans Hospital. "Fine," Kramer exclaimed. "That's what I've had in mind all along."

Brando settled accounts with the Lindermeyers—he remembered everything he owed, down to the last pomegranate—and moved to the hospital. There, for a month, he endured every facet of the paraplegics' bedridden existence; he practiced their exercises, immersed himself in their psychological problems, learned to manipulate a wheelchair. But his hardest task was to gain the acceptance of his wardmates.

Embittered by the shallow sympathy showered on them, the paraplegics looked on Marlon with suspicion; they wondered if he wasn't just another Hollywood "glamour boy." To test his sincerity, they devised an unremitting series of practical jokes. One afternoon, while Brando was resting on the type of hospital bed which can be rolled up at both ends, a patient cranked away until Marlon was tightly wedged between the upraised ends of the mattress, his knees doubled up under his chin.

As the patient wheeled himself from the deserted ward, he

yelled over his shoulder, "Now suffer, you miserable bastard, suffer!"

Every Saturday evening Brando and his hospital buddies repaired to a beer joint near the hospital. Once, as they sat at their usual table, they were accosted by a lady religious fanatic who promised that if they embraced the True Faith they might rise up and walk again.

A glint came into Marlon's eyes and he said, "You mean, if I believe, I'll be able to walk again?" Not waiting for an answer, he pushed back his chair and rose totteringly to his feet; then he dashed out the door and quickly returned with a stack of newspapers, which he peddled up and down the bar. "Now I can make a living again!" he rejoiced.

The men in the wheelchairs roared with laughter and, if any tension still existed between them and Brando, it vanished on the spot.

Marlon was less successful in winning the respect of his fellow cast members. Despite his feeling for the part and his long hours of study, he was ill at ease during rehearsals, and fell back on his old introverted mannerisms. Teresa Wright, Jack Webb, and the other actors grumbled that they couldn't hear him and had no idea of how to react to him in the final performance. Kramer was so apprehensive that on the eve of shooting he asked director Fred Zinnemann to take Marlon aside and instill some spirit into him.

Zinnemann guessed that Brando was insecure about making the transition from stage to screen acting. Later he said, "When Marlon has troubles, he likes to withdraw within himself. It's not easy to reach him . . . it can become quite a problem." Zinnemann sat up half the night with Brando, reassuring him, priming him on the technique of film acting, coaxing him into a relaxed frame of mind. And in the morning, his labors were amply rewarded.

The Men centered on paraplegic Ken Wilocek's relationship with Ellen, the girl he planned to marry before his injury. The first scene Zinnemann filmed was one in which Ellen comes to the hospital to persuade the hostile Ken to proceed with their wedding plans. It was a highly emotional moment which most directors would have staged later in the production, when the actors had warmed up to the camera. But from all reports save one, Brando was brilliant on the first take; the emotion missing in rehearsals now poured forth, stunning cast and crew, and moving Teresa Wright to tears. (The minority brief was filed by Marlon, who said he never "felt" the scene.)

From then on, Marlon was a paragon of cooperation. He always knew his lines, was never late on set, never required endless retakes. Only on the subject of costuming was he temperamental. He refused all studio suggestions for Ken's wardrobe and wore instead clothes he bought at a local army and navy store. These garments were appropriate for most of the film, but not for the wedding scene, in which Ken was to wear a conservative navy blue suit. Marlon repeatedly refused to discuss or be fitted for the suit. As a last resort, the Kramer office asked Mrs. Lindermeyer to see what she could do.

Somehow she managed to get Marlon inside a Beverly Hills department store, but once through the doors, he reverted to type. As they marched along the display cases, he leered like Groucho Marx at all the salesladies, and then, in an elevator, he whipped out a burning match and applied it to his woolen sweater. The childhood party trick retained its old punch; by the time the flame was extinguished, Mrs. Lindermeyer had her nephew out of the store and on his way home.

When he finished *The Men*, Marlon returned to New York for what looked like a permanent stay. For the first time, he leased an apartment of his own, in a well-kept building in the West Fifties, and furnished it in Swedish modern. Only the decor had changed, however; the cast of characters was the same as before.

Marlon's door was always open, whether he was at home or not, and anybody could drop by at any hour. There were always fifteen or twenty drifters loitering about. Some were killing time by reading the dailies; another group might be playing cards in a corner; and there was usually a girl practicing a dance, a comic trying out a routine, an actor learning his cues. Nobody seemed to know anybody else, and no one was looking for an introduction or conversation. Brando was the only common denominator.

Included in Marlon's irregular and scruffy salon were several students from the Actors Studio, a professional workshop founded by Elia Kazan and producer Cheryl Crawford late in 1947. Marlon was one of the original members, along with David Wayne, Tom Ewell, Karl Malden, Montgomery Clift, Patricia Neal, Maureen Stapleton, Eli Wallach, and forty-seven others. The school's original teachers were Kazan and another respected Broadway director, Robert Lewis. (A year or so later Lewis withdrew to concentrate on his own career, and was replaced by Lee Strasberg, who would claim that he played an important part in shaping Brando's early career. This, Marlon said repeatedly, was simply not so. The only teacher to whom he owed anything was Stella Adler, Strasberg's archrival. In retaliation, Strasberg used Brando as an example of the great actor destroyed by Hollywood and self-indulgence.) From its inception, the Studio was dedicated to promulgating the Stanislavsky system which the mass media soon publicized as the "Method."

There are as many definitions and interpretations of the Method as there are disciples of the system, but, put as simply as possible, it might be described as character-building from the inside out; the actor digs into his own experiences, memories, and emotions to duplicate those of the character he is playing. Hard to define, Method acting is easy to spot. The Method actor's performance almost always has a halting, verisimilar coloration, and usually looks like an imitation of Marlon Brando's early performances.

Since he was the first member of the group to reach prominence, Brando was heralded as the original Method actor, and his mannerisms became the totemic emblems by which the school of acting was identified. Each year hundreds of applicants flocked to the Studio to learn to scratch, slouch, and mumble just like Marlon. Though the Studio produced several individualistic actors, its most representative graduates (James Dean is an example) are those who latched on to the surface details of the Brando style (the delaying on cues, the false-start line readings, the suppressed emotion or violence), rode them to success, and leeched them nearly to exhaustion.

In point of fact, Brando is only nominally a product of the Actors Studio—his talent was mature and his style defined long before he began studying there. Moreover, his active membership was brief and his attendance always sporadic. "Though he had good feelings about the school," Kazan says, "Marlon was too erratic, too artistic to be tied down by a regular schedule."

During the run of *Streetcar*, he took part in several of the Studio's scene-study classes, and later staged a few scenes from Ibsen's *Hedda Gabler*. When he returned from filming *The Men*, Marlon took up his studies at the Studio with a momentary zeal that encouraged those who eagerly awaited his Broadway return.

Until then, his fans could see him on the screen of the Radio City Music Hall where *The Men* opened on July 20, 1950. The reviews were generally good, with deep bows accorded Kramer's humanitarian spirit. And arguably, this is his best production. Carl Foreman's script is free of easy pathos and melodrama (though heavy in contrivance and coincidence). The acting of the supporting cast is fine—even Teresa Wright is less whiny than usual. Zinnemann's direction is his usual mixed bag of virtues (taste, intelligence, sensitivity) and defects (stodginess, lack of imagination). His small triumph is in getting the real-life paraplegics to respond and react not to Brando, the man who lived with them for a month, but to Brando, the Ken Wilocek of the film.

The major critical reservations were about Brando's performance, or rather, about his "indistinct mumbling." One reviewer went so far as to speak of a "speech impediment." In keeping with these criticisms, a rumor circulated that Marlon's on-set mumbling forced scriptwriter Carl Foreman to change the main character's name from Williams to Wilocek, the assumption being that only Polish-Americans mouth their words.

From *The Men* to *The Godfather*, the press has printed a lot of nonsense about Brando's mumbling, so perhaps a few blunt facts are called for here, at the beginning of his film career. First, though his "natural" voice has a slightly muddy nasality, he does not mumble in real life unless ill at ease. (Brando once said, "In my own behavior with people, if I didn't trust or like someone I would either say nothing or mumble. I got to be awfully good at mumbling.") Secondly, in his work he never mumbles *unconsciously*; he adopts the woolly delivery only when it fits his character. Thirdly, he can be understood perfectly by any wide-awake spectator with good hearing and a grasp of the English language. If you miss a word here or there, it is because Brando is conveying emotional meaning, not words.

Brando's Ken Wilocek was a brilliant performance. Today, it is almost impossible to recapture the excitement one felt while watching Brando's first film appearance; too much of what was then innovative has been imitated to cliché, and Brando has become too familiar a screen presence for that first shock of recognition to retain its impact. At the time, it was like nothing one had seen before. This wasn't the creamy, homogenized style of Hollywood performance; this wasn't acting in which the jags of reality were honed away— they were still there, sharpened to stab out at the audience. While the raw nerve ends of Brando's playing fooled some people into believing he wasn't acting at all, or that he was acting himself, he was in fact giving a performance of great control and range. He stepped from delicate little moments filled with tiny shafts of insight and light to towering rages that left the audience blistered, keyed up with excitement.

Despite its brilliance, Marlon's performance in *The Men* didn't bring him an instant film following. Perhaps it was too original; perhaps it wasn't glamorous enough, though certainly he looked splendid. (Irene Selznick was right: his broken nose gave him that brute, Humphrey Bogart sexuality that separates the men from the Tyrone Power pretty boys.) Most likely, his impact was limited by the nature of the film. *The Men* didn't appeal to the kind of audience that takes a fanatical liking to a certain actor and thus turns him into a star.

It was the next film that would do that. Shortly after he returned to New York, it was announced that Brando would play Stanley Kowalski in the screen version of *A Streetcar Named Desire*. And, while *The Men* was still playing at the Music Hall, Marlon was packing his two battered grips to return to the West Coast.

·7·
FROM *STREETCAR* TO *ZAPATA*

Marlon Meets the Press: A Brief Scenario

Scene One: A room somewhere in Hollywood. Marlon is being interviewed by Sidney Skolsky-type reporter. "Mr. Brando, do you take a bath or shower?" Marlon thinks fast. "Neither. I spit way out in the air and then run under it." (It's an old burleycue line, but still good for a laugh.)

Cut to

Scene Two: Another room, another interview, another reporter. "Are you crazy, Mr. Brando?" Marlon smiles sweetly. "Only when the moon is full."

Black out. Fade in to

Scene Three: A third interview. A lady columnist enters and stares at Brando. "Why, you look almost like everybody else!" she chirps. Knowing a challenge when he hears it, Marlon walks to the nearest corner and stands on his head.

Slow dissolve to

Scene Four: Close-up of Marlon. He is speaking. ". . . Wish to announce my engagement to Denise Darcel, the French actress who . . ."

Very, very fast wipe.

And so went the opening rounds of Marlon's love-hate battle with the movie press. It began early in the summer of 1950 when he checked in at Warner Brothers for the filming of *A Streetcar Named Desire*. The docility with which he met the press for Kramer was a thing of the past, as was his former tongue-tied uncommunicativeness. Now he had plenty to say, particularly about Hollywood's wholesale invasion of privacy. "I have every right in the world to resist the insipid protocol of turning my life into the kind of running serial you find on bubble gum wrappers," he said. "You can't take sensitive parts of yourself and splatter them around like so much popcorn butter."

The Pop Art imagery of bubble gum and popcorn is typically Brando. His real-life dialogue is a pungent patter composed of prosaic but strikingly vivid childhood references, slightly sodden self-analysis. and blue prep school humor. He can be very earthy. Once, while he was being interviewed in Paris at the Prince de Galles Hotel, a waiter spilled hot coffee on his lap. Brando yelped with pain and then turned to the interviewer and said, "I'll write the headline for this article: Brando Scalds Balls at Prince de Galles."

Considering Brando's contempt for gossip-mongering, he would have been well advised to ban all interviews. He didn't. Instead, he kidded the humorless Hollywood reporters by living up to their worst preconceptions: he was rude, uncooperative, vulgar, and funny. The press, of course, loved it; his insolent ripostes made more colorful copy than any straight answer he might have given, and, in working him over, the columnists outdid each other in coining catchpenny epithets. He was "the Brilliant Brat," "the Hoodlum Harlequin," "a Dostoevsky version of Tom Sawyer." Topping them all was *Time*, which announced, "Where John Barrymore was the Great Profile, Rudolph Valentino the Sheik, Clark Gable the King, Marlon Brando is the Slob."

The more Marlon inveighed against the stupidity of the attention paid him, the more copy he received. He got so much space in the columns that people claimed his disdain for publicity was in fact the clever pose of a publicity-crazed actor. And certainly some of the oddball episodes in Brando's life are open to this charge.

There was, for example, Russell, the most famous raccoon in world history. Exactly when and how Russell entered Marlon's life is unknown, but he was already on the scene back in the Broadway days.

Russell shared an apartment with Marlon and Wally Cox, until Cox decided that three was a crowd. The raccoon had an irksome habit of biting people while they slept and, after being nibbled from head to toe, Cox gave Brando an ultimatum: Russell must be caged at night, or else Cox was moving out. A few days later, Cox took new lodgings.

Brando fed Russell fish. "Watch this!" he said to a friend. He threw the raccoon a fresh bass, then turned on the cold-water spigot in the bathroom sink. Russell scampered in, climbed up on the basin, held the fish under the running water, and delicately tore off tidbits of his dinner until he had devoured the entire fish. "Isn't he smart?" exclaimed Marlon proudly.

Marlon adored the furry creature. "Russell is not only my best friend, he's also my mistress," he said. And he took the raccoon everywhere—to the studio, to dinner parties, to his girlfriends' homes.

Why shouldn't he have a raccoon as a friend, Marlon indignantly asked suspicious reporters. And there was no good reason why he shouldn't, except that raccoons, like cheetahs, pythons, and aardvarks, don't make the most affectionate pets.

Russell was a pesky beast with a talent for indoor sprinting. He streaked around Marlon's living room, smashing into furniture and walls and vandalizing upholstery and curtains with his claws. The debris was something fierce. One day a delivery man arrived at Brando's home with a vacuum cleaner. He took one look at Russell's wreckage and said, "Brother, you need a dump truck, not a vacuum cleaner!"

At the studio, Russell was a real scene-stealer. He ran around the set, knocked over lights, scratched actress Jean Peters's cheek, tore her dress, ripped apart the leather seats of her new convertible. As a result, he got more press coverage than Miss Peters, whom Twentieth Century-Fox had spent five years in grooming for stardom. A studio spokesman told Marlon that from then on Russell must be confined to the actor's dressing room. Brando complied sulkily, and shortly thereafter Russell vanished from the Hollywood scene.

(His end was a happy one. Home in Illinois for a family visit, Marlon let Russell run loose out of doors. The animal promptly went into semihibernation; when his sluggishness passed, so had all his tiny vestiges of civilization. Marlon decided to let him run wild. "I didn't want to break his spirit," he explained.)

Though Brando often claimed to dislike the media's depiction of him as a swaggering stud, he was at least partly responsible for this image. "I can knock off any dame in a couple of hours," he told an interviewer. And he wasn't above staging a noisy, romantic encounter for eavesdroppers. During the filming of *Streetcar*, Shelley Winters dropped by the set to visit her old friend and (according to Miss Winters's autobiography) one-time lover. As soon as he saw her, Brando grabbed her by the arm and dragged her to his portable dressing room, locking the door behind them. "For God's sake, scream!" he whispered, as he shook the walls of the trailer. "Don't you want to help me build my reputation? Scream!"

If Brando did help manufacture the hoopla over his personal life, he was doing himself a disservice. Though the stories about his funky carryings-on made him the most talked-about newcomer in years, they also deflected attention from his considerable acting achievements, turned him into just another personality star, and obscured the conscientiousness with which he pursued his profession. In the early magazine articles there was always the suggestion that he was "difficult," whereas his earliest directors remember him as punctual, efficient, cooperative. When asked recently whether he had ever had any complaints about Brando, Elia Kazan answered, "Complaints, no! *Gratitude*, yes. Marlon always gave me more than I asked. He always gave me more than one hundred percent of himself."

Brando went about the set of *Streetcar* with a black rubber spider which he surreptitiously draped on the shoulders of his terrified lady co-players. Otherwise, he was all business. This was too important an assignment to jeopardize by horsing around.

At first there was some friction with Karl Malden, repeating his Broadway role of Mitch. During the early rehearsals of the poker game scene, Marlon kept horsing around and stepping on most of Malden's lines. "He was the star," Malden said, "and he could get away with it. But he was also a nice guy and probably wasn't thinking of what he was doing to my part. I put it to him straight. I said, 'You've got fifty sides [pages of dialogue] and can toss them away and still register. If I lose one of mine, I've got nothing.' Marlon understood right away. 'I never thought of it that way,' he said. And when that sequence was shot, I got more than was coming to me."

Contrary to popular theory, it is often difficult for an actor to film a role he has played hundreds of times on the stage. He must cut through the layers of tedious repetition to locate the original spark of his performance, and achieve old goals through the new and very different means of the camera. In *Streetcar*, Brando had the added challenge of relating to a new Blanche, and one who was, if not a better actress, a more forceful personality than Jessica Tandy.

Vivien Leigh, who played the role in the sensationalized and unsuccessful London production of *Streetcar*, was always director Elia Kazan's first choice for the movie Blanche, but originally she turned down the offer because she didn't want to leave England. Second choice was Olivia de Havilland, and for a while it looked as if Melanie Wilkes would replace Scarlett O'Hara as Blanche Du Bois. In the nick of time, Miss Leigh reconsidered. Laurence Olivier, her husband, was coming to America to make *Carrie* (based on Theodore Dreiser's novel *Sister Carrie*), and, since she would be accompanying him, she was available to play Blanche.

There's an irony in this: if Laurence Olivier hadn't decided to make a clinker of a movie at Paramount (strictly for the money), screen audiences would be deprived of Vivien Leigh's Blanche, unquestionably the actress's greatest film performance.

Her Blanche Du Bois is the definitive portrayal of unhinged feminine frailty. In a blonde wig styled far too young for her and wearing softly scented chiffon gowns (you can almost smell the jasmine), she looks like a demented caricature of lost, lyrical beauty—Lillian Gish gone totally berserk. By turns she is coy, wistful, meddlesome, exquisite, pitiful, and much more. At the end, when she accepts the asylum warden's arm and speaks her fabled line, "I have always depended on the kindness of strangers," she transcends the melodramatic overtones of the script and lends it true tragic resonance.

She also gives Blanche a tiny spine of strength—this Blanche has teeth and nails and venom. Shrieking and spitting abuse (listen to the way she seethes, "Flamingo? No! The Tarantula Arms, that's where I brought my victims!"), Miss Leigh makes a formidable match for Brando, and he quickens to the challenge.

If anything, he betters his stage performance as Kowalksi. There is a theatrical aura about both his and Miss Leigh's playing which disturbs some viewers, but this is entirely appropriate to the heightened realism of Williams's drama. Both performances are definitive—they are not likely ever to be equaled, let alone surpassed. There's an edge of crude wit to Brando's portrayal, as well as a strange lyric intensity and (particularly in the scenes with Stella) a vulnerability. This may not be the Stanley Kowalski Williams originally envisioned, but Brando's alterations work to the play's advantage.

To a man, the trade journalists predicted that *Streetcar* was a sweep-in to win all the Oscars, particularly in the acting categories. Brando was the odds-on favorite for Best Actor by a wide majority. Therefore, on the night of the Awards, when Humphrey Bogart was announced winner for his performance in *The African Queen*, there was a gasp of surprise, followed by exultant applause; and suddenly it appeared as if no one wanted Marlon to carry Oscar home. (The next day one wag wrote that if Brando had won the Award, he'd probably have used it to scratch Russell's back.)

The snub to Marlon was the more conspicuous since Vivien Leigh, Kim Hunter, and Karl Malden were honored with awards for their work in *Streetcar*. Elia Kazan lost to George Stevens *(A Place in the Sun)* and, in another upset, *An American in Paris* won best picture.

There were several schools of thought about Brando's defeat. One group contended that Bogart won for sentiment or for the cumulative strength of a long string of good performances in the past. Another theory was that the Academy voters were reluctant to lionize an actor who continually talked about returning to the stage. But most people believed it was Brando's maverick disdain for Hollywood that did him in.

Despite the rumors of wild parties and illicit carryings-on, Hollywood in the early 1950s was a small town with a social and moral code as rigid as that of Scarsdale or the Main Line. There were things that were done and not done. When you were making $75,000 a picture (Brando's salary for *Streetcar*) you didn't live in a rented bungalow; you took a villa in Beverly Hills or Bel Air. You didn't wear denims or a blue suit shiny from overpressing; you didn't date secretaries or cocktail waitresses; you didn't eat alone at the Parrot's Cage, a West Hollywood beanery. And if you did do these things, you kept them to yourself.

But Marlon talked, and the film colony wasn't going to give him an award for his candor. Hollywood didn't believe his one-man rebellion was for real; there was everywhere the suspicion that his put-down of the movie *poseurs* was itself a pose as phony as any he was reacting against.

Maybe, maybe not. Dorothy Parker once told an anecdote about walking down a street in Hollywood and seeing an arm lazing out a Rolls-Royce window; the arm was beminked and bejeweled, and its beautifully manicured fingers held a half-eaten bagel. Brando's blue jeans, secretary dates, and Parrot's Cage meals were like that lady's bagel—a reminder that there was something real to chew when the tinsel came too near.

Brando's need for real values sent him back to New York and old friends after each film, a pattern he followed for some years to come. All during the making of *Streetcar* he talked about returning to the stage and the Actors Studio. And true to his word, as soon as the film was finished, he came East; gave his regards to Broadway, bought Edie Van Cleve an orange juice at Schraffts, and told friends about his next film assignment.

It was *Viva Zapata!*, an elaborate biography of Emiliano Zapata, the half-Indian farmer who led the 1910 Mexican peasants' revolt against dictator Porfirio Díaz. Elia Kazan was to direct a screenplay by novelist John Steinbeck, a long-time aficionado of Mexican civilization with a special empathy for Zapata, one of the twentieth century's forgotten heroes.

There was never any question about who was to play Zapata. "I put the project in motion when I learned that Steinbeck was eager to write about Zapata," Kazan says. "But I wouldn't have done so without Marlon for the leading role." And there was never much doubt that Brando would accept this assignment, which promised to sweat from its load of social significance. Steinbeck and Kazan were both politically committed artists; they assuredly wouldn't turn Zapata into an enchilada horse bandit like the Pancho Villa played by Wallace Beery in the 1934 *Viva Villa!*

Viva Zapata! was a daring film to be produced in the Red-scared Hollywood of the 1950s. The House Un-American Activities Committee (HUAC) began investigating Communist infiltration of the movie industry in 1947, an inquisition which spread fear, trembling, and treachery throughout the film community. In the hearings, past and present members of the Communist party were asked to confess their political pasts. Those who refused were sent to prison. Some witnesses freely admitted their Communist affiliation, but refused to inform on their friends, as HUAC requested. They, too, went to jail. Among those imprisoned were such talented men as Dashiell Hammett, Ring Lardner, Jr., Dalton Trumbo, John Howard Lawson, and Albert Maltz.

The industry perfected its own form of punishment: it blacklisted any employee identified in HUAC testimony as a possible Communist. And the major studios rejected any subject that didn't take a positive view of American life. Because it eulogized a hero of the Mexican Revolution, *Viva Zapata!* was wide open to charges of Red propaganda, but Kazan was able to convince Twentieth Century-Fox that the film would be staunchly anti-Communist.

Originally Kazan planned to work on location in Mexico, but he ran up against Good Neighbor opposition. "When the story of Zapata is filmed in Mexico, it will be written and directed by a Mexican and financed by Mexico," a government spokesman said.

The unofficial reason for refusal was government disapproval of Steinbeck's script.

Banished north of the border, Kazan scoured southern Texas for reasonable facsimiles of the scenery of Cuernavaca, Tlaquiltenango, Quila Mula, and the other important towns of the Mexican Revolution. He chose Roma, Texas, a Spanish-American village with a picture-postcard church, adobe buildings, and houses adorned with wrought-iron decorations.

The *Zapata* company began filming in Roma in the spring of 1950. With the exception of Jean Peters (Zapata's wife) and Anthony Quinn (Zapata's brother), the cast was composed entirely of New York actors (which automatically made the film a "class" production). As soon as they felt the sweltering sun of Texas, many of them wished they were back on Broadway. Some days it was 120 degrees in the shade; the heat melted makeup, mascara, and the glue on wigs and mustaches.

Marlon suffered the most, since his was the most elaborate makeup. Before starting the film, he studied portraits of Zapata, and, to enhance his resemblance to the Mexican leader, he flared his nostrils with plastic rings, taped his eyelids, and wore brown contact lenses. The makeup caused him great physical discomfort, and was to bring him little critical praise—too Oriental-looking, said the reviewers. They were totally wrong. Like all Brando's false faces, his Zapata disguise is brilliant; he bears an uncanny resemblance to the Zapata of Diego Rivera's famous portrait.

Marlon's drive for realism brought him into conflict with the wardrobe department. Though Kazan ordered the extras to rub hands, face, and clothes with dirt before facing the cameras, Brando was asked to wear a white ensemble that looked like it had just come off the racks of an Acapulco boutique. He protested, but Kazan insisted he wear the costume. Marlon put it on, muttering under his breath, and then wandered off. When he returned, just in time to film his scene, he was covered head to foot in mud. "I slipped," he said. The ruse didn't work; the scene was postponed until the costume was cleaned.

There were other delays during the location shooting of *Zapata*. Jean Peters came down with dysentery, Brando injured his right knee while on horseback, Russell was around and causing daily havoc, and there were the nude swimmers. Roma, Texas, is on the Rio Grande, the river which forms a boundary between the United States and Mexico. Whenever the company was shooting near the river, a group of Mexicans gathered on their side of the Grande and, as soon as the camera began rolling, they stripped off their clothes, jumped into the water, and swam into camera range. No one was quite sure whether this was political protest or a bid for Hollywood stardom, but Kazan had to appeal to the Mexican authorities to stop further performances by the naked swimmers.

Anthony Quinn has said that in *Zapata* his knock-down, drag-out fight with Marlon was the real thing. Quinn had replaced Brando in the Broadway production of *Streetcar*, and there was a small core of theatergoers who insisted he was the better Kowalski. Quinn agreed—modesty is not one of his strong points. "I thought I'd play Zapata," the Mexican-born actor recalled, "and was really angry when I found out that the part had gone to Brando."

The fight scene was shot several times, and still Kazan wasn't satisfied. Calling a break, the director went over to Brando and whispered in his ear, looking in Quinn's direction. Then Kazan went over to Quinn and said Brando was jealous because he'd gotten better reviews in *Streetcar* and was going to use the scene to work off his aggression. As a result, the two actors went at each other with realistic gusto.

Several Mexicans were employed for extra and bit roles in *Zapata*, and one of them was to become very important to Marlon. She was Movita (née Maria Luisa Castenada), a professional actress who played Clark Gable's Tahitian girlfriend in the 1935 version of *Mutiny on the Bounty*. (She was seventeen at the time.) Afterward, she appeared in a few other American films, but her parts got progressively smaller with each new appearance.

Movita's roles rarely required her to do more than slink around in a sarong or a serape, so there is no way of knowing whether she could act or not. And her beauty is not everyone's cup of tequila; it's the ripe, overblown rose-of-the-rancho look, the kind that suggests flamenco flounces, castanets, and torn peasant blouses. But Marlon took to her at first sight. When the company returned to Hollywood to finish shooting the film at Twentieth Century-Fox's Malibu ranch, Movita went along and moved into Marlon's rented bungalow.

No Hollywood romance—not even Garbo's with Cecil Beaton or Katharine Hepburn's with Spencer Tracy—was ever so successfully hidden from the prying eyes of the movie columnists. The couple appeared in public only occasionally—once they showed up at the opening of the Los Angeles Ice Follies, and a few gossip columnists reported that Movita was sporting a big diamond engagement ring—but usually they saw no one but a few discreet friends. And, unlike some of the women in Brando's life, Movita never capitalized on the romance to further her career. She was content to remain hidden in the shadows of Marlon's private life.

*   *   *

When *Viva Zapata!* opened in February 1953, it was already a subject of controversy. A month earlier Kazan had testified before the House Un-American Activities Committee that he had been a member of the Communist party between 1934 and 1936. Following this admission, he reviewed his entire career to prove that it was clean of Communist propaganda (*Zapata* was cited as "an anti-Communist film") and, at a later hearing, he reportedly identified several friends as card-carrying Communists.

After his testimony, Kazan placed a paid advertisement in the New York *Times* which read in part: "Secrecy serves the Communists. At the other pole, it serves those who are interested in silencing liberal voices. The employment of a lot of good liberals is threatened because they have allowed themselves to become associated with or silenced by the Communists. Liberals must speak out."

Few of Kazan's friends agreed with this self-justification. The director was widely denounced for his cooperation with HUAC, and several of his former collaborators refused to work with him again. Brando was not one of them. Despite his liberal turn of mind, he took no stand against HUAC's "friendly witnesses" (those who "named names") and was to work with many of them in the next few years. Of course, he was not personally involved, but many people he knew suffered from the witch-hunting. Mady Christians, the star of *I Remember Mama*, committed suicide after appearing before HUAC; John Garfield died from a heart attack a few days before his scheduled appearance; and Brando's sister Jocelyn was blacklisted for innocently supporting a Communist-front organization.

While no one discussed *Zapata* in the light of Kazan's HUAC confession, it may well have been responsible for the film's cool reception. It did make a few ten-best lists, won Brando an Academy Award nomination and Anthony Quinn the Oscar as best supporting actor, but most critics were disappointed. The film has no political content to speak of, being neither Communist nor anti-Communist, though its dialogue is a kind of waxwork museum, filled with all the stock liberal clichés of the 1930s. Steinbeck's script is bombastic, episodic, and presents Zapata as one of those noble peasants who wrinkles his forehead to show he is deep,thinking such ponderous thoughts as "Power to the People."

He tries, but there's not much Brando can do with the characterization. He gets through the film on sheer magnetism—and what magnetism! There hasn't been such a display of self-aware male beauty since Rudolph Valentino peacocked his way through the 1924 *Monsieur Beaucaire*. Kazan's pretentious imagery (one continuous quotation from Sergei Eisenstein's *Que Viva Mexico!*) shrivels as soon as the mind receives it, but Brando's face with the drooping, eloquently soulful mustache is alive and vivid years later.

·8·

FRIENDS, ROMANS, MOTORCYCLISTS

ET TU, KOWALSKI? trumpeted a trade journal headline.

MUMBLE MARLON TAKES STAB AT CAESAR, jeered another show-biz publication.

The announcement that Brando was going to play Marc Antony in Shakespeare's *Julius Caesar* gave Hollywood's resident wits a field day. They stumbled Kowalski-like through snatches of "Friends, Romans, countrymen," and stripped imaginary togas off their backs in parody of the T-shirt shorn from Stanley at the end of *Streetcar*.

Only a few of the industry's pundits were perceptive enough to realize that Brando as Antony—Cleopatra's inamorato, in some accounts Julius Caesar's lover—was a shrewd stroke of casting. Undrape him in the flimsiest toga and no one would notice that his elocution wasn't as pear-shaped as the academicians might like.

Brando was apprehensive about accepting this assignment. He had played Shakespeare only in his student days, and he wondered if he possessed vocal resources and training to tackle Elizabethan drama in a larger, professional arena.

Before undertaking the role of Antony, Brando made several Shakespearean recordings at a New York sound studio, and listened attentively while the results were played back. Apparently he liked what he heard; he immediately signed for the film.

A few days later he told a reporter, "No matter how it turns out, I can chalk up my performance as valuable experience."

He took the challenge very seriously. Before production of *Julius Caesar* began in August 1952, he was scheduled for intensive study with Leon Ceparro, MGM's singing teacher, and Gertrude Folger, the studio speech coach. (Miss Folger, a white-haired, birdlike spinster from Boston, got the full charm treatment from Marlon, and remembered him affectionately as "a sweet, thoughtful boy," always sure to send her a Christmas card.) Prior to this professional tutelage, Brando rehearsed alone; he bought a tape recorder and, sequestered up in his New York apartment, he taped, erased, and retaped Antony's speeches. By the time he left for Hollywood, he had definite ideas about how he should "sound" in his grandiloquent scenes.

On his way to the West Coast, he stopped off to see his parents in Illinois. Mr. Brando had invested Marlon's money (as well as his own and some of Miss Van Cleve's) in a cattle farm, the Penny Poke Ranch, located in Broken Bow, Nebraska. (The "Penny" in "Penny Poke" came from Mrs. Brando's maiden name, Pennebaker. Broken Bow sounds like the locale of a Hopalong Cassidy Western, but was authentic.) Marlon hadn't yet seen the ranch, and this stopover marked the occasion of his first visit to his thousand head of cattle.

During the drive to the ranch, Marlon sat in the back of the car rehearsing the "Friends, Romans, countrymen" funeral oration. He had decided that, since Antony delivered the speech to a human wall of Roman plebeians, the sound of his voice would rebound off the crowd and surge back to deafen him. To simulate this effect, he shouted the Shakespearean monologue into a pillow held close to his face. At first the Brandos were struck by the originality of this concept, but, as they approached Broken Bow and muffled blank verse was still heard from the back seat, they wished the pillow was a muzzle.

At the ranch, Marlon continued his vocal exercises. He'd go off to the endmost reaches of the grazing range and keen out his funeral speech to a lazing audience of cattle and tumbleweeds.

Meanwhile, in Hollywood, MGM was working overtime to make *Julius Caesar* the prestige production of the decade. The film was the brainchild of producer John Houseman, an august, doughty-looking gentleman with the stiff formality typical of old guard British theatrical tradition. (He addressed actors as "sir" or by the names of their characters, an affectation that irritated most American players.) In the late thirties, he produced the famous Orson Welles–Mercury Theater modern dress version of *Julius Caesar*, and that production, plus a critically acclaimed *King Lear* (starring Louis Calhern as Lear, Nina Foch as Cordelia, and Jo Van Fleet as Regan), earned him the epithet "distinguished Shakespearean producer and director." The accolade provokes skeptical laughter in certain theatrical circles.

An actor cast in Houseman's production of *Coriolanus* was puzzled by a Shakespearean archaism and asked the producer for an explanation. Houseman struggled with the offending piece of dialogue for a moment, and then said, "I don't understand it either, so we'll just cut it."

It's a rather cavalier solution to the problems of Shakespearean scholarship, but it gave a clean, untangled surface to Houseman's productions. And clarity was undoubtedly the paramount goal in reshaping the text of *Julius Caesar* for the screen.

Having lost a quarter of a million dollars on its last flirtation with Shakespeare, the ostentatious 1936 *Romeo and Juliet*, MGM was very leery about the financial gamble of this new $2,000,000 project, and was using every known production gimmick to bolster box office appeal. There would be stars (James Mason, Louis Calhern, Edmond O'Brien, Greer Garson, Deborah Kerr), elaborate sets, a wide-screen process, and stereophonic sound to sugar-coat the Shakespeare pill. And, as helmsman, the studio selected Joseph Mankiewicz, a four-time Academy Award winner with a down-to-earth approach to filmmaking.

"I'm the oldest whore on the block," Mankiewicz often boasts, and one can't entirely disagree. He's lived profitably through the B. P. Schulberg regime at Paramount, the Louis B. Mayer czardom at MGM, the Darryl F. Zanuck reign at Twentieth Century-Fox, the $34,000,000 coronation of Elizabeth Taylor as *Cleopatra*—a career record that undoubtedly included a few stints of artistic prostitution.

In person, Mankiewicz comes on like a stand-up comic; he purrs and deadpans his way through a dizzying series of quick, clever one-liners. He can be very funny, and so are many of his films *(All About Eve, A Letter to Three Wives)*. The industry considers him a "brilliant dialogue director," which is a polite way of saying his movies often tend to be excessively talkative.

Though not a Broadway veteran, Mankiewicz has been a theater buff since his childhood; his conversation is filled with backstage gossip about the fabled and esoteric stars of theatrical history. He's fascinated by the psychology of the actor and prides himself on his easy working relationship with such supposedly difficult types as ˙Bette Davis, Ava Gardner, Rex Harrison—and Marlon Brando.

Mankiewicz is a close friend of Jessica Tandy and her husband, Hume Cronyn, and was a frequent visitor to her dressing room during the run of *Streetcar*. He met Marlon then and, taken with the young actor's offbeat behavior and extraordinary talent, he filed away the idea of using Brando in some future film project. It was his decision to cast Marlon as Antony and, while most of the MGM executives looked upon this casting as a publicity coup, Mankiewicz was confident that Brando would play the role brilliantly.

Mankiewicz's appreciation of fine acting led him to cast John Gielgud as Cassius, the chief conspirator in Caesar's assassination. One of the noblest of Britain's titled actors, Gielgud is especially revered for the bravura precision of his vocal technique. Cadaverously thin, with the sharp, deceptively benign features of a hooded falcon, he was the ideal "lean and hungry" Cassius, and the role had brought him enormous acclaim on the British stage.

Hollywood society preened itself for Gielgud's visit, the social occasion of the season; in anticipation, the Beverly Hills hostesses decanted the sherry, dressed up the poolside buffets with the best silver and damask, and dusted off the butler from central casting. Brando was as excited as everyone else, but he didn't attend any of the galas; he wasn't interested in chatting with Gielgud, he wanted to watch him act.

As soon as rehearsals began, Marlon haunted the set, surreptitiously appearing whenever Gielgud was scheduled to read a scene. Once he asked the Englishman to record two of Antony's speeches on his tape recorder. Gielgud accepted, and was astonished to find Brando's dressing room a littered library of tapes and recordings of Laurence Olivier, John Barrymore, Maurice Evans, and Ralph Richardson. Marlon explained that he was studying these records to improve his diction.

"Brando's very deferential to me," Gielgud wrote to a friend. "He's a funny, intense, egocentric boy. . . . He's very nervous and mutters his lines and rehearses by himself all day long. . . . I think his sincerity may bring him to an interesting performance. His English is not at all bad . . . but I think he has very little sense of humor."

Later Marlon asked Gielgud to advise him on the interpretation of a speech. Gielgud was reluctant to poach on what was clearly the director's terrain, but when Mankiewicz approved the tutelage, he readily coached Brando.

"Marlon's difficulty was that he didn't really know the whole play," Gielgud said. "But he was very quick . . . I talked to him for a couple of hours, and the next morning he came down to work, and he'd put in everything I'd suggested, and executed it most skillfully. I wasn't in any other scenes with him and the director never asked me to interfere again, and Marlon didn't ask me, so I didn't like to press it. I don't know whether I could have helped him."

One day, Gielgud asked Brando, "Why don't you play Hamlet?" Coming from one of the great Hamlets of the twentieth century, the question itself was a compliment.

Marlon was taken aback. After a moment, he asked hesitantly, "Would you direct me?"

"Yes," Gielgud answered. But nothing came of the project. "I think Marlon felt he had too much to lose," Gielgud later said with obvious regret.

After *Julius Caesar* opened, several critics were so impressed by Brando's Antony that they, too, suggested he think about Hamlet. Marlon wouldn't commit himself. "I think when an actor plays Hamlet, it somehow puts a period to his career," he said. "There are too many other things I want to do and a lot of things I still have to learn before I try that."

Besides double-talk (*Hamlet* is a turning point in most actors' careers, not a swan song), there's also sane self-judgment in Marlon's remarks. It's no easy jump from Antony to Hamlet, especially when the Antony is as middling as Brando's. Visually, it's a striking performance: he struts and sulks through the film in such splendor that his prosy line readings go unnoticed—the first time around. Watch the movie again, pay attention to his vocal delivery, and the big speeches sound monotonous; they're played on one continuous note of fiery conviction, with little attention to Shakespeare's meter or emphasis.

Brando was bedeviled by vocal problems during the production. Shouting through take after take, he lost his voice several times, and thus played havoc with Mankiewicz's tight shooting schedule. Mankiewicz had hoped to finish the film in three weeks, but it took considerably longer. While waiting for Brando to recover, the director killed time by photographing crowd scenes and the glories of MGM's recreated Roman forum.

(The decor received heaps of praise and won an Academy Award for best art direction. But the final word on these settings came from Vittorio De Sica, the great Italian director and actor. While visiting MGM, he walked down one of the Roman streets constructed for *Caesar*. "Ah, what realism!" he murmured. "It looks exactly like modern-day Ferrara!")

A knowledgeable Shakespearean director (there was no such creature in Hollywood) might have guided Marlon toward a more resourceful and colorful reading of the role, but Mankiewicz was quite pleased with Brando's Antony; it suited his forthright, uninflected interpretation of the play. The two men got along well, and for a while Mankiewicz harbored the hope of directing Marlon in another Shakespearean film.

In the late 1960s, Mankiewicz met Brando at a party. "Why don't you get yourself in shape and we'll do *Macbeth*," the director said.

A gleam came into Marlon's eye. "Do you think I could do it?"

"Yes," Mankiewicz answered. "But you'd have to go into training." Marlon grinned.

And that's the last anyone has heard about Marlon Brando and Maggie Smith in Joe Mankiewicz's *Macbeth*.

During the filming of *Julius Caesar*, Brando was unusually cooperative about granting interviews to promote the film, but he often played games with his interviewers. Sometimes, when a reporter phoned to schedule an appointment, Marlon answered in the Chicano accent he had perfected for *Zapata* that Señor Brando had left yesterday for Tasmania.

Marlon is notorious for his telephone disguises; his phony accent has ranged from Japanese through German to Italian, depending on the nationality of his current film role. He also likes to travel incognito. Wearing a snap-brim hat, dark glasses, and trench coat, he's been seen checking in at hotels as Lord Greystoke, Tarzan's ancestral name.

Once they had penetrated Marlon's disguise, the interviewers got their appointments, but there were more charades to come. Brando took one writer for a hair-raising spin on the Los Angeles freeway and then for a sunbath at Muscle Beach. The reporter got lots of sand up his pants (Marlon forgot the beach towels) but nothing new or sensational to tell his readers. Brando now had a portfolio of anecdotes about his past— Shattuck, the Lunts, Russell the raccoon, the Birmingham Veterans Hospital—and he thumbed through it whenever an interviewer pried into his current personal life. A reporter who met Brando while he was being fitted for a toga did happen upon one previously unknown intimate detail: Marlon wore purple bikini-style undershorts.

In 1952–53, Brando was living in a rented ranch house near the Pacific Palisades. By then Russell was running wild through the Illinois countryside, and only Movita was around to keep Marlon company. This San Andreas romance had its full share of seismic upheavals, but the quakes left Marlon and his señorita with their feet still on the ground, and no one the wiser for all the emotional stress. It was, as it had been since its beginning, a very private affair. On the few occasions Marlon appeared in public, he was alone and often moving so fast no one recognized him.

For several years, Marlon had been a motorcycle enthusiast. Back in his Broadway days, he used to weave madly through the crawling Manhattan traffic on his sleek chrome two-wheeler, arriving at the stage door just in time to don his makeup and costume. Now he had taken to tearing around Los Angeles on his motorbike, dressed in the leather and chain style typical of cyclist speed addicts. Occasionally, he stopped at a squalid juke joint frequented by *pachucos*, the California-Mexican variety of juvenile delinquent. To stay in the bartender's good graces, he'd order straight whiskeys, pretend he was drinking them and then, when no one was looking, he'd pour the rotgut on the sawdust floor.

One night, the Los Angeles narcotics squad raided the café and lined up the most likely pushers and addicts. In the confusion, Marlon was swept along with them. The police frisked him, checked his arms for needle marks, and then released him, apparently unaware of his movie-star identity.

Marlon's latest surge of motorcycle mania was part of his preparation for a new film, *The Wild One*, which began shooting early in 1953. The movie was based on a real-life incident which took place on July 4, 1947, in Hollister, California: a group of four thousand motorcyclists marauded into the small town, camped down for the night, and tore the place apart before leaving the next day.

At first, Brando was enthusiastic about the film. "There are so many kids who are confused today," he said, "and the problem hasn't yet been intelligently articulated in entertainment." He hoped *The Wild One* would explore the reasons "why young people tend to bunch into groups that seek expression in violence."

The picture did not live up to his expectations, as he himself later admitted. He cited it as one of the biggest disappointments of his career. It was produced by Stanley Kramer, whose position in the Hollywood hierarchy had dropped considerably since the days of *The Men*. His last few films had been critical and financial flops, and he was harassed by front-office interference by his distribution company, Columbia Pictures. These business problems kept Kramer from supervising the preproduction planning of *The Wild One* with the scrupulous attention he had expended on his earlier films.

The Wild One doesn't examine youthful violence—it makes it look like fun. In the film's most famous sequence, Brando is struggling inarticulately to get to first base with a very proper waitress who is frightened by his leather and his iron insignia. "Man, you're too square," he tells her. "I have to straighten you out. You don't go to any one special place . . . you just *go* . . . the idea is to whale, to make some jive. . . . Do you know what I'm talking about? . . . you got to *whale*."

Most kids who watched the movie didn't know exactly what he meant—there's a legend that Marlon improvised most of his dialogue—but whatever "whaling" was, it sure sounded more exciting than finishing high school or holding down some dumb job. As a result, *The Wild One* swiftly became a cult film for teenagers, a status that led to its being severely censured by concerned citizens for its promulgation of "antisocial behavior among the young."

The film's penultimate sequence shows Brando being brutally beaten by a gang of motorcycle samurai. *Crunch, zam, zap* go the fists into Marlon's gut, and yet he still finds the breath to taunt, "Come on you guys! My old man hits harder than that!" It was both the ultimate gay S&M fantasy, and the first of those punishing, masochistic finales which conclude so many Brando films—"the obligatory messianic scene," as one critic has written.

One of the first American movies to strike gold by depicting the glamour of brutality, *The Wild One* is also the progenitor of that sleazy motorcycle genre that proliferated during the late fifties and sixties, and which reached its zenith with *Easy Rider*. It's strictly a B movie, but it's earned a footnote in any film history book.

Shortly after finishing *The Wild One*, Brando told reporters he might retire after one more film, maybe *Pal Joey*. (The movie wasn't made until 1957, when Frank Sinatra starred in a vulgarization of the superb Rodgers and Hart musical.) "One more film and I'll have made my pile," Marlon said. "My father and mother are taken care of. I have a thousand head of cattle on my ranch in Nebraska, which will soon bring me an income of eighty thousand a year. That will be enough. I'll enjoy life. Any acting I will do will be on the stage."

On another occasion, he talked about chucking everything for a beachcomber's life on a Pacific island, where he'd concern himself exclusively with "eating and sleeping and the reproduction of the race."

In the next few years Brando announced his forthcoming retirement every six months or so. No one took him seriously, but Brando meant what he said—at least on the day he said it. Later, when his spirits picked up, he'd coast back into the old picture-making routine, but once on the job, he'd again feel depressed and dissatisfied. Acting was beginning to leave him unfulfilled, and the hollow sensation, which grew worse as he grew older, was to become a chronic ailment of his middle years.

In the spring of 1953, Brando fled to New York, not in search of a stage role as he hinted to reporters, but to escape domestic vicissitudes. He and Movita had been quarreling and Marlon decided they needed a continent between them until things settled down. Stubbornly, Movita followed him East and moved into his Manhattan apartment. Marlon allowed her to stay, as he was about to leave for Europe.

A few days before his scheduled sailing, he was meandering around Greenwich Village and ran into Valerie Judd, a costume designer he had known in his Broadway years. He asked how things were going. Rotten, she said; she was out of work, as were many of Marlon's old buddies.

It was a point of honor with Marlon to do everything he could to help his friends. A few years earlier, he had taken Wally Cox, then still a silversmith, to meet Edith Van Cleve, and had asked her to find him a job in show business. "I told Marlon that though Cox was very nice and probably quite talented, he had no experience in acting and consequently there wasn't much I could do," Miss Van Cleve remembered. "Marlon understood that. I don't think he expected me to do anything, but the story's a typical example of his loyalty."

After talking to Valerie Judd for a few minutes, Brando hurried uptown to the MCA building. When Edie Van Cleve returned from lunch that day, she found Marlon sprawled on the floor of her office, thumbing through the pages of *The Players Guide* (a casting agent's directory to Broadway players). He informed Edie that he was temporarily postponing his European trip to act in summer stock. Miss Van Cleve was flabbergasted. "I would never have dared to ask him to play the straw hat circuit!" she said. He was going to star in a production utilizing the talents of his old Broadway buddies, who were to receive all profits of this four-week tour.

Miss Van Cleve told Marlon he'd need a business manager. Absolutely not, Marlon replied; he didn't want any third party cutting into his friends' take. He asked Edie to make all financial arrangements.

"I told him I simply couldn't undertake such a chore," Miss Van Cleve said. "I knew that when word got around that Marlon Brando was going to play the summer circuit, there would be hundreds of offers, and to sift them down to four engagements would take time and tact. To make things more difficult, he was very particular about where he played—he only wanted to appear on a certain part of the Eastern seaboard, the Connecticut–Long Island–Cape Cod area. When I promised him I'd find a producer/business manager who'd work for love and just a little money, he agreed." She suggested Morton Gottlieb, one of Marlon's old friends, who thereby gained his spurs as a theatrical producer. (He was later to promote *Sleuth* and *Same Time, Next Year* to Broadway and Hollywood fame.)

For his return to the stage, Marlon chose George Bernard Shaw's *Arms and the Man*. In keeping with his desire to make the production a showcase for his friends, Brando elected to play Sergius, the less personable of the play's two leading male roles, and gave Bluntschli, the better part, to his friend William Redfield, a well-known Broadway juvenile and one of the original members of the Actors Studio.

Redfield was blessed with a jack-of-all-trades talent; he danced and sang a little, was adept at both comedy and heavy drama, and was popular with TV and radio fans. At the time of *Arms and the Man*, he was holding down a lucrative job on a network soap opera, and was reluctant to abandon it for a skimpily salaried stock assignment. Brando eventually won him over by matching his weekly TV salary, an arrangement which made Redfield the highest paid member of the *Arms* company by several hundred dollars.

Other members of the cast included Janice Mars, a cabaret singer and sometime actress who was very thick with the Tennessee Williams–William Inge set; Carlo Fiore; and Sam Gilman, the most discreet and therefore the most durable of Marlon's long-term friends.

After a walk-on career on- and off-Broadway, Gilman played a bit role in *The Wild One*, and during the filming he formed a silent brotherhood with Marlon. When asked about Brando, Gilman speaks of his friend's sense of humor and wacky pranks, and then goes mute. Pressed further, he'll tell you to talk to Marlon; he says he hasn't anything derogatory to report.

The tour of *Arms and the Man* opened in early July 1953 at the Theater-by-the-Sea in Matunuck, Rhode Island. The company then played Falmouth on Cape Cod, Ivoryton, Connecticut, and finally wound up at Framingham, Massachusetts. At each leg of the journey, the reviews were good and the business sensational. And there was the usual summer stock romance: Marlon and Janice Mars were a minor item along the straw hat trail.

Brando didn't take the tour very seriously. Two shows out of eight he was on top of his performance; the rest of the time he just walked through the play. A group of vacationing Boston matrons accosted Billy Redfield in Falmouth and complained about Marlon's performance. "Does he think we're deaf and dumb?" they asked belligerently.

Redfield told Marlon about the reproach. Marlon didn't care. "Man, don't you get it? This is summer stock!"

When the show closed in early August, Marlon and Redfield sailed for Europe on the *Liberté*. They were to be gone for two months or longer. At the moment, Brando had no definite plans or commitments, though there were rumors that he was about to sign for the film version of *Mister Roberts*.

Henry Fonda eventually played *Mister Roberts* on screen as he had on stage. It was no great loss for Marlon—he really wasn't right for the part. And his next film was far more important than this mild-mannered military comedy. Shortly after his return from Europe, he started work on Elia Kazan's *On the Waterfront*.

·9·
TERRY MALLOY,
A CLASS CONTENDER

On the Waterfront originated in Malcolm Johnson's series of Pulitzer Prize–winning articles about crime and corruption among New York's unionized dockworkers. Kazan read Johnson's pieces, saw a film in them, and asked Arthur Miller to fashion a screenplay from the material. Miller backed out after Kazan testified before HUAC; though the director's testimony was never made public, it apparently implicated Miller. Kazan then asked novelist and screenwriter Budd Schulberg to work on the project. Like Kazan, Schulberg had also "named names" for HUAC, and his script became a justification of "stool-pigeoning" on one's buddies.

Kazan and Schulberg peddled the film at all the major studios, but with no buyers. (Darryl Zanuck turned it down because he considered it too drab a subject for CinemaScope, his secret weapon against TV competition.) Finally, Sam Spiegel, an independent producer, agreed to finance the picture and allowed Kazan to film it in authentic New York and Hoboken locations.

Frank Sinatra was Kazan's first choice for the leading role. "Sinatra can be a very good, serious actor when he's working for a director he respects," Kazan said. "I thought he had the right look and personality for the part." It was also a strong commercial piece of casting. Sinatra had just completed his sensational comeback performance in From Here to Eternity, and there was stiff competition for his services. He wasn't interested in *Waterfront*.

Brando said he wasn't very interested in the film, either; he claimed he accepted it only because he needed the money. Though he was still living frugally, Marlon was now in a high tax bracket—his salary had risen to about $200,000 a year—and despite what he had said a few months earlier, the cattle ranch wasn't paying off as quickly as he'd hoped. He may have been pressed for money, but that wasn't the only reason for his disparagement of the Kazan film.

His plaint "I'm only doing it for the money" (which was to be heard again and again in the years ahead) seems to have been a form of self-protection: by saying in advance that he was playing a role just for the salary, he was in the clear if the film bombed; he had already forewarned his fans that it would probably be a bust.

Most actors cast in an obvious piece of drivel convince themselves that with a little rewriting, some nice costumes, and the sunburst of their personality, the sow's ear will miraculously become a silk purse. Not Marlon. Perhaps he was too intelligent, perhaps he was a born pessimist; whatever the reason, he always had gnawing doubts about the worthiness of every project, even about *Waterfront*, one of the shining moments of his career.

Once he signed on for the film, Brando became cooperative—for a time, anyway. He took a real interest in the search for the actress to play the leading role in the film, and agreed with Kazan that Eva Marie Saint—a TV and stage actress best known for her luminous performance in Horton Foote's *A Trip to Bountiful*—was the ideal choice. And he also agreed to work with Kazan and other members of the *Waterfront* cast at the Actors Studio on improvising scenes based on Schulberg's script before the picture went into production.

In exchange for these courtesies, Marlon requested and was granted a favor of his own. His friend Carlo Fiore (with Brando's financial and moral support) had just licked a bad heroin habit, and was now looking for a steady job. Marlon asked that Carlo be hired as his stand-in and dialogue coach. It was an on-and-off, made-to-order assignment that would keep Fiore afloat for the next several years.

Once shooting started, Marlon's mood changed dramatically. He was in a desperately unhappy frame of mind while making *On the Waterfront.* Asked if he knew what was bothering Brando, Kazan said, "Personal problems." Well, yes, but what *kind* of personal problems? No answer.

There may have been other factors, but Marlon's bad times were at least partly caused by a seemingly irreparable rupture with Movita. She was fed up with his sudden fits of distemper, and moved out without leaving a forwarding address.

Despite his unhappiness and the freezing temperatures of a Hoboken winter, Marlon tried to be cooperative. Eva Marie Saint remembers, "Working with Marlon was a beautiful experience. *Waterfront* was my first movie, and he was so kind to me, such a gentleman. It was a cold winter, and when we were on location he always made sure I would have a warm place to sit down."

Marlon and Rod Steiger had problems filming their famous car scene, which took many takes before Kazan decided to "print it." At first Brando couldn't remember his lines, and then, when he was in command of the words, Steiger began to cry. "Steiger's one of those actors who loves to cry," Brando once said, with unconcealed disdain.

For years there have been rumors of a long-lasting feud between Brando and Steiger. But in 1973, Steiger wrote a beautiful, well-reasoned letter to the New York *Times* to defend Brando against a scurrilous attack by one of the newspaper's interviewees. The hatchet, if it had ever existed, had apparently been buried.

About working with Brando in *Waterfront,* Kazan once said, "At that time, he was an unhappy, anxious young man, who doubted himself. He was solitary, proud, oversensitive. He was not someone particularly easy to get along with, and yet he was a wonderful and lovable man, because one felt that nothing protected him from life, that he was in the midst of it."

Late in 1972, Kazan reclined on the foam rubber, Korvette convertible couch in his cramped office above Broadway's Victoria Theater (now demolished), and reminisced about Brando. "Marlon's a lovely, warm man," he said. "He's probably the gentlest man I've ever met in my life. Oh, sure, he's got problems, but he recognizes them and he never, never tries to hide them. I wish we could have worked together after *Waterfront*, but it never panned out." (Kazan later offered Marlon roles in *Baby Doll*, *A Face in the Crowd*, and *The Arrangement*.)

How did he feel about Brando's performance in *Waterfront*? "I've said it before, and I still think it's the finest thing ever done by an American film actor," Kazan answered.

He might get some argument on that estimate, but not much. Maybe it's not the best, but Brando's Terry Malloy has always been recognized as one of the great, seminal screen performances.

In the film, Terry Malloy, a former boxer turned longshoreman, witnesses the murder of a recalcitrant docker arranged by union boss Johnny Friendly (Lee J. Cobb). At first, Terry refuses to speak out about what he has seen. Then he falls in love with the victim's sister (Eva Marie Saint); his slowly awakening conscience is worked over by a Catholic priest (Karl Malden); and his brother, Charlie (Rod Steiger), Friendly's lieutenant, is murdered. This sequence of events leads Terry to testify before the Crime Commission. He is brutally beaten by Friendly's henchmen—in the second of Brando's "obligatory messianic" scenes—but staggers to his feet and leads the stevedores back to work.

Budd Schulberg's script derives from the Group Theater–Clifford Odets tradition of socially relevant drama; it's agitprop melodrama, diluted by a tender love story and an upbeat, not very convincing, ending. (When Schulberg turned his script into a novel, he had Terry Malloy killed in the final chapter.) Kazan's direction is at its most frenzied. He keeps whipping up the emotions with the delicate touch of a pile driver, and you're forced to respond to his skill, even if you don't respect it.

Brando gives the film its class. He doesn't indulge in any actorish gestures or pauses or intonations, and yet his performance is filled with small grace notes—the entirely natural (and yet brilliantly inventive) way he puts on Eva Marie Saint's glove in a shy love scene; the poignancy he wrings from one monosyllable, "Wow!" when his brother threatens to have him killed; the heart-rending despair behind the word "contender" in his often-quoted speech, "Oh, Charlie, Charlie, I could have had class; I could have been a contender; I could have been somebody, instead of a bum, which is what I am."

The film is often remembered for that speech alone, or for the "Damn!" Brando spits at a priest—the first time the four-letter word was heard in an American movie since Rhett Butler mentioned it to Scarlett.

Never before (and rarely since) has Brando been so warm and gentle and vulnerable on screen. His delicate and awkward moments with Miss Saint are among the finest and most erotic love scenes ever done in an American film.

As Brando became more successful, the roles offered him became less interesting. His skyrocketing salary put him outside the reach of low-budget producers with controversial or risky projects. Mostly, he was offered vacuous epics, dispirited musicals, warmed-over Broadway ephemera—the sort of escapist stuff he once scorned. Now he played it, partly because he was handsomely paid, partly because he wasn't given an opportunity at anything better.

After finishing *On the Waterfront*, he made his first whopping mistake by agreeing to appear in Darryl F. Zanuck's $5,000,000 spectacle *The Egyptian*. Brando was cast as Sinuhe, a brilliant young surgeon who gives up everything for a high-class Mesopotamian strumpet. When the lady catches the Babylonian pox, Sinuhe becomes disenchanted and, after curing his paramour (free of charge, a studio synopsis points out), he returns to treating the poor.

The role was prime Victor Mature beefcake, and even the most die-hard Brando fans felt uncomfortable imagining

Marlon wearing an Egyptian tunic as he prowled around the Sphinx. Maybe Brando was also afflicted with such painful images because he quickly backed out of the project.

In the donnybrook that followed, it was never clear whether Brando had read the script before taking on this foolish assignment, but apparently his initial acquaintance with its heady contents came at the first rehearsal. Present on this unhappy occasion were director Michael (Casablanca) Curtiz, a mad Hungarian noted for his malapropisms ("I'm at the pinochle of my career," he once said), his whip-cracking discipline, and total lack of humor; Darryl Zanuck; and Bella Darvi, a Polish actress and Zanuck's current fair lady, who was cast as Nefer, the Babylonian whore.

Miss Darvi was born Bella Weiger. Zanuck coined her stage name by combining the first three letters of Darryl with the first two letters of Virginia, the name of his long-suffering wife. With all Hollywood snickering behind her back, Mrs. Zanuck played the gracious hostess to Bella for several months, and probably would have continued to do so if her daughter hadn't ordered her to evict the Polish concubine.

At the rehearsal, Brando gave no indication that he was unhappy. But that night Jay Kanter (Brando's film agent) called Zanuck at home. "Marlon's left for New York," Kanter said.

"Why?" Zanuck asked.

"He doesn't like Mike Curtiz," Kanter answered. "He doesn't like the role. And he can't stand Bella Darvi."

"He can't do this to me!" Zanuck shrieked.

Brando wasn't intimidated. He got his psychiatrist, Dr. Bela Mittelman, to issue a statement that he was too ill to work. No one was fooled, certainly not Darryl Zanuck, who immediately filed a $2,000,000 breach of contract suit. Marlon's role in The Egyptian was offered to James Dean, who turned it down, and then to Edmund Purdom, who accepted.

Kanter and the MCA legal staff worked overtime trying to settle the case outside the law courts. Finally, Twentieth Century-Fox agreed to drop charges if Marlon would star (without salary) in the company's forthcoming production of

Desirée, a historical romance about a French demoiselle Napoleon loved before, during, and after Josephine.

Brando wasn't thrilled by the prospect of portraying a lady novelist's marzipan conception of Napoleon, but he had no real choice. It was either *Desirée* or the law courts.

As soon as he checked in at Twentieth Century-Fox, Marlon started to balloon in weight. During *The Wild One* he put on ten pounds, lost most of it for *Waterfront,* but gained almost twenty while playing Napoleon. He explained that when he was unhappy in a role, he ate compulsively; consequently, he was to overeat a lot in the next fifteen years, and his weight was rarely at the regulation mark of 165 pounds.

Marlon hated his *Desirée* assignment and threatened to quit. The studio said that if he walked off the picture, he'd be thrown in jail. "The only good thing you can say about the twerp is he doesn't smoke marijuana," cracked a Fox executive. Probably MCA warned Marlon to toe the line: a repeat of the *Egyptian* incident could ruin him. No one in Hollywood was going to hire an actor who repeatedly sabotaged multimillion-dollar productions.

So Marlon lowered the war flags and sailed smoothly into the preproduction stages of *Desirée.* It could not have been an easy time for him, since there had been another upheaval in his personal life. On March 31, 1954, while visiting relatives in Pasadena, California, Dorothy Brando died suddenly of a heart attack. Brando has never spoken of his mother's death, and no one has had the insensitivity to question him about his feelings at that time, but his grief must have been deep.

Once into production, Marlon apparently relaxed and enjoyed himself. He liked Jean Simmons, who was playing Desirée and hating every minute of it; they shared a mutual addiction to chewing gum, and ruined many takes by forgetting to remove the spearmint before walking into camera range.

Marlon was also friends with his Empress Josephine, that exotic and charming courtesan, Merle Oberon. Later, after Miss Oberon had married Italian industrialist Bruno Pagliali and established herself as one of the doyennes of Hollywood, Marlon frequently attended her small, elegant dinner parties.

To play Napoleon, Brando got out his well-stocked makeup kit. He built up his nose, combed his hair into spit-curl bangs, and girthed himself with an unneeded foam rubber waistline. When he was done, he posed next to one of the famous hand-in-vest portraits of Napoleon; there's a striking resemblance, though Marlon's the handsomer of the two.

In the film, he spoke in a husky whisper with British accents that reminded one critic of Claude Rains. But to other ears, he sounds like a cross between Joan Greenwood and Hermione Gingold.

"Most of the time I just let the makeup play the part," he said, and most of the time he does, but he seems to be having a royal good time behind the disguise. (Laurence Olivier is a great admirer of Brando's *Desirée* performance. He once said it was the best Napoleon he's ever seen. Perhaps when he made this statement he had not seen Albert Dieudonné in Abel Gance's classic 1927 film.) This is the first of Brando's burlesque walk-throughs, and there are several hoots in watching him camp it up. There's a wonderfully witty little scene in which Napoleon raps his naughty sisters on the forehead with a baton, and some real Sarah Bernhardt panache when he snatches the crown and enthrones himself.

Just before the release of *Desirée, Time* magazine featured a cover story on Brando entitled "Too Big for His Blue Jeans?" The reference was to Marlon's talent, not his figure, and the gist of the argument was that Brando had reached the end of the Kowalski-Malloy line, but what next? Where would he find roles worthy of his talent?

By 1954, Hollywood was in sorry shape. When Brando arrived there at the end of the forties, the big studios were inching toward more controversial filmmaking, but the HUAC witch-hunting put a stop to that. Then the studios lost their audiences to TV, and they answered the competition in the only way they understood: they began spending money lavishly and foolishly. The pictures got wider, longer, louder, more colorful, more star-crammed. It was the era of Marilyn Monroe wiggling her eight-foot CinemaScope derrière, of wide-screen Trevi Fountain travelogues, Gray-Flannel-Suit morality plays, and Biblical epics like *The Robe*.

It was an era when *Marty* passed as a masterpiece, when *On the Waterfront* was the most "intelligent" film in several seasons.

Consequently, it looked as though there would be several more *Desirées* in Brando's future. And the industry Cassandras predicted that Marlon would keep walking through them on makeup alone, until there was nothing left of his talent. Or he might go the Gary Cooper–Henry Fonda–James Stewart route, and be sapped of his originality and vitality by playing roles like Abe Lincoln or Mr. Deeds or Mr. Smith, finally winding up as one of those well-loved old codgers who are good for nothing but broken-down cowboy roles.

Either way, it was a dismal prospect.

·10·
BRANDO IN LOVE

Many women had flitted in and out of Marlon's life, but for a long time he managed to keep his romances fairly well hidden from the press. This was to change when he fled to New York to escape *The Egyptian*. While there, he began a relationship that was to supply the gossip columnists with juicy items for several months to come.

The young lady was named Josanne-Mariana ("Josie") Berenger. She was petite (an inch under five feet) with cropped, raven hair and the toothy, gamine appeal of the young Leslie Caron.

She was nineteen years old, and was the daughter of a fisherman who lived above Henri's Bar in Bandol, France, a small town on the Riviera.

When she was seventeen, she caught the eye of Moise Kisling, a Polish artist, and became his model. Through Kisling, she met many wealthy Americans; one of them (a psychiatrist) brought her to New York as his children's tutor.

The psychiatrist had many friends in the theater world. Josie liked the theater; she decided to try her hand at acting. She took classes. She even claims to have finagled a role in a José Ferrer production, though there's no record of her Broadway appearance in any theater yearbook.

Through her theater connections, she wangled an invitation to a posh cocktail party where she met Brando. They left the party together.

For their second evening together, he told her to prepare

dinner for three. The additional guest (who leaked this anecdote to Sheilah Graham) was a girl Marlon had been seeing prior to his meeting with Josie Berenger.

Perhaps this was one of those peculiar tests Marlon reportedly likes to set for his girlfriends; or perhaps it is an example of the kind of deliberate humiliation he is said to inflict on all the women in his life. However she may have interpreted it, Josie accepted the insult without complaint, and from then on her evenings with Brando went unchaperoned.

Josie accompanied Marlon to the West Coast for the filming of *Desirée*. She hung around the set for several weeks, looking timid and unobtrusive, and then in June 1954 returned to France to inform her parents that she was affianced to Marlon Brando.

When Marlon told his friends he was going to marry Josie, they were openly skeptical. They remembered the crank engagement to Denise Darcel, and concluded that a marriage announcement from Marlon was nothing more than a practical joke.

In late October 1954, Brando sailed on the *Île de France* for Paris. Upon arrival, he found refuge with *Paris Match* editor Hervé Mille, an old friend. Josie joined Marlon in Paris and then, a few days later, they traveled to Bandol.

When they arrived in the small village, the couple was noisily welcomed by literally hundreds of photographers and reporters, all of them milling around the entranceway to Henri's Bar. Marlon and Josie fought their way upstairs to the Berenger apartment (where Brando was given the living room couch as a bed), and later that day publicly announced their engagement. They emerged once or twice, dressed in identical boat-neck striped jerseys, and strolled around Bandol; and one evening the lovers motorbiked to nearby Monte Carlo for dinner and gambling.

The newspapers took the romance with a large grain of salt and treated Josie rather shabbily. No one spelled it out, but there was always the insinuation that Mlle Berenger was a gold-digging hussy with career ambitions in place of a heart.

Josie's reputation sunk lower when a Paris art dealer got

hold of the Kisling portraits and displayed them in his gallery window. There was Josie in the altogether. Parisians queued up daily to walk past the undraped charms of Marlon's fiancée, and the American tabloids had a field day with the incident. Today, when *Playboy* has made starlets' breasts a coffee-table commonplace, it's difficult to understand what all the brouhaha was about. But at the time, at least in America, posing nude for an artist was one step above "acting" in a stag film.

(History has a way of repeating itself with the most interesting variations. The uproar over Josie's nude portrait was nothing compared to what occurred in January 1973, when *Time* published a still from *Last Tango in Paris*, which showed Brando simulating intercourse with a French actress. Within twenty-four hours, the photograph was the subject of nationwide TV debate; Johnny Carson almost drooled over the idea of Brando doing all the things they do in the hard-core flicks. And ABC's Harry Reasoner denounced Brando for selling pornography as art.)

If there were widespread doubts about the durability of the Brando-Berenger romance, Marlon did little to squelch them. At the end of his visit to Bandol, he sent Josie back to New York (the press made it sound as if he were relegating her to a convent), while he traveled on to Italy. He said his trip was strictly business—there were several film offers he wished to discuss.

Business trip or not, the reporters asked, shouldn't Josie travel with him? No answer.

A year or so earlier, Brando had been invited to co-star with Ingrid Bergman in Luchino Visconti's lush, operatic *Senso*, written by Tennessee Williams, but the film eventually starred Farley Granger and Alida Valli. Whatever movie deals he discussed in 1954 never materialized.

When Marlon returned to New York that winter, the romance was still in high gear. "This is not a publicity stunt," he told the reporters who flocked aboard the *United States*. "I do intend to marry the girl in the summer." The journalists asked him why he had chosen a French girl to be his wife. "In choosing a wife," Brando answered irritably, "I don't think it's important to question her nationality, providing she's not Joe Stalin's cousin."

Later, the couple snuggled and smiled for photographers outside Brando's new home, a small flat in the Carnegie Apartments in New York's West Fifties (a building famous for its show business tenants), and occasionally appeared together in New York's darker night spots.

By a wide margin, there are more photographs of Marlon with Josie than with any other woman in his life, and each snapshot brought the romance a step closer to its finish. Apparently, Brando thought Josie was a little too eager to talk to the press (though she never said anything to embarrass him), too willing to pose for her picture, too career-conscious.

Brando never publicly abrogated their engagement, and as late as spring 1956 Josie was still insisting that she and Marlon would soon be wed. She was then sharing a modest apartment with a girlfriend in Los Angeles, and working as a salesgirl to pay her rent and acting school tuition. She received no money from Marlon, she said; she wanted to make it on her own. When asked point-blank, she admitted that she hadn't seen Brando for some time, but added that they often talked on the phone.

The interview was a cruel joke, since everyone knew that Marlon had been dating for several months. He was applauded for dancing a torrid mambo with Carmen Amaya, a Spanish flamenco specialist, at New York's La Zambra Café, and was seen about town with a number of exotic beauties.

Jerri Gray, a cabaret and musical-comedy dancer (she played a bit role in Sammy Davis's *Mr. Wonderful*), was Brando's secret playmate in this period. *Confidential*, the widely read exposé rag, first revealed the story of this racy romance, complete with a photograph of Brando on which he had scrawled his devotion to Miss Gray. The article is composed mainly of innuendo and a few quotes from Miss Gray, who describes how, on the night they met, Marlon banged on his bongos while she stripped to her scanties and raced through an interpretive dance. About Marlon's prowess as a lover, she was vague, but enthusiastic.

This true-confession item titillated readers with two scandalous facts. First, Brando was carrying on with Jerri Gray in the early days of his engagement to Josie Berenger, and, the real corker, Miss Gray was black. This was several years before interracial liaisons and marriages were casually accepted by the theater world.

Marlon's most frequent post-Berenger companion was Rita Moreno, for a while the favorite contender in the Brando matrimonial sweepstakes. Though she never became Mrs. Brando, Rita was the girl Marlon returned to when his other love affairs went sour. Today they are still friends, and, whenever he is in New York, he drops by to see Rita (now Mrs. Leonard Gordon) and her daughter, Fernanda Lu.

When Marlon met her, the Puerto Rican–born Moreno was a minor Hollywood player who danced in the background of MGM musicals and pouted provocatively in poverty-row Westerns. She was a neurotic, unhappy girl, as she herself once admitted: "Some people hide their feelings with a lot of noise, and that was my style."

If she made a lot of noise, it wasn't about Marlon. When questioned about her famous boyfriend, Miss Moreno would look blank, and then begin discussing racial prejudice, the plight of underdeveloped nations, or some other serious social problem. She may not know Brando, people joked, but she certainly talks like him.

On one rare occasion Miss Moreno was a bit more open. "You have to understand that when you're going with Marlon Brando, particularly back then, you didn't dare open your mouth about it," she said. "You'd get in trouble with Marlon. We were both private people anyway. And he just didn't like to be talked about.

"There's really nothing much to say about it now," she went on. "I went with Marlon for a long time. It's very well known that Marlon always liked very fiery-looking, sexy

Latin girls. That's the kind of girl that attracted him. But that's for Marlon to straighten out, really."

"If anything, Marlon's a romantic about women," explains one of Brando's men friends. "Nothing seems to shake his faith that he will find someone ideal. His tastes run to exotics—Latins, Polynesians, Orientals. He'd like his ideal to have sloe eyes, an inscrutable expression, and, if possible, he would prefer to meet her in a setting that included incense and tom-toms."

With few exceptions, the women in Marlon's life have all been the sarong or serape type, dark-haired vixens who seem to have stepped out of the sinister shadows of a Charlie Chan thriller.

There was, for example, France Nuyen, a Marseilles-born actress of French and Chinese parentage, who played the leading role in the Broadway production of *The World of Suzie Wong*. She and Brando made all the gossip columns for a few months. They vacationed incognito in Haiti—he traveled as "Dr. Miles Graham, dentist from Omaha," and she was "Tiny Vanna." During their holiday, Miss Nuyen, a tempestuous sort, got headline attention when she biffed a peeping Tom photographer.

She went to Hong Kong to make the film version of *Suzie Wong*, and then a few weeks into the production she was replaced by Nancy Kwan. The official reason for her dismissal was "nervous exhaustion"; confidentially, it was reported that she was too fat to play a Hong Kong daughter of joy.

This inside story blamed Marlon for Miss Nuyen's advanced state of avoirdupois. Back in the States, he was seeing other girls, and, distraught by reports of his infidelity, France started to eat compulsively.

Whether Marlon was really responsible for her overeating is debatable. Once, at Sardi's restaurant, she was seen lunching on a huge steak, an overly generous serving of cannelloni, a basket of rolls, and a whipped-cream dessert. On that occasion, there was no romantic justification for her gluttony.

Marlon flew East to meet Miss Nuyen as she waddled off the plane from Hong Kong, and there was a brief reunion in

New York. And that was the end of the affair. Brando returned to California and Barbara Luna, the woman responsible for increasing France Nuyen's calorie intake.

Miss Luna was a half-Hungarian, half-Philippine chorine who made a career of playing Liat (the "Happy Talk" girl) in touring productions of *South Pacific*. (Miss Nuyen played the same role in the film version of the Rodgers and Hammerstein musical.) A dark-haired, Eurasian-looking beauty, with big eyes and apple-round cheeks, Miss Luna was only a background attraction both in movies and in Marlon's love life.

So was Marie Cui, a lank and leggy Philippine dancer, but she made the most of what was, at best, a very brief relationship with Marlon. In the early 1960s, she filed a paternity suit against Brando, claiming he was the father of her four-month-old daughter, Maya Gabriella Cui Brando. Eventually the case was thrown out of court—blood tests proved that Brando couldn't have fathered the child.

There was never much doubt about the outcome of this case. Whatever Marlon's shortcomings as a husband or lover may be, he is a devoted and conscientious father—whether the offspring are legitimate or not. Rita Moreno ended her discussion of Brando with this bit of unsolicited praise: "He's a lovely man. And by the way, he's a *wonderful* father. Next to my husband, he's the best parent I've met."

If Brando had been the father of Miss Cui's child, no doubt he would have willingly owned up to his responsibility.

·11·

ALL SINGING! ALL DANCING!
ALL WRONG!

In August 1954 the New York *Times* carried the following squib:

> Marlon Brando, dressed in full regalia for his role of Emperor Napoleon, whistled his own accompaniment as he did a competent time step today on the set of *Desirée*.

Perhaps Brando wanted to call attention to his song-and-dance talents, which so far had been sadly neglected by the Hollywood producers. If so, his bid for attention did not go unnoticed for very long. "GARBO LAUGHS," the MGM publicists puffed, "and now BRANDO SINGS!" which was the studio's way of announcing that Brando was to appear in the film version of the Broadway musical, *Guys and Dolls*.

It was going to be a big, splashy, $5,000,000-plus production; $1,000,000 alone had been paid for the film rights to the musical, an adaptation of Damon Runyon's arch "fables" of New York touts, tootsies, and floating crap games.

"Brando was my first choice for the role," said producer Sam Goldwyn. "His acting talent is so great he can easily adapt to any sort of role. Singing and dancing is only a question of a little more projection."

It was well known within the industry that prior to Brando,

Goldwyn had considered Gene Kelly, Cary Grant, and Burt Lancaster for the role of Sky Masterson, a Broadway sharpy who falls hard for a Salvation Army lass.

Marlon took on *Guys and Dolls* because he longed "to do something in a lighter color." Was he nervous about the singing? he was asked. "I know I can carry a tune, if the handles are big enough," he said. "But I've never sung anything that could be heard outside a shower. The idea scares me, but I think it's part of an actor's job to try new things."

Though the press wasn't told, there was a strong possibility that Marlon's songs would be dubbed by a trained singer. To determine whether a vocal double was needed, Brando auditioned for Frank Loesser, the composer of *Guys and Dolls'* splendid score.

The audition was held in a Los Angeles recording studio a few months before the film's January 1955 shooting date. Marlon took a deep breath and then crooned a chorus of "I'll Know," a love ballad from the show. (Brando's other songs in the film included "Luck Be a Lady" and "I've Never Been in Love Before.") When the recording was played back, Marlon winced and muttered, "Sounds like the mating call of a yak."

Loesser was favorably impressed. "It's an untrained voice, but has a pleasing, husky baritone quality," he said. "He isn't playing the role of a singer, but a gambler who bursts into song occasionally. With hard work—he can do it."

Brando went into training with Leon Ceparro, the MGM vocal coach with whom he had worked during his preparations for *Julius Caesar*. Ceparro was a testy sort, and finicky about whom he taught; once when a Slavic beauty with more bosom than talent applied for lessons, he gave her a withering glance and then snapped, "Wonders I can work, not miracles."

But he liked Marlon. "Mr. Brando has an opera singer's palate," Ceparro rhapsodized. "He can sing a top B flat without effort. That is a tremendous feat after only a few weeks of training!"

Two or three times a week, Brando appeared at Ceparro's studio, cleared his throat, and engaged in about fifteen minutes of scales. Then he and Ceparro took a breather and were soon discussing sports—usually boxing. These confabulations inevitably led them to square off for a little exhibition boxing. It was a cozy pupil-teacher relationship, but unfortunately it did little to improve Brando's bathroom baritone.

As part of his preproduction regimen, Marlon also took dancing lessons from Michael Kidd, the small, comic-faced Broadway choreographer who was staging *Guys and Dolls'* musical numbers. Kidd expressed delight with his pupil. "Marlon moves like a prize fighter—very light on his feet," he said. "A little heavy for ballet, but you'll be agreeably surprised when you see him on screen."

A little heavy is a little bit of an understatement—on screen Marlon looks like a hippo dancing. But the ballet classes did help him strip off the excess weight he had gained while making *Desirée.*

The questionable distinction of turning *Guys and Dolls,* one of the sprightliest and most literate of Broadway musicals, into a cacophonous film catastrophe must be shouldered equally by Sam Goldwyn and director Joseph L. Mankiewicz. Mankiewicz was an obvious bad mistake for this assignment. He had no experience in the very special craft of staging musicals; his pacing (all important in song-and-dance films) was often sluggish; his visual sense was undistinguished; his brand of humor was several shades too worldly for the tawdry innocence of the Runyon world.

Then there's the almost perversely misconceived casting. Jean Simmons was chosen for Sarah Brown, the Salvation Army lass; the part was conceived for a singer with operetta ambitions, but Miss Simmons had no vocal training of any kind. Frank Sinatra was signed for Nathan Detroit, a borscht belt comic role with very little singing attached to it. A couple of songs were hurriedly written for him, and the speed shows.

Miss Adelaide, the musical's fourth major character, went to Vivian Blaine, who created the part on Broadway. A wise choice, but by this time Miss Blaine had impersonated the chronically sneezing chantoosie so often that in the film she overplays the role by rote. And Mankiewicz doesn't help. In misguided appreciation of her big comic scenes, he almost pushes the camera down her throat.

Inside the industry, Mankiewicz was admired for taking on a trio of actors as "temperamental" as Brando, Sinatra, and Jean Simmons (who, though not publicized for it, was often stubborn and outspoken). But there were no flare-ups. Everybody got along just fine, says Mankiewicz.

About Sinatra, Marlon reported, "Frank is the kind of guy, when he dies, he's going to heaven and give God a bad time for making him bald." This was the nicest thing he was ever to say about Sinatra. Despite Mankiewicz's claim of all being calm on the set, the two actors avoided each other whenever possible. Sinatra believed, justly, that he should have been cast as Masterson, who gets to sing all the show's best ballads. Reportedly his aversion for Marlon continues to this day—he can't hear the name Brando without going into a towering rage.

Fortunately most of Marlon's scenes in *Guys and Dolls* were played with Jean Simmons, his chewing gum pal from *Desirée*. Once again they kept chewing before the camera, until Mankiewicz brought on set a huge trash can labeled PLEASE DEPOSIT CHEWING GUM HERE! Between scenes, Marlon and Miss Simmons relaxed by joking about the off-key harmony of their love duets.

It was no laughing matter. In a review entitled "Sam, You Made the Film Too Long," *The New Yorker* critic wrote that Brando sang "through a rather unyielding set of sinuses" while looking for assurance from Jean Simmons, who "unfortunately is always a half-tone off-pitch." That's a little unfair to Miss Simmons; she's only about a quarter-tone off the mark, and she has some style and charm—rare commodities in this musical disaster area. But about Brando's vocalizing, the critic hits it on the nose.

"I've never had so much fun as working on this film," Jean Simmons told reporters. Warm and friendly working relationships, however, don't necessarily make good films, as any

Hollywood veteran will tell you, and as *Guys and Dolls* sadly demonstrates. It grossed $8,000,000, not quite enough to show a profit on its large initial investment.

Nobody had a good time working on the freezing Hoboken locations of *On the Waterfront,* and yet it won all the important film awards for 1954. That year the Academy Awards presentation was held while *Guys and Dolls* was in production, and Marlon left early to attend the evening's festivities. After all the minor awards had been distributed, Bette Davis strutted on stage and opened the little white envelope from Price, Waterhouse. "Marlon Brando," she announced in a cracked whoop.

"I'm thrilled Marlon won," Miss Davis said later. "He and I have a lot in common. He, too, has made a lot of enemies. He, too, is a perfectionist."

Probably many people expected—perhaps hoped—that Marlon would do or say something outrageous, but he was on his best behavior. The only shock that night came from a very pregnant Eva Marie Saint, who accepted her award as best supporting actress by gasping, "I think I may have the baby right here." There were a few titters from the audience and a rash of reproaches in the next day's press.

After the Awards ceremony, Marlon attended a dinner dance at Romanoff's restaurant. He posed politely with Grace Kelly, the year's best actress for *The Country Girl.* "Kiss him, Grace," a photographer yelled. "Kiss Marlon!"

"I think Mr. Brando should kiss me," Grace answered, with just a trace of frost in her voice. And, with a sly little grin, Marlon leaned over and bussed the future princess's cheek.

There was a certain undercurrent of disappointment that Brando had acted so true to Hollywood form. Suddenly, in certain quarters, there was a wave of nostalgia for the old, insubordinate Brando, and a disheartened acknowledgment that in the last year he was beginning to conform.

"I'm sick to death of having people come up and say hello, and then just stand there expecting me to throw a raccoon at them," Marlon said late in 1954.

And, in accordance with his words, he began to shed the

gaudy trappings of his old image—there were no more publicity pranks, no more mudslinging at the Hollywood phonies, no more blue jeans. Now he dressed with gangster chic; he wore dark shirts, light ties, continental suits. His new look (maybe the *Guys and Dolls* influence) wasn't the height of *Town and Country* elegance, but along the Hollywood–Palm Beach–Las Vegas circuit, it passed muster.

There are several possible explanations for this change in Brando. First, at age thirty-one, he was too old to play the kid-rebel game any longer.

Next, he had probably outgrown his psychological needs for the game. He told Edith Van Cleve, "My analysis has helped me. I'm more at peace with myself now."

Finally, the Oscar may be a meaningless award as far as artistic merit is concerned, but financially it is a real windfall. It can double, sometimes triple, an actor's salary. There may have been pressure (from Jay Kanter, from MCA) on Brando to cool it until after the Academy Awards.

The film industry accepted this third proposition as explanation for Brando's model behavior. And the public also questioned his sincerity.

There's a strong backlash involved in winning the Oscar. Almost from its conception, the Academy Awards ceremony had been laughed at by all the bright and clever people, and by the 1950s it had about as much class as the Miss America Pageant. That Brando deserved the award, that there wasn't another actor within twenty qualitative furlongs of his performance, that everyone was really rooting for him, made no difference. When he stretched out his hand to accept an eighty-dollar (the hockshop value of an Oscar) statuette, Marlon became a member of the Hollywood establishment, and for an actor who had made his reputation on insurrection, that was apostasy.

By now Marlon had been a film star for five years, and the movie public was beginning to take him for granted. A star's first reign of popularity never lasts much longer than five years; then there's often a lull. Brando needed a sensational new role if he was to hold his fans, some of whom were already seeking new favorites.

Several Brando imitators were now reaching prominence. Paul Newman (who, like Brando, was discovered by Maynard Morris) made his first film, *The Silver Chalice*, in 1954. It was a terrible movie, and Newman's performance was poor; but, made up and photographed to resemble Brando, he caught the fancy of teenage girls. Newman was so embarrassed by his first movie that he rushed back to Broadway, where he played the Brandoesque hero in *The Desperate Hours*.

When he returned to the screen (as Rocky Graziano in *Somebody Up There Likes Me*), he was still doing the Brando bit, though he was sweeter than Marlon, smoother, and a lot less scruffy. He always seems to be sporting the colors of Andover or Yale, even when playing a convict or pool shark. Very quickly he began to develop his own, highly likable style, and has had such success with it that today it is hard to remember why he was ever pigeonholed as a pipsqueak Brando.

Perhaps if he had lived longer, James Dean might also have found his own direction, but as it stands, the record shows him to be the most flagrant and successful of the Brando imitators. Dean made his dynamite screen debut in the 1955 *East of Eden*, after a brief career in TV and on the stage. So few people saw his Broadway appearances—one was a quick flop and Dean quit the other a few weeks into its run—that a legend has grown that he was brilliant in both. He wasn't. There was something very perverse about those performances; they were a series of tics and whines, and they were colored by a groveling masochism. You couldn't take your eyes off him, but you weren't sure you ever wanted to see him again.

Elia Kazan, *East of Eden's* director, may have been responsible for Dean's blatant aping of Brando. (Kazan didn't like Dean—he once referred to him as a creep—and reportedly took him on only because he thought he could manipulate the actor into giving a star performance.) But pre-Kazan, Dean was already walking in Marlon's footsteps. He hero-worshipped Brando so openly that his devotion became an inside joke of the theater crowd.

Marlon was not amused. Asked if he thought Dean copied his style in *East of Eden*, Brando answered, "I have great respect for his talent. However, in that film, Mr. Dean appears to be wearing my last year's wardrobe and using my last year's talent."

Later he said, "Dean had an idée fixe about me. Whatever I did, he did. He was always trying to get close to me."

Dressed in denim, leather jacket, and boots, Dean zipped around Hollywood on a motorcycle, looking sullen and untouchable; he was rude to Louella and Hedda, uncivil to the movie society, uncooperative with the studio bosses. All that was missing from the déjà vu picture was a raccoon.

Somehow, Dean had gotten Marlon's private telephone number, and was forever calling, asking for a private meeting. Brando refused to answer the phone, or if he did, he disguised his voice and gave Dean his not-at-home routine.

One night, the two finally met at a party where Dean was "throwing himself around, acting the madman" (Brando's words). Marlon took him aside, talked sense to him, urged him to undergo analysis. But neither analysis nor Brando's fatherly advice helped Dean. Sixteen months after the release of his first film, he died in a car crash (he was driving a Porsche at eighty miles per hour), a fatal accident that has been interpreted as "suicide by default." Dean was nearsighted and wasn't wearing his glasses when he crashed.

After Dean's death, his fans staged the most spectacular wake since the funeral of Rudolph Valentino; there were séances, rubber death masks, and other morbid rites and totems.

Commenting on the hysteria, Brando said he wanted to make a documentary about Dean to show his fans what he really was—"just a lost boy trying to find himself. That ought to be done and I'd like to do it—maybe as a kind of expiation for some of my own sins. Like making *The Wild One*."

A surprising number of people who otherwise have good taste prefer Dean to Brando. A spokesman for this group (a young woman who came of movie age at about the time Dean was making his film debut) puts it this way: "I always thought Brando was gross and animalistic—those thick-corded arms, heavy lips, and paunchy belly were repulsive to me. But James Dean was small and delicate and sensitive."

This statement gets at the basic difference between the actors: Brando displayed a brute, potentially threatening sexuality, whereas Dean was the boy-man who could be understood and mothered.

Pertinently, the comment also discusses the men only in terms of their physical presence; that is, as movie stars, not as actors. Talk to a Dean fan about Brando's superior acting talent, and you'll get a blank stare, as if you were talking gibberish.

At the time Dean was electrifying the public with his moody, withdrawn, and paranoid portrayals, Brando was getting lost along the avenues of big-time movie stardom. After *Desirée* and *Guys and Dolls* came *The Teahouse of the August Moon*, another expensive, instantly disposable movie in which Brando gives one of the few embarrassing performances of his career. Most of his fans felt like the young man who, after seeing the film, left the theater and said, "It's going to be hard, but I'm going to try to forget I ever saw that movie."

Teahouse had been a successful novel, and then a Pulitzer Prize–winning Broadway smash, but never, in any form, was it more than a tired businessman's think-piece. A wispy fantasy, it tells of how a group of Japanese villagers bamboozle the United States armed forces into building a teahouse for the local geishas. Behind the wind chimes, bamboo screens, and gauzy settings was a gentle reprimand: Leave off the foolish attempts to Americanize occupied countries. It was precisely this theme and his attraction to Oriental culture which attracted Brando to the picture.

Sakini, the play's major character, is a wily, pixilated Japanese interpreter, and he should be played by a somewhat fey actor. David Wayne had winged through it on stage like an Oriental Peter Pan. It was a ridiculous part for Marlon, but Lord knows, he tried to play it as written.

As soon as he signed for the film he went on a starvation regimen, and eventually got his weight down to 140 pounds. When he did eat, it was in a local Japanese restaurant, where he sat for hours eating and studying the movement, posture, and speech of the waiters.

(There is one compliment that can be paid Brando's Sakini. He gets the movement down pat, and does some wonderfully comic, articulate things with his legs.)

In the picture, Marlon had to speak both Japanese and Oriental-style broken English. To master the dialogue, he got out his tape recorder and asked a Tokyo native to record his speeches.

"I had to learn Japanese by rote, copying inflection," Brando said. "I have no feeling for the words. I'm flying blind as far as that's concerned. To learn broken English was just as difficult. I learned by listening to Japanese speak English. My broken English is not too genuine. If it were too accurate, no one in the United States would understand it. So I edited the broken English I heard to keep just enough of its flavor."

To create an authentic façade for Sakini, Brando worked with famous makeup artist Keyston Weeney. His tear ducts were filled in by pasting a rubber lid around the eyes, and a cosmetic base was applied to accentuate his cheekbones and deemphasize the flesh of his cheeks and jowls. And, as the crowning touch, there was a black, straw-textured wig. It took Mr. Weeney an hour and a half to apply this makeup, which is none too successful. A critic said Brando looked like Fu Manchu, but actually he's the spitting image of Jerry Lewis in *Geisha Boy*.

Teahouse was scheduled to be shot entirely in Japan—the exteriors in Nara, a small town near Kyoto, and the interiors at the Daiei Studios in Tokyo. Director Daniel Mann and his troupe, which included Glenn Ford, Eddie Albert, and Louis Calhern, arrived in Japan in February 1956, and shot about twenty percent of the film before the rainy season set in. After two weeks of sunless weather, Mann decided to pack up and go home—a very expensive decision, since he had to import several Japanese actors who figured prominently in the already completed footage.

Back in Hollywood, new complications arose. Louis Calhern died unexpectedly and two weeks of shooting were lost before a replacement—Paul Ford—could be found; then all Calhern's scenes had to be reshot with Ford. Then the two starring actors declared open warfare on each other. Glenn Ford accused Brando of trying to upstage him, while Marlon openly derided Ford's "habit of flapping his arms like a chicken wing" to express deep emotion. Director Daniel Mann kept reprimanding them for behaving like "contentious children," but the children went on acting contentiously for the entire production.

Brando's interest in Oriental culture grew stronger during his short stay in Japan, and his life-style in the next few years was to exhibit this fascination. He was later to buy a home in the Los Angeles area—his first admission to permanent California residency—which he decorated in Japanese style, complete with wind chimes, temple gongs, tatami mats, and other Eastern artifacts.

He began reading Lao-tzu and other ancient Chinese and Japanese philosophers, and brought conversations to a stand still by quoting the cryptic sentences of these holy scholars.

Shortly after *Teahouse* opened at the Radio City Music Hall (November 1956), Brando visited New York and dropped in at Edith Van Cleve's office. He told her about his enthusiasm for Japan—"I can't wait to go back," he said. "I'd like to live there some day." Then he asked her if she had seen *Teahouse*. She nodded yes. What did she think? he wanted to know.

"Well, Marlon," she answered diplomatically, "I thought it was very entertaining."

"It's a shame," he said. "I'd hoped that at least some of the magic of the play would have come across on screen."

·12·

SAYONARA, AUF WIEDERSEHEN

In 1955, Marlon formed an independent filmmaking company, Pennebaker Productions—named in tribute to his mother, Dorothy Pennebaker Brando. It was then both voguish and financially sound for superstars to become their own producers. The dual capacity guaranteed the star-producer a larger slice of a film's profits, and also gave him a better break with the Internal Revenue Service.

There was a third benefit, and probably one which greatly appealed to Brando: the star-producer was, at least nominally, in artistic control of his films.

On the debit side, the actor-producer carried a back-breaking work load. He had to seek out properties, package and finance them, and then negotiate distribution. He couldn't cast himself in anything daring or unconventional unless he was sure it would show a profit. Consequently, the actor who announced he was turning producer "to do the kind of serious films the big studios don't produce" was deluding himself. Usually, he wound up playing the same old roles—or worse.

"The first picture has to make money," Brando said. "Otherwise, there won't be another." He decided the initial Pennebaker production would be a Western of the *Shane* or *High Noon* variety. Specifically, it would treat the plight of the American Indian, a subject dear to Brando's heart. "Today the Indians are a broken race of people," he said. "The white man took his culture away and destroyed his philosophy of life and morality. We challenged the precepts on which he based his religion and destroyed the very kernels of his existence."

Six months passed, and no further word on the Indian film. Then, in March 1956, Brando left Los Angeles with his Pennebaker business associate, George Englund, and writer Stewart Stern, for Honolulu, the first leg of a twenty-thousand-mile survey of Southeast Asia. The purpose of the trip, Marlon explained, was to develop a scenario for an adventure film based on what happens to United Nations employees when they are transplanted to foreign environments. The project, which was tentatively titled *Tiger on a Kite*, never materialized, though Brando later made something similar to it, the 1963 *The Ugly American*, a film written by Mr. Stern and directed by Englund.

Marlon went back to his Western idea, but after being kicked around by various associates and writers, it no longer had its American Indian twist; instead, it was growing Topsylike into the story of a Western outlaw, someone like Billy the Kid, according to one report. Brando jotted down notes for the scenario, and handed them over to a writer for further development. Two hundred thousand dollars' worth of writing talent came and went, and still there was no shooting script, not even a passable first draft.

The money was coming out of Marlon's pocket, and it hurt. So he went into his "I'm only doing it for the money" routine, and signed for *Sayonara*, a blockbuster mix of travelogue and deep-think melodrama.

Sayonara's script was hewn out of a sprawling James Michener novel, which for months captivated straphangers in the New York transit system. Set in the last days of the Korean war, the novel exposes the U.S. armed forces' bigoted attitude toward miscegenation. Its hero, a battle-fatigued jet ace, travels to Japan for "R and R" (rest and rehabilitation), and there falls in love with a Japanese dancer. He's a West Pointer and thereby an archconservative, and he goes through a lot of soul-searching and cultural conflict before the bittersweet ending: unable to face the hardships that lie ahead, the lovers end their romance with a rueful *sayonara*.

That's the way the novel ends, but Marlon wasn't buying it. If he made the film (and he wasn't too enthusiastic), he insisted that the pilot marry his Japanese lady friend. With that finish, the film would be "worthwhile"; it would take a stand against American racial prejudice. There would have to be one additional change, Marlon later added. His character must be from the South. This would make the hero's internal battle with his own bigotry all the stronger. (It would also present him with a new technical challenge—he had yet to be asked to master a Southern drawl.)

Joshua Logan, *Sayonara*'s director, agreed to honor Brando's conditions, but Marlon still stalled on signing a contract. Then, just as Logan was ready to look for another actor, Marlon said yes. Logan asked him why he decided to come aboard.

"I like you," Brando said. "I like the tender way you took the dead leaves off that plant while we were talking yesterday."

Probably he also liked the terms of his contract. He was paid a flat $300,000, plus a percentage of the gross. He made a small fortune on the film; *Sayonara* was one of the top moneymakers of 1957–58, grossing over $10,000,000. Until *The Godfather*, it was the most profitable of Brando's films.

As an added attraction, the movie was to be made in Japan, a country Marlon was longing to revisit. A month before the film's January 1957 shooting date, he was already settled in at the Miyako Hotel in Kyoto. It was predominantly a Western-style hotel, but Brando elected to stay in one of the few suites furnished in the traditional Oriental manner. During his stay in Japan, he went native—his only reversion to Western culture was at mealtimes.

Before his trip to Japan, Marlon slimmed down to 170 pounds, and then undid his good work by constant overeating in Kyoto. Except for seaweed and raw fish, most Japanese dishes fall into the starchy, deep-fried, or sautéed categories, but they're not nearly as rich next to the Oriental concept of American cooking. Marlon was served gargantuan helpings of steak, spaghetti, potatoes, apple pie à la mode—and, bite by bite, he puffed up. And though he is carefully photographed in the film, there's no mistaking the swell of belly beneath his artfully tailored Air Force uniform.

Brando loved the Japanese. "They kill me," he said. "They really kill me. The kids too. Don't you think they're wonderful? Don't you love them—the Japanese kids?" And the Japanese returned his love. The chambermaids tittered coyly while turning down his bed or passing him in a corridor. And outside the hotel, there was always a crowd waiting to shout "Herro, Marron!" as he rushed toward the studio limousine.

The role of the Japanese dancer was first offered to Audrey Hepburn, who said she didn't see herself as a twentieth-century Madame Butterfly. After her refusal, there was a "worldwide" talent search, and, wonder of wonders, the lucky girl was found almost on the doorstep of Warner Brothers Studio. She was Miiko Taka, a sixty-dollar-a-week clerk, discovered at the annual Nisei Carnival in Los Angeles. With lightning speed she was screen-tested, and the "brilliant" results were broadcast throughout the trade-press world.

On set, Logan almost tore his hair out in getting a presentable performance from Miss Taka. And he beat feet and head against the wall while coaching Red Buttons and Miyoshi Umeki (both to win Academy Awards) in *Sayonara's* most prominent supporting roles.

Logan was one of Broadway's most admired directors—he had put together such smashes as *Mister Roberts, South Pacific,* and *Fanny.* His theater work is in the David Belasco tradition: he does small things in a great big, sensationally overproduced way. In a Logan production you can expect—and usually get—anything from an on-stage swimming pool to Jane Fonda climbing a twenty-foot wire fence to escape her would-be rapists.

His stage work, however, is overshadowed by his three-ring-circus film productions *(Picnic, Bus Stop, Fanny).* And *Sayonara* is one of his gaudiest and most entertaining creations. It's a grab bag of a film, so full of assorted goodies—a lush theme song, dancing, puppets, Ricardo Montalban as a Chicano–Kabuki, vaudeville, heartbreak, laughter, tears, picture-postcard scenery—that one barely notices that it runs a good thirty minutes longer than necessary.

Brando and Logan didn't agree on the interpretation of many key scenes, and days were lost as they argued out a compromise. One of the controversial scenes showed Brando discovering the double suicide of Red Buttons and Miyoshi Umeki. Marlon wanted to build this moment into a violent outburst of anger: he'd look at the dead bodies, bang his fists into the door, and then rip the room into a chaos of debris.

Logan said he didn't want any theatrics; he'd like a quiet expression of deep grief. "That's stupid and ridiculous!" Marlon exclaimed.

After a long debate, he agreed to try it Logan's way. In the film he pushes through a silent crowd, looks at the bodies and murmurs, "Oh, God!" As Marlon later admitted, Logan's staging was highly effective.

Because of the long-winded debate, the film went way over schedule. Sometimes it seemed as if they'd never finish. And then, with only three days' shooting left, Marlon arrived on set with his right arm in a sling. Logan almost fainted. "Is it broken?" he asked.

"I think so," Marlon answered. He explained that the accident had occurred during a wrestling bout with his stand-in, Carlo Fiore.

"Can you remove the sling for a few minutes of shooting?" Logan asked. No, Marlon replied, the doctor warned that if he removed the sling, he'd be maimed for life. Logan was beside himself. Since Brando was in every remaining scene, there was nothing to do but postpone filming until his recovery.

"If I arrange the camera so the sling won't show, do you think you could move your fingers a little?" Logan pleaded.

"Well, I guess so," Marlon answered. And then, doubled over with laughter, he pulled his hand out of the sling and wriggled his fingers violently.

"That little prank," Logan said, "took ten years off my life."

While making *Sayonara*, Brando rarely fraternized with the company. Between takes, he sat apart from his co-workers, reading philosophy and jotting down notes for his Western screenplay, now titled *A Burst of Vermilion*. After work, he stayed close to his hotel suite and socialized mainly with his own personal entourage, which included a secretary, a personal makeup man and his wife, and Carlo Fiore.

Once in a while Brando and Fiore went out to investigate the question of whether geishas did more than pour tea and titter. And occasionally they entertained friends in Marlon's rooms. One of the visitors was to do a lot of damage to Brando's reputation; Carlo warned him to be prudent, but Bud just wouldn't listen.

And so—enter Truman Capote, bearing a quart of vodka and an assignment from *The New Yorker* to write a profile of Brando. They had met before at a Broadway rehearsal of *Streetcar*, and in his *New Yorker* piece (published November 1957, a month before the opening of *Sayonara*), Capote implies that their friendship was, at best, casual. Therefore—except for that bottle of vodka—it is surprising that Brando made so staggering a number of imprudent remarks, all of which Capote recorded with poisonous accuracy.

Throughout the article, Brando comes off as childish, perverse, antisocial, neurotic, pretentious. There's no analysis of Brando's talent—in fact, the inference is that he's just another movie star who equates success with money. But the really damaging section of the interview concerns *Sayonara* and Joshua Logan. Here Capote plays it both ways. He sneers at *Sayonara* (the Japanese hate the novel, he says), pokes fun at Logan's enthusiasm for the project, but then pulls a long face when Marlon scoffs at the director.

"I'm going to walk through that part, and that's that," Brando told Capote. "Nobody knows the difference anyway." He goes on to say that in one scene, he did everything wrong he could think of—rolled eyes, grimaced, used irrelevant gestures. When he finished the scene, Logan smiled and said, "It's wonderful, Marlon. Print it!"

When Marlon's unhappy in a production, says a friend, he looks for a scapegoat. He takes out his frustrations and doubts on the script or his co-star or the director—sometimes with justification, sometimes not. Back in the days of *The Eagle Has Two Heads,* he singled out Tallulah Bankhead. Now it was Josh Logan's turn.

By the time the article appeared, the film was in the can, and Brando had forgotten his Logan frustrations. He was deeply distressed by the publication of his drunken, supposedly off-the-record outburst of self-indulgent griping. "What am I going to do?" he asked Edith Van Cleve. "I never meant any of those things!"

"I don't know, Marlon," she replied. "But you must do something. Logan's a very sensitive man and I'm sure he's terribly hurt."

Brando wrote Logan a note of apology, saying that several times during the production he thought he was in the hands of an idiot, but the finished film proved Logan's judgment to be sound.

The critics concurred with Marlon's opinion. They liked the film and praised Brando's performance as one of his best. (It won him his third Academy Award nomination.) And though his Lloyd Gruver is a warm, often touching portrayal, it's fun, not top-notch Brando. At his best, he's sly and slightly mocking. Never quite stepping outside the context of the film, he's always teetering on the verge of walking through it.

Logan was a gentleman about the whole Capote incident. After receiving Brando's apology, he spoke understandingly of the actor's motivation in denigrating his directors or co-workers. "Marlon's a very special man," he said. "His trouble is he believes everyone is trying to belittle him. He hates authority. He distrusts anyone with power—the producer, the director, the writer, the politician in Washington."

Not everyone was ready to forgive and forget. It's impossible to judge how much damage Capote's article really did, but certainly it played an instrumental part in souring the press on Brando.

From Japan, Brando traveled to Germany for the filming of *The Young Lions,* an adaptation of Irwin Shaw's epic World

War II novel. With long-winded glibness, Shaw juxtaposed the stories of two Americans—one of them a Jew (Montgomery Clift), the other a Broadway playboy (Dean Martin)—with a portrait of Christian Diestl (Brando), a German ski instructor turned Nazi. At the end of the book, the three men cross paths and the German kills the Jew; then the American playboy stalks down the German, and shoots him in the best B movie tradition.

In the film, the German (Brando) raises his rifle against the Jew, pauses, lowers it, and is shot by the playboy. This new ending raised a lot of eyebrows.

In 1957, the world still wasn't ready for a soft-hearted Nazi, and the whitewashing of Shaw's puppet blackguard was chalked up against Brando. "No star wants to play a villain," went the outraged litany. "No actor will risk being unsympathetic."

At a press conference in Berlin, Brando declared, "Irwin Shaw wrote his great book while war hatreds were still white hot. We hope they have cooled. The picture will try to show that Nazism is a matter of mind, not geography; that there are Nazis—and people of good will—in every country."

"Mr. Brando speaks more like a statesman than a movie actor," a German journalist observed dryly.

The main point of public interest in *The Young Lions* was the first joint appearance of Marlon and Montgomery Clift, the two young geniuses of 1940s Broadway and Hollywood. At the beginning of his career, Brando was often likened to Clift, though there was never more than a surface similarity. Both specialized in playing troubled young men victimized by an indifferent society, but Clift was softer, frailer, more intellectual, and his acting had a minimum coat of conventional Broadway polish. (His great hero was Alfred Lunt, with whom he appeared when still a child actor in *There Shall Be No Night*.)

By 1957, Clift was in bad shape. A year earlier, he had attended a dinner party at Elizabeth Taylor's Beverly Hills home and, driving away afterward, had crashed into a telephone pole. There lingers an unsubstantiated rumor that he was drunk—in those days, he was often drunk.

The accident left Clift's face a battered and bloody pulp, which even the best plastic surgeons couldn't reconstruct. When he returned to the screen in *Raintree County,* the public was deeply shocked to see this once angelically handsome man transformed into an expressionless wraith. Surgery left his face immobilized, and he seemed to move and react through a slow-motion fog of anesthesia. Once, when he went backstage to visit Lynn Fontanne (Mrs. Alfred Lunt), she stared at him, and gasped, "Oh, my poor child! What have you done to yourself?" Around the world, audiences stared and gasped in similar pained disbelief.

Clift and Brando first met in the late forties during the Broadway run of *Streetcar.* One day Marlon and Wally Cox were motorcycling up Madison Avenue when Marlon abruptly turned in to the curb. He dismounted and walked over to a young man standing by a shop window.

"Hey, aren't you Montgomery Clift?" Marlon asked.

"Yes," Clift said. "And you're Brando. I recognize you from *Streetcar.*"

"People tell me I remind them of you," Marlon said.

"Oh?" Clift replied.

Brando gave the other actor a long stare. "Yes. But I don't see it." And then he turned on his heel, remounted, and roared off.

The two men admired each other—at least for public consumption. "One year, Marlon and I were both nominated for Oscars—he for *Streetcar* and I for *A Place in the Sun,*" Clift recalled. "I voted for him. I thought him that good. But Humphrey Bogart won, anyway."

In private, they harbored the usual professional jealousy. And at this time, Marlon was still (if barely) in the seat of power; in *The Young Lions,* he got all the good lines, all the pretty girls (Barbara Rush, May Britt, Liliane Montevecchi), and the full brunt of Clift's resentment. On the set, Monty turned to a friend and said, "Look at Marlon! He can't stand not being sympathetic! He's turning that bastard Nazi into a martyr!"

They had only one scene together—Brando's death scene. According to the script, after he is shot, Brando staggers down a hill and then keels over. Marlon wanted to season the ending with some histrionic salt—he suggested to director Edward Dmytryk that he die on a bundle of barbed wire, his arms outstretched.

Clift was outraged. "If Marlon's allowed to do that," he said, "I'll walk off the picture."

"When Monty's around," said a bystander, "there's only room for one Jesus Christ!"

Dmytryk said Marlon was charming and cooperative throughout the production. "He got the idea it was a serious picture and buckled down." *The Young Lions* is not an important film, but it is entertaining, thanks mainly to Brando. With his corn-silk blond hair and in his well-tailored uniforms, he looks splendid, and his portrayal of the idealistic Christian Diestl is, if not a great performance, certainly an exhibition of star acting at its most charismatic.

After two months of location shooting in Paris, *The Young Lions* unit moved to Borrego Springs, California, where filming was completed in September 1957. Then Brando, who had been working steadily for almost a year, announced he was going off on a holiday. For his fans, it was to be a very long vacation. There was a two-year, twelve-day interval between *The Young Lions* and the release of Marlon's next film, *The Fugitive Kind*.

·13·

MISADVENTURES

On "Hollywood Squares," a once-popular TV celebrity quiz game, comic Paul Lynde was asked: "Marlon Brandon named his first son after one of his favorite screen roles. What is his son's name?"

Lynde thought a moment and then replied, "Well, he must have called him either Desire . . . or . . . Waterfront."

Christian (for *The Young Lions*) Devi Brando was born in May 1958, seven months after his parents were married.

The first Mrs. Marlon Brando, Jr., was Anna Kashfi. She said she was a Darjeeling-born Buddhist who had made her American screen debut in 1956, in *The Mountain*, a Spencer Tracy fiasco.

Brando met this sari-clad houri shortly after her arrival in Hollywood, but their romance didn't become serious until Anna was hospitalized for tuberculosis. Marlon visited her frequently and was gentle and considerate. Miss Kashfi decided she had found the perfect husband. "Anna was deeply in love with Brando, and did what she felt she had to do to get him to marry her," recalled one of her friends. "She knew that more than anything else he wanted children."

The wedding was originally scheduled to take place in Arizona at the beginning of October 1957, but at that time the state barred interracial marriages. The ceremony finally took place on October 11, 1957, in the living room of the Lindermeyer home, where Brando had stayed when he came to the Coast for *The Men*.

Brando didn't want the press to know about the wedding until the ceremony was over, but how could he buy a ring without telling the world of the forthcoming event? He asked Sam Gilman to do the honors, and Gilman was happy to comply. Then, at the last moment, Marlon decided to do the purchasing himself. No one would recognize him, he claimed.

He did his shopping in downtown Pasadena, and was promptly mobbed. He was wearing a Hindu robe—hardly the most inconspicuous garb. A friend says Brando believes any disguise—no matter how superficial—renders him unrecognizable, and is always flabbergasted when spotted beneath his sunglasses and funny accents.

Shortly after the wedding, a London newspaper identified Anna Kashfi as Joanne O'Callaghan, the Calcutta-born daughter of a couple now living in their native Wales. For some time, the O'Callaghans had been wondering whatever happened to Joanne.

The English reporters quickly pieced together a Kashfi biography. Of Welsh parentage, she had been born in India and educated there in a convent school. Then at age thirteen her parents took her back to Wales. She finished school, worked for a time as a waitress and a clerk in a butcher shop, and then went to London to become a model or an actress. She was spotted by a talent agent who recommended her for the role in *The Mountain*. Edward Dmytryk, the director of that film, later stated that he had known Miss Kashfi's real name was Welsh, but assumed she was Anglo-Indian.

Kashfi then offered a revised edition of her life story. She was the illegitimate by-product of an alliance between Devi Kashfi, a Calcutta architect, and Selma Ghose. When she was two years old, her mother married an Englishman, William Patrick O'Callaghan, thereby incurring the wrath of her family, which disapproved of miscegenation. She had been educated at the Kurseong Roman Catholic convent and had not put foot on English soil until she was eighteen.

When reporters asked Brando to clear up the confusion, he snapped, "No comment."

They kept pestering Miss Kashfi for an interview, but she stalled. She asked Marlon what she should say.

"Tell them the truth," he replied.

"You son of a bitch," she yelled. "When you're asked, it's none of their business, but *you* want *me* to tell them the truth!"

For all of its very brief duration, the marriage was tumultuous. Both parties were at least partly responsible for the constant warfare. By her own admission, Kashfi drank too much and took too many pills. She was also inclined to temper tantrums, some of them not unjustified.

"During the time I was married to Marlon," Miss Kashfi said, "he would take off at all hours, day or night, without explanations, and sometimes wouldn't return until three or four A.M. When I asked him where he had been, he told me it was none of my business . . . and that he intended to lead the life he had led before we were married."

Later, Brando testified that at the time of the marriage, he fully intended to divorce Miss Kashfi within twelve months.

On September 25, 1958, less than a year after the wedding ceremony, the couple was legally separated and, on August 22, 1959, they were divorced.

As settlement, Marlon was ordered to pay Miss Kashfi $500,000—an immediate cash deposit of $60,000, with the remaining payments spread annually to 1970—plus $12,500 yearly in child support. After the divorce, Miss Kashfi never made another movie.

Anna was granted custody of Christian, with Marlon being allowed visitation rights. Brando wasn't happy about this arrangement, which immediately led to angry confrontations between the parents. On November 19, 1959, they were again facing a judge, who ordered them "to stop molesting and harassing each other."

And for a few weeks they did. Then in January 1960 they were back in court, with Brando requesting full custody of Christian. The previous Christmas he had tried to visit his son and Miss Kashfi had barred the way. Why? the judge asked. Kashfi replied that she was "humiliated and embarrassed" because Marlon was escorting Barbara Luna, his current flame.

The judge told Miss Kashfi she must permit Brando to entertain Christian at his home from five to seven P.M. on Wednesdays and Saturdays. "I want to impress upon you the necessity of good faith . . ." he said. But neither parent really listened.

The following May they were back on the witness stand. Marlon said Miss Kashfi was withholding visitation rights and he requested that she be held in contempt. Kashfi let fly with a few contemptuous words of her own—and she didn't wait for the court stenographer to record them. At recess, she cornered Brando and in a low voice called him one four-letter name after another, ending with a shout, "You ——— slob!"

Later, on the witness stand, the judge reprimanded her for evading his questions. "Isn't that too damn bad!" she replied. "I'll not be shouted at!" Then she picked up her purse and flounced out of the courtroom.

And that was only the beginning of a courtroom drama that was to go on for many years.

During this period of paternal anxiety, Brando was also beset by Pennebaker problems. He was still struggling with his Western, now titled *Ride, Comanchero!*, and had a rough draft, when Paul Newman made a Billy the Kid film, *The Left-Handed Gun*, which bore glaring similarities to the script Brando had evolved. There was no choice—Marlon was forced to scrap much of his material, and seek out fresh ideas. (Eventually, he was to buy three novels and borrow plot incidents from each. The basic source material was *The Authentic Death of Hendry Jones* by Charles Neider.)

In the meantime, Pennebaker had acquired other properties and, as it turned out, its first production did not star Brando. The initial release was *Shake Hands with the Devil*, a drama about the 1920 Black and Tan warfare in Ireland, with James Cagney and Don Murray in the leads. The company also bought *Paris Blues*, a story of American jazz musicians in

France. Brando thought he might star in this picture, hopefully with Marilyn Monroe as his co-star. Miss Monroe was then trifling with an offer to play Holly Golightly in *Breakfast at Tiffany's*, but she liked the idea of working with Marlon. She agreed to do *Paris Blues* if Brando co-starred, but he stalled on committing himself. (When Pennebaker produced the film in 1961, it starred Paul Newman and Joanne Woodward.)

To help shape his Western, Brando hired director Stanley Kubrick *(Dr. Strangelove, A Clockwork Orange)* on a six-month probation period. At the time, Kubrick had just won his place in the Hollywood sun with *Paths of Glory*, a pacifist melodrama about World War I. He had an undeniable flair, was bright, hip, and young. At face value, he seems the kind of fellow Marlon would like, but the two never got together on this project.

As soon as Kubrick scanned the confused *War and Peace*—sized script Marlon handed him, he knew it would take more than six months to straighten it out. Still, he showed up regularly at Brando's home for a singular series of conferences with Marlon, associate producer Frank J. Rosenberg, and an assortment of journeywork screenwriters.

To call meetings to order, Marlon sounded a large Japanese gong, just like the loin-clothed lackey at the beginning of a J. Arthur Rank movie. At first the conferences were so heated that Marlon often boomed on the gong to gain the floor. Then, as the weeks dwindled away, enthusiasm boiled down to apathy and finally there was more poker playing than film discussion.

Kubrick complained to Brando, "We've spent six months on this film, and I still don't know what the story's about."

"It's about the three hundred and fifty thousand dollars we've already spent," Marlon answered. The two men dissolved their partnership "by mutual consent."

Later Kubrick said he thought Marlon always wanted to direct his movie himself, and was slowly building up the nerve to take the plunge. With Kubrick quitting the film only two weeks before its December 1958 shooting date, Marlon found the incentive he needed. Either he directed himself or once again he would have to delay one of the most postponed productions in film history. He chose the first course.

Asked why he wanted to direct, Brando said, "I've got no respect for acting. By and large, acting is the expression of a neurotic impulse. I've never in my life met an actor who was not neurotic—not that it's bad to be neurotic, it's just not satisfying.

"Acting is a bum's life, in that it leads to perfect self-indulgence," he went on. "You get paid for doing nothing and it all adds up to nothing. . . . Acting gives me no satisfaction, which is why I'm considering stopping as an actor. The creative satisfaction I seek comes from creating—that means functioning in other areas . . . the principal benefit acting has afforded me is the money to pay for my psychoanalysis."

If you slice through the pseudopsychiatric palaver about actors and their neuroses, there's a real clue as to why Brando was seeking a toehold behind the camera: screen direction offered him a measure of artistic control he could not command as an actor.

In film, it is the director who gives an actor's performance its rhythm, its continuity, its climaxes, its ultimate place in the design of the film. He can make an actor look very bad by cutting away from him at strategic moments, by bad camera placement, by a hundred other insensitivities. After the release of *The Young Lions,* Brando complained that if all of his performance had been seen (the film was severely cut in the editing stages), there would have been no criticism of the one-sidedness of his sympathetic Nazi.

Once Marlon spoke about Hollywood directors and divided them into two categories: those who understand the actor's problems and those who don't. "John Ford would never have me in a picture because he directs from the director's point of view, not the actor's. He isn't interested in actors. . . . Alfred Hitchcock is another. He tells the same story over and over again, not from the human point of view, but from the point of view of camera angles.

"Then there are the directors who are capable of both. George Stevens is one of the best and so is Kazan."

Did he intend to emulate Kazan and Stevens? "To want to be like anybody else is a mistake," he answered. "I'd rather follow my own intuition."

By the time he went into production, Marlon had already spent $1,250,000 on *One-Eyed Jacks*, the title definitely chosen for his film. Budgeted at twelve weeks and $2,500,000, *One-Eyed Jacks* was six months in production and eventually cost $6,000,000. Since a film must gross two and a half times its cost before it shows a profit, *One-Eyed Jacks* needed a box-office take of $15,000,000 to break even. At this time, only a handful of movies had ever made that kind of money.

Brando's cast included Karl Malden, Katy Jurado (a Mexican actress with whom Marlon had earlier had a brief romance), Ben Johnson, Sam Gilman, and Pina Pellicer, a delicate, sloe-eyed actress who played the lead in a Mexican production of *The Diary of Anne Frank*. She was highly touted as "a major discovery," and under Brando's loving direction she turned in a spirited performance.

Besides helping her with her acting, Marlon coached her in horseback riding, tutored her in English, and made love to her whenever the schedule permitted. He also dropped her as soon as the picture was finished. She returned to her native country, made two Mexican films, and committed suicide in December 1964.

Throughout the shooting, Marlon was self-indulgent about squandering time and money; no detail was too insignificant to escape his attention. For a seacoast sequence, he kept cast and crew waiting for days until the Pacific whipped up breakers that met his standards. (Most of the film was shot on location near Monterey, California.)

He demanded fully rounded performances, even from his bit players. "Think!" he shouted to extras about to witness a flogging scene. "Think of the horrible things in your own lives and then the camera will photograph the horror in your faces." He scanned the bored faces of his players and yelled,

"Besides, there's a three-hundred-dollar bonus for the man who looks most horrified!"

In *One-Eyed Jacks*, Marlon had to play a very sloshy drunk scene. Drunks, he said, were never played convincingly. So he decided he'd really get drunk for the scene. He and Sam Gilman swigged away at a bottle of bourbon until they were both blotto, and then they reeled into camera range. After several lost-weekend takes, the cameraman stopped loading his camera, but Brando and Gilman continued to lurch through a series of sodden improvisations.

The showpiece of the film is the sequence in which Brando is bound to a hitching post and horsewhipped. Marlon staged this scene as though he were De Sade plotting the final orgy at the Chateau de Seligny: he demonstrated exactly how the bullwhip was to be brandished across his back, and artfully arranged the camera angles to emphasize the tortured beauty of his face and torso. And the meticulous planning paid off: in the finished film, the flogging scene is powerfully, almost sensuously shot.

Brando's affection for self-punishment was now becoming something of an inside joke: "You want Marlon for a picture? Well, just write in a scene where he's beaten up. He likes to be beaten up."

Marlon was well into production before he discovered a theme for his film. As he explained it, the film's title referred to man's two-sided nature. While most men show only their good face to the world, there's a reverse side which, like that of playing cards, remains unseen.

The theme is worked out with some pretty heavy symbolism. With one blue eye and one brown eye, the Rio Kid (Brando) is an easily identifiable and much-feared bank robber of the Old West. As the film begins, he's turned over to a posse by a treacherous partner (Karl Malden). After five years in jail, Rio goes in search of his betrayer and finds him working as a sheriff in a border town; he's changed his name, rather symbolically, to Dad Longstreet, and he's a respected pillar of the community. Rio doesn't expose him, but he's not

Brando with Teresa Wright
in his first film,
The Men (1950)

Brando and Vivien Leigh in *A Streetcar Named Desire* (1952)

"Getting those colored lights going": Brando and Kim Hunter in *Streetcar*

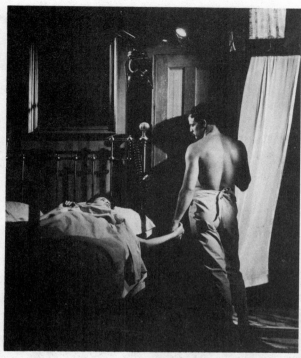

With Jean Peters in
Viva Zapata! (1952)

The Funeral
Oration from
Julius Caesar
(1953)

Ready for some "whaling": *The Wild One* (1954)

With Jean Simmons in *Désirée* (1954)

"Luck Be A Lady": *Guys and Dolls* (1955)

Visiting James Dean on the set of *East of Eden* (1955).
The two actors are surrounded by a technician and three
supporting players from the film

"I could've been a contender" : Brando and Rod Steiger in
On the Waterfront (1954)

Sayonara (1957)

Director Edward
Dmytryk gives Brando
some last-minute
instruction during
the filming of
The Young Lions (1958)

Brando and
Anna Kashfi on
their wedding day

With Anna Magnani in *The Fugitive Kind* (1960)

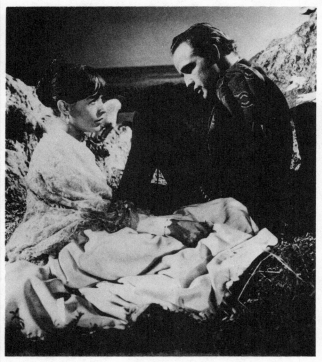

With his protégée
Pina Pellicer in
One-Eyed Jacks (1961)

willing to forgive and forget. As revenge, he seduces Dad's stepdaughter (Pina Pellicer), only to fall in love with her.

Brando wasn't sure about the ending. One day he thought Rio must die and on the next, he granted him clemency. In the film, Rio rides off into the sunset—a finish forced on Marlon by his distributor. He didn't like it, but never described an alternative ending.

The shooting script for *One-Eyed Jacks* ran almost two hundred pages (about four hours of shooting time), and Marlon didn't blue-pencil while filming. (If anything, he expanded; he used lots of improvisation, and improvised performances tend to be loose and pause-inflated.) But after 133 days in production, Marlon crept past the finishing line and called together his cast for a champagne celebration.

Dressed in tails, top hat, and a magician's cape, he emceed a comedy routine by Mort Sahl. "I want to notify you officially that this picture is completed because we ran out of money," Sahl quipped. Everyone laughed, even Brando, but the joke was too true to be funny.

Once again Brando was crying poor, and this time with reason. The preproduction costs of *Jacks* came out of his pocket, which was already being pinched by Anna Kashfi's alimony payments. And, just when an incoming buck would have been welcome, the family business skidded into the red.

Four years after Mrs. Brando's death, Marlon Senior married Anna Parramore, a twenty-eight-year-old divorcée; in other words, Marlon gained a stepmother who was four years his junior. The newlyweds settled in the Los Angeles area, and the elder Brando went to work as manager of Pennebaker Productions. (He was to remain an executive of the company until his death in July 1965.)

Deprived of Mr. Brando's supervisory hand, the Penny Poke Ranch suddenly and mysteriously began to lose money. The supposition was that the hired hands were slowly and skillfully cheating their bosses, and, with no real alternative, Marlon Senior decided to sell out—at a considerable loss.

In their new roles as business partners, Marlon and his dad

presented a cozy front to outsiders. Mr. Brando liked to joke about the confusion of having a famous son with an identical moniker. Whenever "Marlon Brando" was listed on an airline passenger list, the stewardesses preened in anticipation of meeting the celebrity guest and were unpleasantly surprised when a grey-haired nonentity claimed his seat.

Once, when Brando Senior opened some "personal" mail intended for Brando Junior, Marlon was furious. "Why don't you change your name?" he yelled at his father. "It was my name before it was yours," Marlon Senior replied good-naturedly.

But beneath the friendly surface, there were still deep currents of resentment—at least on Marlon's side.

According to British writer H. A. L. Craig, a close friend of both Brandos, the two men railed at each other in private. Marlon cursed his father for "ruining" his mother, and constantly picked at old childhood wounds. He called his father almost daily, and after one conversation Mr. Brando said, "Why is my son afraid to talk to me? I hear it every time he opens his mouth." Then he put his hands to his ears, implying, Craig thought, that he neither expected nor wanted an answer.

With the liquidation of the Penny Poke Ranch, Marlon was largely responsible for his father's welfare—another financial (and, one imagines, emotional) drain. There were any number of things Brando could have done to make a fast killing, and easiest of all would have been a promotional endorsement. But back in the *Streetcar* days he had chided Jessica Tandy for lending her name to advertising, and now he wavered, but remained true to his old, self-righteous attitude.

"I called him to say he had received a fifty-thousand-dollar offer to do a TV commercial for Love Cosmetics," Edith Van Cleve remembered. "He didn't have to say anything, as I recall, he just had to stand there and kiss or be kissed by a model who was dousing herself in eau de cologne. After I outlined the offer, Marlon said, 'Well, tell them I'll think it over, but frankly, I find the whole idea very embarrassing.' We both laughed and that was the end of that."

Brando compromised in other ways. He put aside the editing of *One-Eyed Jacks* to film a role he had formerly turned down as a stage comeback. It was Val Xavier, the snakeskin-jacketed troubadour of Tennessee Williams's *Orpheus Descending*. To play it, he was guaranteed a million dollars, and even considering the salary, it was one of the worst mistakes of his career.

He could have been playing Lawrence of Arabia. Producer Sam Spiegel announced that Brando was to star in his film biography of T. E. Lawrence, but apparently he wearied of waiting for Brando to finish *One-Eyed Jacks*. In a huff, Spiegel said he was going ahead with an unknown in the leading role. (Peter O'Toole got the part.) Brando told friends he had never agreed to play Lawrence—it didn't fit into his schedule.

Brando should have squeezed it into his schedule somehow. Without casting aspersions on O'Toole's fine performance, one may surmise Marlon could have been splendid in the part, and, who knows, that one triumph might have staved off his 1960s washout.

·14·
MARLON DESCENDING

In the mid-1950s Brando finally admitted that he had no intention of returning to the stage. "Why should I?" he asked. "What's so hot about New York? What's so hot about working for [Broadway producers] Cheryl Crawford and Robert Whitehead?"

To explain this sudden about-face, he developed a wide-ranging series of defenses. Movies paid better than Broadway, he said; they reached a far wider public; they might someday become a potent factor in the "moral development" of the people.

Once he admitted that he couldn't stand the deadly routine of a Broadway run. "In the theater, they expect you to freeze a performance and play it the same way night after night. I could never face that again."

Then he added, with a shrug of the shoulders, "Besides, there aren't any roles for me."

People really hooted at that one. Brando, they said, could have any role he wanted. And while, yes, he probably could, what roles on Broadway were worth his attention?

Here's a representative sample of plays Marlon has turned down over the years: *The Rape of the Belt*, an English comedy about Hippolyta, Hercules, an assorted mythological bedhoppers; *Ready When You Are, C. B.!*, a one-set, six-character farce about love and apartment-sharing on Riverside Drive; *Poor Richard*, a Jean Kerr loser; and *Scratch*, Archibald MacLeish's torpid retelling of *The Devil and Daniel Webster*.

He was offered his pick of revivals. One producer came forward with the pipe dream of staging *The Cherry Orchard* with Brando, John Gielgud, and Ina Claire. The American Shakespeare Festival in Stratford, Connecticut, wanted him to do Hamlet on carte blanche terms. And Sol Hurok in conjunction with General Electric said, pick a classic, any classic, and we'll tour it for sixteen weeks in the elite of American regional theaters.

Brando refused them all. He didn't believe America had the tradition or the personnel for producing the classics. (And in the early 1960s, he had a valid point. Those were the years that saw Alfred Drake as Iago, Katharine Hepburn in a Gilbert and Sullivan version of *Twelfth Night*, Elia Kazan's ignominious production of *The Changeling*.)

"There were many, many other offers," Edith Van Cleve recalled. "I diligently sent the scripts to the Coast, though I knew Marlon wasn't interested. I'm sure that most of the time he didn't even read them. Sometimes he'd send them back with regrets; sometimes his secretary returned them; often I never saw them again. He must have a cellar full of unopened manuscripts."

Tennessee Williams wanted Brando for the male lead in the four plays he wrote after *Streetcar*, but Marlon refused, saying the roles were too close to Kowalski. Williams didn't take four no's for a definite answer. In 1955, he dragged an abandoned play from his trunk and rewrote it to fit the talents of Brando and Anna Magnani.

In its original version, the play was called *Battle of Angels*. In 1942 Margaret Webster produced it with Miriam Hopkins in the leading role, and, while on the road, she decided it wasn't ready for Broadway. She closed it "for alterations" in Boston, where audiences were scandalized by the heavy-breathing love scenes. Williams never got around to revising the play; instead, he started afresh with *The Glass Menagerie*, then *Streetcar*, and onward with his string of 1950s hits.

A dry run of creativity sent Williams back to the play, which he retitled *Orpheus Descending*. Val Xavier, its guitar-slinging hero, is one of Williams's holy losers; he knows the world is corrupt (he's been a teenage hustler), knows there's nothing he can do about it, knows it's best not to try, and yet, through love, he's sucked into confrontation with an unbeatable evil.

Val wanders into a bayou backwater and meets Lady Torrance, the frustrated wife of the town lout. "I NEED YOU!!!" Lady shouts at Val, "TO GO ON LIVIN'!" (It's a play heavy in exclamation marks.) It's an invitation Val can't refuse, and of course Lady becomes pregnant ("Hang the tinsel and Christmas lights on me, there's life in my body!!" she cries). But just before the final curtain, her husband shoots her and masterminds the murder of Val.

Marlon read the play and told Williams he didn't understand Val's motivation and therefore couldn't accept the part. "You can't play a void," he said. Williams rewrote the play according to Brando's vague suggestions, and then altered it again. Brando was still dissatisfied.

"I have no intention of walking on a stage with Magnani," he told Truman Capote. "Not in that part. They'd have to mop me up."

A few months later Anna Magnani also backed out, pleading an insufficient grasp of English. When the play opened on Broadway in March 1957, it starred Maureen Stapleton and Cliff Robertson. Poorly reviewed by the critics, it limped through a two-month run, and its closing marked the funeral rites for Williams's fashionable reputation.

The industry welcomed the announcement that Brando and Magnani were to film *Orpheus Descending* (retitled *The Fugitive Kind*) with predictions of Italo-American warfare. Magnani was called La Lupa, the She-Wolf, for her temperamental pyrotechnics and electrifying, peasant-real performances. If she chose, she could mop up both screen and set with Marlon.

The Fugitive Kind was filmed in a New York studio in the summer of 1959 under the direction of Sidney Lumet, a former actor (he replaced Marlon in *A Flag Is Born*) who switched to directing in the halcyon days of live TV drama.

By the time of *The Fugitive Kind*, he had three film bombs behind him, and even his biggest fans despaired that he was stepping way out of his class in opting to referee such a heavyweight cast.

Besides Brando and Magnani, there was Joanne Woodward as Carol Cutrere, a plantation aristocrat turned slut. (Miss Cutrere doesn't have much to do with the plot; she stands around, half-dressed and fully crazed, spouting lines like "Wi-i-i-ld things leave thar sk-i-i-ins behin'!!!" Maybe she serves as the Greek chorus in this riffraff retelling of the Orpheus myth.) Miss Woodward wasn't the temperamental type, but, as a former Academy Award winner, she was entitled to her share of the red carpet.

The supporting cast featured Maureen Stapleton. She played Lady Torrance on stage, and some people felt it was crass of Lumet to ask her to support Magnani in the film version. But Miss Stapleton didn't take offense.

The Fugitive Kind was her second film, and she was still at sea when it came to acting for the camera. Brando taught her a valuable lesson. "I had a scene with Marlon where we walked up a hill," she remembers. "The camera was at the top of the hill, and we're at the bottom, and they waved at us to start up. I'm reacting all over the place, and Marlon says, 'Cool it,' and I said, 'What do you mean?' And he answered, 'The camera isn't even turned on; I'll tell you when to start acting.' So we walked on, and I asked, 'Now, Marlon?' and he said, 'Not yet.' Well, when the camera was almost on top of us, he said, 'Okay, act!' And that was the day I knew there was a lot I had to learn about screen acting."

Early on in the production, Brando was commuting between New York and California. Every weekend, he flew to the West Coast where he worked continuously on the editing of *One-Eyed Jacks* until it was time to return to New York and *The Fugitive Kind.* But the pace became too debilitating and he was forced to turn *Jacks* over to professional cutters.

This enforced separation from his brainchild soured Marlon on the Williams film. He had never been very enthusiastic.

Once again the playwright had overhauled the script and once again he had failed to bring Val to life. With nothing to stimulate his imagination, Brando walks through the film, leaving a shadow of indifference behind him. And since it's Williams and Brando together again, one can't help but remember Kowalski; the comparison is devastating.

He does have one stunning scene—his first in the film. It's in a courtroom, and in a three-minute monologue, Val describes where he's been and where he's going. Here Marlon has his old magnetism, and he does some surprising things with Williams's dialogue; but then, just as one's about to bring out the superlatives, the performance goes dead. It's heavy and cumbersome—a joyless self-parody of past glories.

Though Marlon and Magnani both have their moments individually, their teamwork never generates much electricity. There were wild tales that Marlon drove Magnani to distraction by blowing his lines in take after take, but if so, the Italian actress had forgotten all about it.

"Marlon's a fine fellow," she said. "I'm terribly fond of him, I admire him. His only fault is he plays the star too much."

The two fought over billing—both wanted first listing in the film's credits. One afternoon, when the actress was down in the dumps (personal problems, she said), Brando went up to her and started to needle. "I know why you're blue. I know."

"Be quiet, Marlon," she said. "You don't know anything."

"You want your name to come before mine in the credits. Why?"

"Because it's my due," she answered.

"Because you're an ambitious woman," Marlon said.

"And what do you call yourself?" Magnani shot back.

(A compromise was worked out on the credit question. In America, Marlon's name came first. In Italy, Magnani got first billing.)

When *The Fugitive Kind* was finished, Brando returned to Hollywood and *One-Eyed Jacks*. Though he made a yeoman's effort, he couldn't take more than an hour out of the excess footage, and Paramount, which put up most of the production money in exchange for distribution rights, refused to release the film until it was shorn of another forty minutes. The battles that ensued were ugly and unrewarding; Paramount finally took the picture away from Brando and carved it down to regulation size. In release, *Jacks* ran two hours and twenty-one minutes. It was, say his friends, a traumatic experience for Marlon.

Throughout the 1950s, Marlon frequently made the lists of the ten top-grossing stars. Then, in 1959, he didn't appear in any films, and therefore automatically dropped off the list. He wasn't to rejoin the big-money elite until 1972, the year of *The Godfather*.

In the early sixties, Brando would have made (if there were such a thing) the list of the ten biggest losers—in fact, he would have been its number one attraction.

First came *The Fugitive Kind*, which was a terrible fiasco. Audiences and critics attacked it with a hostility that isn't entirely explained by the poor quality of the film; it's bad, but not *that* bad. Suddenly everyone was bored by Williams's Southern Gothic decadence; by Anna Magnani's earth-mother realism; most of all, by Brando's poetic hooliganism.

Once Brando had touched the nerve of his time, but the times were changing, and here was Marlon still doing his old routine. And the kids who quivered with recognition while watching *The Wild One* were now sophisticated enough to scoff at their former teenage idols.

"An actor's like a household pet," Brando remarked. "People think of us much like they think of their favorite cat or dog. When you have a pet you talk about it as if it were something special. You become emotionally involved with the animal and you endow it with qualities and characteristics it might not have. It is the same with an actor. You have one or two emotional experiences with him and you begin to trust him . . . but once you have fulfilled people's expectations, they demand you live up to their next fantasy, and the next."

Early in 1960, *The Fugitive Kind* was sneak-previewed at a second-run theater in Manhattan. By performance time—eight P.M. on a Sunday—the theater was mobbed with all New York's bright young people. There were rumors that the stars were going to attend, though only Tennessee Williams and (if memory serves) Joanne Woodward turned up.

Silence prevailed during Brando's first scene, but then, as the clumsily staged and painfully slow film inched along its predictable course, the audience grew restless and chatty. The guffaws began when a very sturdy Joanne Woodward mentioned her "fragile arms and birdlike body." A few minutes later, there was pandemonium as Miss Woodward, in a scene with Brando, sunk to her knees and out of frame, her head somewhere in the vicinity of Marlon's crotch. After that, there was too much noise to hear the dialogue on the screen.

Following the preview, the entire audience waited in the lobby to boo Tennessee Williams as he left. The playwright cheerfully hissed back and a few kind souls applauded his futile gesture. That was the only round of applause *The Fugitive Kind* ever received. When the film opened in April 1960, it played to near-empty houses. Exhibitors reported that audiences walked out in droves.

It took Paramount another year to prepare *One-Eyed Jacks* for release. It opened in March 1961, to generally favorable reviews. The critics liked Brando the director; they praised his sweeping visual style, his skill with actors, his offbeat handling of the Western format.

They were honorable, but not money-in-the-bank, reviews. *One-Eyed Jacks* never returned a dime on its $6,000,000 investment—eventually it grossed $4,500,000—but it did garner a large underground following. And it's the quintessential cult film—perverse, slightly incoherent, open to all sorts of iconographic or psychosexual interpretations.

The *One-Eyed Jacks* enthusiasts will tell you that the maiming of Rio's gun hand is tantamount to castration, that his affair with Dad Longstreet's stepdaughter is nothing short of incest, that his relationship with the Sam Gilman character is fraught with homosexual innuendo. All true, all meaningless. In short, it's the kind of horse opera that leads Ph.D. candidates to write theses on (this is not a fabricated title) "The Classic Mythology of The Modern Western Genre."

There's one thing to be said for Brando the director: He knows how to photograph Brando the actor. His Rio is less a feat of acting than a farrago of Byronic posturing, and sometimes (maybe because there's so little self-humor), he's slightly silly. But the lush, wide-screen close-ups have an electrifying, egotistic grandeur; they're a whole picture show in themselves.

To date, *One-Eyed Jacks* is Marlon's only directorial effort. As he predicted, when the first film doesn't make money, there is no second chance.

· 15 ·

BRANDO ON THE *BOUNTY*

Next came the Waterloo of Brando's career—the $26,000,000 version of *Mutiny on the Bounty*. It wasn't meant to cost that much, and some claim it would have sailed across the finish line at $20,000,000 less, if it hadn't been for Marlon. He vehemently disagrees, and he went to court to clear himself of this widely credited vilification.

Prior to the Brando version, the true-life story of H.M.S. *Bounty* had been filmed twice. In 1933, an Australian company made *In the Wake of the Bounty*, but outside Sydney and Melbourne few people saw it. Then, two years later, MGM produced *Mutiny on the Bounty* with Clark Gable, Charles Laughton, Franchot Tone, and Movita. An immediate success, it was to become one of the most beloved movies of all time.

In the 1960s, the poverty-stricken Hollywood studios were looking over their production backlog for possible remake material. In this way they skirted the astronomical prices being asked for best-selling novels and Broadway smashes, but still had the assurance of a property with pretested name value. *Mutiny on the Bounty* was a natural: it was a title everyone recognized, and offered unexplored vistas for the wide-screen, color cinematographer.

The *Bounty* remake was produced by Aaron Rosenberg, an ex-All-American football player with lasting gridiron tastes. He made his fortune by grinding out Westerns, sea sagas, and

Tony Curtis romances that nobody remembers, but everyone once paid to see.

One day, director John Sturges suggested Rosenberg revamp *Bounty* for Brando (as either Bligh or Fletcher Christian). "Great idea!" Rosenberg said, and immediately asked Brando's agent to feel out Marlon's reaction. And he hired Eric Ambler, the British suspense novelist, to fashion a screenplay.

"Marlon's interested," the agent reported, "but he doesn't want to redo the old picture. He'd like to emphasize the period when the mutineers reach Pitcairn Island. He wants to get across the message that the way our society is constituted, people can't live without hate, even in a paradise."

Rosenberg approved Brando's interpretation, a cue for Marlon to vacillate as to whether or not he would take on the assignment. After a few months of dickering, Rosenberg decided to search for another superstar.

But when Ambler handed in his script, Rosenberg decided to send it to Marlon on a long shot. No, Brando said, definitely no. And then he asked the producer to drop by for a chat.

At the conference, Marlon said he'd play Fletcher Christian if Ambler would skimp still further on the adventure sections of the script and place major emphasis on the Pitcairn segment. Rosenberg agreed, and also assigned Marlon consultation rights on that part of the picture. With that guarantee written into the fine print, Marlon signed a contract paying him $500,000 in advance against ten percent of the gross, with a provision of $5,000 per day if the film went overtime.

Rosenberg's first mistake was in initialing that overtime clause. Before the production ended, it added an additional $750,000 to Brando's base salary.

Brando's contract specified an October 15, 1960, starting date, as did those of his co-stars Trevor Howard (Bligh), Richard Harris, Hugh Griffith, and the film's director, Sir Carol Reed. In choosing Reed—he made *The Fallen Idol, Odd*

Man Out, The Third Man—Rosenberg was telling the world that his *Mutiny* would be a thinking-man's spectacle with psychology as well as swashbuckling. The English director wasn't the Cecil De Mille type; his forte was character and plot development.

Sir Carol arrived in California several months before *Mutiny*'s October starting date. He and Rosenberg stopped by Brando's Beverly Hills home, but Marlon wasn't in a *Mutiny* mood. Instead, he spent two hours trying to promote a film biography of Caryl Chessman, the executed rapist. (Chessman was then on the tip of every liberal tongue, and Marlon was constantly rehashing the case. On the night Chessman was executed, Brando went to San Quentin and picketed outside with the other mourners.) When Rosenberg refused to replace *Mutiny* with the Chessman story, Brando lent an ear to the day's business. Yes, he'd accompany Reed and Rosenberg to Tahiti, the site selected for the filming of *Mutiny*; and, yes, he'd help them choose a Polynesian girl for his leading lady.

Papeete, the capital city of Tahiti, was the spearhead of the *Mutiny* operation and the three men settled in at its only "first class" hotel, sadly misnamed The Grand. Auditions were held there to select the native cast members. After the minor roles were filled, sixteen local *vahines* were invited to compete for the role of Maimiti, Fletcher Christian's concubine—Marlon was allowed the honor of plucking the most promising blossom from this lei of beauties.

One by one, he took the girls into a secluded room and announced he was about to jump from the window. He wanted to study their reactions to his suicidal threat, with the role going to the most unexpected response.

The test was a bust. All the girls reacted in the same way: they giggled. (The Grand Hotel was only two stories high.) Finally, Marlon picked Tarita Teriipaia, a nineteen-year-old employed as dishwasher and waitress in a local hotel. (Her last name was eliminated in the film's credits.) She giggled less than her competitors.

Meanwhile, in faraway Nova Scotia, a 118-foot replica of the *Bounty* was being built by the Smith and Rhuland shipyard at a cost of $750,000. On the outside, it looked like the original *Bounty;* inside it was equipped with diesel engines, electricity, and dressing rooms. When the ship was completed, it would be sailed from Nova Scotia to Tahiti.

On October 15, 1960, cast and crew were assembled and on salary, but neither *Bounty* nor script arrived on schedule. Smith and Rhuland missed their deadline—the ship wouldn't arrive in Tahiti until late November. With the help of scenarists Borden Chase and William Driskill, Eric Ambler had finished another draft of the screenplay, but no one was satisfied with it. Rosenberg fired the three writers and asked Charles Lederer, a veteran Hollywood scenarist, to revise the script from scratch. Lederer said it wasn't possible to complete the job by November. Okay, Rosenberg replied, write as we shoot—just stay a day ahead of the shooting schedule.

The *Bounty* was now on the high seas. On its way to Tahiti, there were two fires; the ship rolled frighteningly in the heavy swells; and the sailors suffered appallingly from seasickness. Before Papeete was sighted, there was almost a real-life mutiny on this make-believe *Bounty.*

Back in Hollywood, the MGM executives were tearing their hair out. Every time there was a delay in production, MGM stock fell—often as many as ten points in a single day. Already the executives were preparing to delegate the blame, and Brando was prime candidate as scapegoat. Because of the Capote interview and the delay on *One-Eyed Jacks,* Marlon now had a reputation as a troublemaker, and MGM was unscrupulous enough to exploit it to the company's advantage.

Cast and crew arrived in Papeete a few weeks before the *Bounty.* In 1960, there were fewer than three hundred rooms suitable for tourists on the entire island. MGM took over two-thirds, paying as high as $300 a month for the choicer quarters. It requisitioned three large warehouses for lights, cameras, costumes, sound equipment, props, and other paraphernalia. Practically all the island's spare transportation was leased by the company, and hundreds of local workers were employed regularly, while thousands of natives were hired for journeywork.

The Tahitian government was enraged by MGM's monopolization of the island's labor force. Tahiti was then in the midst of a building boom, and the local businessmen complained that *Mutiny*'s heavy demand for labor was driving up wages. And there are unsubstantiated reports that the Tahitian bluestockings disapproved of the company's moral standards.

Marlon lived in a "villa," described by one journalist as "a straw hut of epic proportions," and, according to another reporter, there were several handmaidens in constant attendance. Brando promptly fell in live with Tahiti—it was the South Sea Eden he envisioned in his retirement fantasies. He learned the *tamuré*, a native welcoming dance; discovered an appreciative audience for his bongo drums; and generally lived it up as a white god beachcomber. The only vestige of Western civilization he craved was the Sunday *New York Times*, flown in to him at a cost to MGM of $27.94 a week. Back in Hollywood, this petty detail was entered in the studio brief against Brando. So was his insistence on motorboat transportation. Why, MGM asked, couldn't he sail out to location with the rest of the cast?

Production began in earnest on December 4, 1960. At first, filming went smoothly, if slowly. Reed was a highly professional but meticulous director, and the MGM executives were troubled by his snail's progress. Later Brando defended Reed by saying: "Carol couldn't in all conscience go ahead without a full script so he delayed shooting crucial scenes."

What happened next is subject to angry, wildly contradictory testimony.

MGM claims that after a few weeks of filming, Marlon told Rosenberg he didn't see himself as Fletcher Christian; instead, he thought he'd like to play John Adams, the sole survivor of the *Bounty* mutiny.

The cameras stopped while this request was relayed to California. A belligerent, irreparable veto was wired back to Tahiti, and Brando meekly continued as Christian.

Absolutely not true, Marlon insists. He never asked to switch roles.

For some reason there was a hiatus in the production, and shortly after shooting was resumed, the rainy season hit Tahiti with gale force. It rained for seventeen straight days and, with no sunshine expected for several weeks, Rosenberg decided to pack up and return to Hollywood for an early start on interior filming. When the rains ceased, the *Mutiny* company would return to Papeete to finish the outdoor scenes. This round trip voyage would, of course, add a couple of million extra to the budget (and cause another stock-market plunge for MGM).

On arrival in Hollywood, Carol Reed left the production. Some say he was stricken with gallstones and asked to be removed; others insist he was really fired. The MGM publicists hinted that Brando was behind the Englishman's dismissal, and the cast, strongly pro-Reed, was incensed. To extricate himself from this web of deception, Marlon called together cast and crew and announced, "I don't give a damn what the press says about me concerning this matter, but I do care about what you people think. My loyalties are torn. . . . I'm fond of Carol, but the argument doesn't concern me, and I had nothing to do with it."

Reed confirmed that Brando was blameless in this awkward situation. Rosenberg told reporters, "It's very unfortunate. Sir Carol worked in a very special way. We figured if he continued at his rate, we would be another year and a half just in the shooting." He went on to say that most of Reed's footage would be scrapped.

Marlon claimed that MGM on several occasions requested him to seize Reed's command, but he refused. Maybe so; still, it's hard to believe that anybody would ask Brando, with the titanic disaster of *One-Eyed Jacks* just behind him, to guide this sand-barred production into safe waters.

Lewis Milestone replaced Reed. He had some distinguished films among his credits, including *All Quiet on the Western Front* and *Of Mice and Men*, but quality was a happy accident in his films. He was an old Hollywood pro—the traffic manager type of director who's setting up the next take while finishing the last. There are reports that Brando personally selected Milestone because of the pacifist spirit of several of the director's films. If so, he made a bad mistake.

"Do such and such," Milestone ordered.

"Why?" Brando inquired.

Milestone was the first director who actively and vocally detested Brando. "Did you ever hear of an actor who put plugs in his ears so he couldn't listen to the director or other actors?" Milestone asked reporters. "Whenever I tried to direct him in a scene, he'd say, 'Are you telling me or are you asking my advice?'"

One of Brando's friends dismissed the earplug story as a vicious misinterpretation of the facts: "It's ridiculous because Marlon has always kept plugs in his ears when he was studying a script. He has to concentrate completely, and he finds he can't with all the noise that is made on a set or a location. . . . Of course, he removes them if someone speaks to him."

Milestone says Marlon rarely talked to him. If Brando had an objection to a scene or an interpretation, he argued it out with Rosenberg or Charles Lederer. "Sometimes the three of them haggled over a line for hours before a camera would turn," Milestone said. If they reached a stalemate, the trio resorted to "democratic process" (Milestone's term): Marlon got one vote, Rosenberg and Lederer a half each.

When the company returned to Tahiti in March 1961, the big trouble began. The MGM spokesmen said Brando's barefoot beach orgies brought him to the set bleary-eyed and unprepared, demanding "idiot cards," those dialogue reminders actors place around the set or on their person to stimulate their faulty memory.

Often Marlon took excessive liberties with his lines, much to the disgust of his co-stars. "Sometimes I'd stand there with egg on my face," Trevor Howard said. "I didn't know whether he'd finished a line or not."

Line retention wasn't Marlon's long suit; neither was fidelity to an author's text. Like many actors (both good and bad), he exercises the right to revise lines that trip his tongue or offend his inner ear. And there are writers who say he knows best. "I learned more about dialogue writing from Brando than from anything else in my career," said one screenwriter. "The little changes he made, his pauses, an adjective he dropped—it was a revelation. Ninety-nine percent of the time, his changes were an improvement over the script."

During *Mutiny*, Brando became angry when accused of bad memory. "There were twenty-seven scripts for the movie," he said. "It was impossible to memorize them. . . . Everybody was just beside themselves with confusion, desperation, disappointment, disgust."

Charles Lederer managed to stay at least a day ahead of schedule until the return to Tahiti. A few days later, his aunt, Marion Davies, lapsed into a terminal cancer illness, and Lederer rushed to her bedside, wiring his daily labors to Papeete in time for the next day's filming. Sometimes the cables cost a thousand dollars or more and sometimes they didn't arrive on schedule. When the telegraph failed them, Brando and Rosenberg second-guessed Lederer; they filmed each scene from every possible angle, hoping that one would meet Lederer's blueprint.

Lederer wrote eleven drafts of the Pitcairn Island sequence, and finally, he thought it was right. So did Rosenberg. They presented it to Brando. He was outraged.

"This isn't what I asked for," he shouted. "It doesn't show man's inhumanity to man. I wanted to draw a parallel with what's going on in Africa today."

Through gritted teeth, Rosenberg told Marlon to write his own ending. Three weeks later, Brando delivered his version of the concluding segment. Marlon's finale had Fletcher Christian sitting in a cave, contemplating man's inhumanity to man, while outside the *Bounty* sailors rape, loot, and murder the Pitcairn natives. In effect, Brando had written himself out of any active part in the concluding reels. As tactfully as possible, Rosenberg said he was going to use Lederer's version.

"You're making the biggest mistake of your life," Marlon

said. But then, in a surprising spurt of compliance, he agreed to do as told.

Now the problems really began—if you believe the MGM contingent. They say Marlon began to add homosexual overtones to his role in an attempt to sabotage the entire production.

There was a well-publicized encounter with Richard Harris, the hot-blooded Irish actor, then at the beginning of his film career. In his one big scene, Harris sets fire to the *Bounty* and Brando reprimands him with a floor-crushing blow.

Instead of belting Harris, Brando flicked his co-star's face with a gentle, fanlike tap. Taking the gesture as an insult to either his virility or his acting ability, Harris was enraged. He kissed Marlon on the cheek. The director requested a retake played in strict accordance with the action outlined in the script.

Once again, Marlon merely tapped his opponent's face. "Shall we dance, Mr. Christian?" Harris roared, and then stomped off the set, asking not to be recalled until Brando was ready to play the scene as written.

Brando apologized. "Don't talk to me," Harris yelled. "If it happens tomorrow, I'll kiss you, I'll dance with you, I'll jump on your back." The next day it happened again. Harris walked off the set and refused to return for three days.

After the sabbatical, Brando approached Harris and said, "Dick, you shouldn't have done it. I'd like you to know this. I am the star of this picture. You're opposing me. Remember, I'm a big *star.*"

This anecdote was Harris's letter of introduction to the American press—it got him a lot of coverage. It doesn't ring true. In the finished film, Brando plays Christian as a Restoration dandy from the outset; that was his interpretation of the role—he saw Christian as an aristocratic fop who achieves manhood through his ordeal on the *Bounty*.

And this interpretation has historical pertinence. One of the most recent studies of the *Bounty* suggests that both Bligh and Christian were shipboard homosexuals, and that the key to the mutiny "lies somewhere in this forbidden darkness."

When Rosenberg saw the rushes of the final Tahiti footage, he realized it couldn't be used. But he went ahead and assembled a rough cut. When he saw it, he despaired of ever getting the film into release. Then, to the producer's amazement, Marlon phoned and asked to see the film. "You know, that's a pretty damn good picture—but the ending is lousy," he said after the screening. He proposed that they put together a new, brief Pitcairn Island ending and offered to forgo his $25,000-a-week salary for an additional two weeks of shooting.

Rosenberg put Charles Lederer and Ben Hecht to work on a rewrite that would be staged on the MGM lot. Milestone was asked to direct, but refused. Rosenberg pleaded and eventually the director agreed to supervise the final scenes as long as he didn't have to go near Brando or the camera. During the filming he sat in a dressing room, reading movie magazines, while messengers relayed his orders to the set.

"It was terrible," Richard Harris said. "It was like being on a ghost ship with no captain." But, at long last, the film was finished. Sort of.

No one was happy with the revised ending. The film was shown to several of Hollywood's bright idea men, and some, Billy Wilder included, came up with promising suggestions.

By then, *Mutiny's* expenses had mounted to about $25,000,000, and MGM called a halt to further revisions. The picture might have been the most expensive production in history, except that the Elizabeth Taylor *Cleopatra* was simultaneously chalking up even bigger expenditures.

During *Mutiny*, the press worked Marlon over almost daily. Article after article accused him of "petulance," "unprofessionalism," "temper tantrums." He was charged with wasting $6,000,000 of MGM money, and with destroying the Hollywood system of film production. He was, said one piece, persona non grata in Tahiti because of his licentious deportment.

Marlon denied all allegations, and slapped a slander suit on the publisher of a particularly defamatory article. Brando's professional life was at stake, and desperate measures were needed to save his career.

The problem was this: All big Hollywood productions are heavily insured against every known calamity—against death, earthquake, bad weather, illness, delay, ad infinitum. The insurance companies scrupulously investigate every production they warrant, and keep careful tabs on the health and capabilities of all major stars. Brando's bad publicity on *Mutiny* automatically made him a high-premium risk. And, if the insurance companies blackballed him, he would be virtually unemployable in the film industry.

Aaron Rosenberg stood behind Brando. "Marlon gave us a rough time," he admitted, "but he felt we weren't living up to the agreements we had made with him about the basic concepts of the picture. Besides, with an actor like him . . . you must allow him to make his contributions to the script and direction. Otherwise, he can't work."

Joseph Vogel, MGM's president, also defended Brando. He cited "delay, the late delivery of the reproduction of the *Bounty,* bad weather in Tahiti, and the resignation of the original director" as the major contributory factors of the film's astronomical cost.

But exoneration came too late. Public and industry alike were steadfastly convinced that Marlon deserved sole blame for the *Bounty* fiasco.

Mutiny on the Bounty opened in November 1962 to poor reviews, with the lion's share of the catcalls going to Brando. Trevor Howard and Richard Harris were highly praised, though both turn in dull performances. Howard gives Bligh a no-nonsense interpretation—he's all British restraint and dour psychology, and how one longs for some Charles Laughton theatrics.

With his hair groomed into a pony tail and wearing hip-snug white breeches, Brando looks piggy. His face is waxen, his eyes tiny, and his body bloated—during the production his weight went from 170 to 210—and in the action and romantic sequences he's torpid and ungainly. But early on, when he's playing the aristocratic dandy, he is exuberantly funny, the only splash of style in this spiritless saga.

MGM opened *Mutiny* on a reserved-seat, advance-price basis, and eventually grossed $9,800,000: not bad, considering the reviews, but it needed about $60,000,000 in ticket sales to break even.

This was Brando's third big loser in a row. In the eyes of the industry, he was no longer a major box-office attraction.

·16·

SONS AND LOVERS AND WIVES

Much to everyone's amazement, Marlon attended the Hollywood première of *Mutiny on the Bounty* at the Egyptian Theater. It was a benefit performance for the Thalians, a charity organization headed by Debbie Reynolds, which cared for emotionally disturbed children by building and staffing clinics. "I don't ordinarily come to these things," Brando said, "but I want to do all I can to help the Thalians."

The real surprise of the evening was the lady hanging adoringly on Marlon's arm: she was Movita, the second Mrs. Marlon Brando. This was the couple's first public appearance since the surprise announcement of their marriage a few months previously.

The secret wedding, which took place in 1960, caught most everyone off guard. The gossip columnists were predicting that any day Marlon would marry Rita Moreno. Perhaps Miss Moreno thought so, too; it was at about this time that she swallowed an overdose of sleeping pills while staying in the home of Alice Marshak, Brando's secretary. One of the few people aware of Movita's legal status was Anna Kashfi, and she learned about it when Marlon telephoned her the news from Tahiti.

"I knew sooner or later my marriage [to Movita] would be found out," Marlon commented. "I thought it would be fair, honest, and considerate of me to tell her [Kashfi] rather than for her to find it out through gossip . . . it was a distressing time for both of us."

Public disclosure of the secret marriage came in another round of the custody battle over Christian in June 1961. Marlon was then in Tahiti with the *Bounty* and he flew to Los Angeles for the hearing. On the witness stand, he admitted that Movita was his wife and that they had a son, Mika. Movita was pregnant at the time of their marriage, but afterward they led separate existences. "I've never lived with Movita since," Brando said. "And I've had no sexual relations with her since the baby was conceived."

Both Mrs. Brandos were pregnant when they faced the altar, and Hollywood wits said Marlon only married the women he impregnated. But that wasn't strictly true. Back in Papeete, Brando was keeping company with Tarita, his *Bounty* co-star, and she, too, was to bear Marlon a son, Tehotu.

This scandalous tidbit was also revealed in court testimony. Between 1961 and 1965, Brando and Kashfi engaged in a series of lurid custody suits, and in each session another piece of dirty linen was hung on the line.

At one hearing, Kashfi told the judge she had come to Brando's house and found him in bed with a nude woman (Maria Cui). Was he in the habit of having ladies in his home for sexual reasons? Brando was asked.

"I have ladies in my home for many purposes, including sexual," Marlon answered, "but I would not like to give the impression that people are invited to my home primarily for sexual reasons."

Brando then told his version of the nude girl incident. "Miss Kashfi," he said, "broke into my house and jumped on the bed and started pulling the girl's hair out. The girl, terrified, beat it. Then Anna started wrecking the house. When she heard the taxi drive up, Anna ran down to try to catch the girl before she left. I followed along, with Anna biting me, hitting me, scratching me, and swearing at me. Finally, I said, 'Anna, this is enough. Go home.' She refused, so I took her and turned her over and spanked her as hard as I could."

At another hearing, Miss Kashfi accused Marlon of being an unfit father, and to prove her case she dredged up some ancient history of his *Mutiny* carrying-on. She also claimed she had been stabbed three times by her husband's "henchman," and that he was continually consorting with other women while their child was in his custody.

She didn't like it one bit when Marlon introduced Christian to Tarita and Tehotu. "It's very disturbing for Christian when illegitimate children and mistresses are flaunted in front of him all the time," she said.

What did Marlon tell Christian about Tehotu? the judge asked. "I explained to Christian that Tehotu was his brother," Brando replied.

Why hadn't he divorced Movita? the judge asked. "Because there had been ample stress these last few years," Marlon explained. "I thought it best for Christian's sake not to stir already muddy water."

He went on to say that Tarita and Tehotu had returned to Tahiti, the implication being that he had sent them home only to please Miss Kashfi. He wanted Christian, Mika, and Tehotu to play together as brothers.

Brando had a few lurid tales to spin about his ex-wife, and they were of a much younger vintage than his Tahiti adventures. Once while Miss Kashfi was caring for Christian, the boy telephoned Marlon to report that his mother was "ill," and Brando, accompanied by police sergeant Ed Hall, went to Miss Kashfi's fashionable Brentwood hotel, obtained the key to her apartment, unlocked the door, and found her under the influence of barbiturates. He scooped up Christian, and beat a hasty retreat.

Miss Kashfi's version of the incident was considerably different. She said Marlon and "a friend" broke down the door and awakened her and Christian, both of them enjoying a deep sleep. Then Marlon grabbed his son, paused long enough to "give that grin of his," and yelled, "Now you'll never get him back!"

After her testimony, Sergeant Ed Hall took the stand and substantiated and enlarged on Marlon's story. Following Brando's departure, Miss Kashfi, clad in a sheer nightgown and light robe, ran screaming and fighting through the hotel lobby, while "breaking everything in sight." She slapped several innocent bystanders, and rapped Hall "with a mean left hook." She was handcuffed, dragged to the police station, and later released on $276 bail.

"Miss Kashfi keeps a fully loaded revolver in her home and carries it around and plays with it while under the influence of barbiturates," Brando maintained. "She is capable of doing great harm to herself and our son."

The judge awarded custody of Christian to Marlon, but said the child must live with Brando's sister Fran Loving, a resident of Mundelein, Illinois. Though Fran was undoubtedly a conscientious guardian, it was at best a compromise arrangement as far as Marlon was concerned.

Miss Kashfi was tried and convicted of assault and battery on a police officer and ordered to pay $200 or spend twenty-nine days in the Los Angeles County Jail. She screeched and yelled, but finally shelled out the $200.

Needless to say, she soon had Brando back in court. A few months later, she regained custody of Christian, and that's the way things stood for several years.

But the hiatus in his legal battle with Miss Kashfi wasn't the end of Marlon's courtroom appearances. For a while it seemed as if every time he left his home, he was greeted by a process server. In 1967 Movita filed a separate maintenance suit against Brando for $500,000. (It was eventually settled at a lesser sum.) A year later, he was involved in a suit concerning some remarks he had made about the slaying of a Black Panther member in Oakland, California.

And then, at the end of 1969, Anna Kashfi grew greedy. Her term of alimony was coming to an end, and she requested the court to order a continuance of her allowance. Marlon explained to the judge that he had already paid Miss Kashfi $500,000—the settlement allotted by the court at the time of their divorce. The judge awarded Brando an unqualified victory—not only did he deny Miss Kashfi's request for additional alimony, but he also granted Marlon joint custody of Christian. And so there was another ceasefire for two years.

Then it's 1972. Christian's a boarder at the exclusive Ojai Valley School, near Santa Barbara, California; Anna is in

California; Brando's in Paris preparing for *Last Tango*. He receives a phone call from the Ojai headmaster who says Anna took the boy from the premises a day or so earlier. Brando begins to check the whereabouts of his son. He hears a rumor—reportedly circulated by Miss Kashfi—that Christian is "skin-diving with friends in Mexico."

Brando didn't believe it. He hired a private detective to locate his son, and two weeks later, when he got the report, he was on the next plane to California.

In the meantime, Anna Kashfi was arrested in El Centro, California, on a charge of disorderly conduct. When taken into custody, she and an unidentified lady friend were creating a ruckus on a bus by refusing to let anyone sit near them. (Witnesses say the ladies were several sheets to the wind, but these allegations went unsubstantiated.) At the time of her arrest, Miss Kashfi said she was on her way to join her son.

But where was Christian? A Mexican newspaper printed a story in which Brando said his son had been kidnapped. The next day, Marlon vehemently denied ever making such a statement, and the newspaper retracted the item. Still, as it eventually unfolded in court, the history of Christian's disappearance sounded suspiciously like a "staged" kidnapping.

Marlon's detective, Jay Armes of El Paso, Texas, was called the Super Shamus because of his crack record as a tracer of lost persons. And with very few clues to guide him, he did a Superman job of recovering Christian. He made a few calls to friends at three Mexican border crossings. From them, and from other information he picked up after arriving in California, Armes concluded that the abductors had already crossed the border in a red Volkswagen, and were heading for Baja California.

The detective rented a helicopter and spent three days flying over the Baja area, finally spotting a red Volks in a deserted stretch of the coast near the small fishing village of San Felipe.

Backed up by the Mexican police, Armes returned and found the car located near a campsite. A naked twenty-one-year-old girl was lying in a sleeping bag, and lingering about were six men and a second woman—all of them dressed as hippies.

Inside the tent, Armes found Christian cowering under a pile of dirty clothes. He looked undernourished and was ill; he was having trouble breathing because of a sinus infection. The boy was confused and frightened—he thought Armes was trying to kidnap him—and he tried to escape on three different occasions. But finally the detective deposited him safely with Marlon, who by this time had arrived from Paris.

Armes said that one of the men related that Miss Kashfi paid him $10,000 to "hide the boy for a little while." A second man said Kashfi offered each of the eight partners $10,000 each, and implied that she would get the money from Brando. In concluding, Armes added that the campsite was stocked with enough supplies for a three- to four-month stay.

Barry Rose, Miss Kashfi's attorney, branded Armes's testimony "a super con job"; such accusations aren't worth answering, he shouted, "because they are totally false . . . pure fiction." And then, he pleaded softly, "She did not kidnap the boy. She loves her son and wants to see him safe."

The judge rapped his gavel and gave Marlon temporary custody of Christian. Brando took his son back to Paris and enrolled him in a school there.

Miss Kashfi accepted the defeat with her customary good grace. "This baby is my whole life," she moaned on exiting from the courtroom. "I bore him. Where the hell was Marlon Brando when the child was being brought up? I am not through fighting! I will subpoena the judge and the whole damn court!"

She didn't go quite that far, but she did file a crime report with the Los Angeles Police Department and slapped a $200,000 assault and battery suit on Marlon. She claimed that an unnamed man, an employee of her husband, attacked and injured her when she went to Brando's home to pick up some of Christian's belongings.

Miss Kashfi's suit was dismissed, and a few months after the kidnapping case she relinquished full custody of their son to Marlon in an out of court agreement. There were to be further hassles, but Brando was to retain guardianship of his son.

Marlon has successfully kept his other children out of the limelight—so successfully, in fact, that no one is sure how many little Brandos he's fathered.

An Italian reporter once asked Brando how many children he had. "Several," he answered. "My children are flowers in a great meadow of love." (Marlon's a natural mimic; when he talks *to* an Italian, he talks *like* an Italian.)

His other children have all been carefully protected; only Christian has been thrust into the public spotlight. And certainly Christian's unwarranted celebrity must have been very distressing to Brando.

In a morose photograph of father and son, they are marching to a Santa Monica courthouse in March 1972. Frail, dark-haired Christian (he looks like his mother) has arms crossed against his chest; his head is bowed. A very hefty Marlon stares straight ahead, his face frozen into an expressionless mask; there's only the slightest hint of anger and pain.

·17·

THE UGLY AMERICAN

AND OTHER MISTAKES

In March 1962, several months before *Mutiny* was released, Marlon was back in Hollywood working on the "modestly budgeted" ($4,500,000) *The Ugly American*, a Pennebaker production for Universal release. Several of Brando's forthcoming films were to be released by Universal.

Universal was the hack house of the major Hollywood studios. With a history dating back to the Stone Age of the American film industry, it had survived for over four decades by grinding out B pictures. But by 1960, TV was sating the public appetite for double bill rubbish, and the company entered the valley of the shadow of bankruptcy. Then, just in the nick of time, MCA, the talent agency that managed Brando, maneuvered an intricate merger which made Universal a satellite of its powerful empire.

For many years, MCA and the other managerial companies had held sway over the industry. When the agencies complained, the studios cowered. For example, when Twentieth Century-Fox announced Brando, Montgomery Clift, and Tony Randall as stars of *The Young Lions*, MCA informed the studio that it wanted Dean Martin, one of its clients, in the Randall role. Fox quickly complied. If it hadn't, the agency might have pulled Brando and Clift, both under MCA contract, off the picture. In effect, the agencies and not the studios were casting Hollywood films.

MCA had been producing TV shows for several years, a conflict of interest that qualified as monopoly under the Sherman antitrust laws. The government ordered the company to divest itself of one of its branches, and after looking at the books, the MCA executives decided to scrap the management side of the business. Then it expanded its production activities by absorbing Universal Pictures.

Therefore, after fifteen years, Brando was forced to sever relationships with the agency that had nurtured his career from the outset. But the parting wasn't a clean break. MCA found new ways to retain Marlon's services.

Jay Kanter, Brando's former MCA agent and close friend, went to work at Universal in a high-power position, eventually becoming one of the big wheels in the company's machinery. Though no longer guiding Brando's career in an official capacity, he still retained the actor's loyalty and attention. Undoubtedly he was largely responsible for bringing in Brando as a Universal star. There was no official tie at the time of *The Ugly American*, but a year later Marlon sold Pennebaker Productions to MCA-Universal for $1,000,000; a deal which included Brando's services for an undisclosed number of films.

This was the first time Marlon had signed a multiple-picture deal, and though it rid him of a heavy financial burden (all the Pennebaker productions had lost money), it proved to be a bad mistake. MCA valiantly tried to raise the level of Universal production, but failed nine times out of ten. Through mismanagement, or bad luck, or penny-pinching inexperience, the company turned out multimillion-dollar pictures that looked as if they were churned out of a subway photo booth. Top-grossing, award-winning talents came to Universal and immediately struck out, turning in the biggest duds of their careers. Marlon was no exception: his Universal films were to be the worst of his career.

The best of the lot was *The Ugly American*, based on the best-selling novel by Eugene Burdick and William J. Lederer, which lashed out at American mishandling of foreign aid to

Southeast Asia. The film kept the title, character names, locale, and general skepticism of the book, but threw most of the plot away, replacing it with some of the material fashioned for *Tiger on a Kite*, the UN movie Brando was developing for Pennebaker back in 1957.

The Ugly American begins as newspaper executive Harrison Carter MacWhite (Brando) wins a diplomatic appointment to Sarkhan (a mythical Asian country), where his main job is to insure the progress of Freedom Road, an international highway which the United States is promoting despite local resistance. MacWhite's chief opponent is his former wartime buddy, Djeong, now the leader of a people's revolt in Sarkhan. By the film's end, MacWhite has lost his Eisenhower assurance that American knows best, and begins to spout the liberal clichés of the Great Society.

It's a well-made script, though not very lively, and depressingly elementary in the development of its central political conflict. A high-power director might have gotten some velocity from it, but George Englund drives it forward at a snail's pace.

In this period Englund was one of Marlon's closest friends, though from surface appearances they had little in common. Tall, handsome, with big, piercing blue eyes, and something of a ladies' man, Englund exuded an air of well-educated good breeding and sported a wardrobe of Brooks Brothers suits. Yet there was another side to Englund: he was the scion of a show business family, and he inherited their no-nonsense professionalism. His straight-shooting honesty was exactly what Marlon would have looked for in a business associate.

Brando may well have used Englund as a model for Harrison Carter MacWhite. In real life, he was already copying the director's style. From the gangster chic of the *Guys and Dolls* period, he had gone straight to gray-flanneled, Sulka-tied conservatism. He had also adopted Englund's elaborate phraseology. After Englund, "prevaricate" replaced "lie" in Marlon's vocabulary.

Many people assume the colorations of those near to them,

but Marlon, being the fine actor he is, by some accounts actually became George Englund. Or so say some Hollywood observers.

Through Englund, Marlon met America's former First Lady, Jacqueline Kennedy. The introduction occurred at an Embassy Row restaurant in Washington at the beginning of 1964. Mrs. Kennedy arrived with sister Lee Radziwill a few minutes early for the appointment, and was promptly scurried to a dark, secluded section of the restaurant. Marlon arrived with George Englund, who was about to stage a benefit pageant for the Kennedy Foundation, and the quartet spent an elegant two hours over *haute cuisine* and civilized conversation.

These were Marlon's conservative, outwardly conforming years. He rarely showed up at premières or poolside parties— at least not when columnists or photographers were present—but his life-style could hardly be faulted by the Hollywood establishment. He lived in a resplendent house atop a hill on Mulholland Drive in Beverly Hills—the guides on bus tours of movie stars' homes always pointed it out to the tourists, though there wasn't much to see. Once the residence of Howard Hughes, the Brando manor was an impenetrable fortress against the outside world.

More than ever before, Marlon guarded his privacy as a sacred possession. Interviews were strictly limited to professional or philosophical questions. There were no personal revelations about his wives or his children. He didn't talk about whom he knew or counted as friends. But a surprising number of people mentioned him as their friend, seemingly incompatible Hollywood-types like Debbie Reynolds.

There are stories that show him as the same incorrigible Marlon. At a party, he once stuck a piece of paper in his shoe, crossed his legs, and waited until someone's curiosity forced him to bend over and look at the missive. "What the fuck are you looking at?" it read.

But in public, Brando was often as stiff and proper as the junior statesman he plays in *The Ugly American*. Masquerading behind pencil-thin mustache, Dunhill pipe, and slimming pin stripes, he's the spitting image of a bull-necked, Ivy League conservative—only there's too much of a twinkle in his eye. Brando scores comic points by playing his recently acquired polish off against his old slob image. He's as aware of the incongruity as we are, and by elbowing us to say he sees the humor, he lets us enjoy the joke.

Later, he disappears into the role, and the fun promptly stops. Played straight, the ugly American is a part for Gregory Peck or some other pompously sincere face and voice.

The film dies when Brando's performance goes serious. Visually, there's nothing to look at; except for some on location background photography in Thailand, the film was shot on the Universal back lot, and the elaborate construction of an Asian village isn't convincing. And there's no one in the supporting cast who stands out. The best of the lot is Jocelyn Brando, Marlon's sister.

Jocelyn came to Hollywood in the early fifties to play an important role in Fritz Lang's *The Big Heat*. Though lacking superstar charisma, she is a highly competent actress, and might have had a profitable career playing Martha Hyer–type second leads. But her reputed Communist past caught up with her and she was blackballed by the motion picture establishment. Ostracized by Hollywood, she appeared in a few Broadway flops and turned up frequently on TV (she was a staple in the casts of *Alfred Hitchcock Presents*) without adding impetus to her career.

Brando cast his sister in *The Ugly American* to break the blacklist blockade set up against her. By 1962, this hardly qualified as a daring gesture—Hollywood was busy burying its witch-hunting history—and it didn't help Jocelyn. Her career remained in low gear.

When *The Ugly American* opened in spring 1963, it was welcomed with lukewarm praise. The critics rather enjoyed it, but doubted if their readers would respond to such a "didactic film lesson" in international diplomacy. And so, another box-office bust was billed to Brando's account.

Still, it was a triumph compared to his next Universal production, *Bedtime Story.* Prior to release, it was called *King of the Mountain*, but under any name, it stands as the nadir of Brando's career. Written by Stanley Shapiro, Doris Day's favorite scenarist, it is the story of an aging Casanova (David Niven) who passes on his secrets to a young rival. Brando plays a Rock Hudson role, and has neither the wooden style nor looks for it. Euphemisms like "portly" or "plump" won't do—in this film, Marlon's unmistakably fat. He looks like he's carved out of sun-tanned Crisco, and that's hardly the proper image for a romantic hero. He has some fun impersonating a mad Hapsburg, but for the rest, he's coarse and flat.

The film is incredibly crass. The intern Casanova keeps trying to elicit sympathy by feigning to faint, then explaining, "I haven't eaten for six days—I'm saving money for my grandmother's operation." (Considering Marlon's appearance, the ploy makes no sense.) Then, to win the heroine (Shirley Jones), he sits in a wheelchair, pretending to be a paraplegic. This was, of course, a deliberate, demeaning reference to Brando's first film, *The Men.* What could Marlon have been thinking of? Was he so disgusted with his career that he could mock his own achievements? Possibly, but for a man supposedly committed to the cause of the underprivileged, this ridiculing of the handicapped was shabby behavior.

Stanley Shapiro says Marlon was a model of cooperation during production. David Niven agreed. Marlon said that when he saw the first rough cut, he thought the film was a riot. Then he saw it again and sobered up. Maybe he resaw it at a critics' screening. The reviews were the worst of his career.

After *Bedtime Story*, Marlon flew to Tahiti to visit Tarita and Tehotu. Tarita's film career ended with *Mutiny*, but because of her alliance with Brando, she is a major tourist attraction and minor celebrity of the island. She lives in a pretty white house surrounded by tropical foliage, with a foreign car and a motorcycle—a *mise en scène* created by the natural beauty of Tahiti and Marlon's taste for fast motion. His relationship with Tarita was to endure for many years, and has been blessed with (at least) one other child, a girl named Tarita Cheyenne.

"At first I was upset when Marlon didn't marry me," Tarita once said. Then she paused and added, "But now I think it's best this way." She wears a plastic turquoise ring on her wedding finger, a present Marlon bought at Disneyland. And she wears it with forty-carat diamond pride. One visitor reports that above her double bed hangs a picture of Marlon and across it lies a fabulous black mink coat with a French couturier label. "Everything I want, I've got," she told a visitor.

Marlon has a penchant for prolonged relationships, even when they are stormy and riddled with unpleasantness. He frequently returned to Movita, and for a period prior to their final separation in 1967, they lived together off and on, and were to conceive another child, Rebecca. The relationship finally ended, according to the Hollywood gossips, because Movita "cheated" on Brando and turned his home into a sleepy hacienda complete with chickens roosting on the kitchen windowsills.

The marriage was finally annulled in 1968 on grounds that Movita was still legally married to a previous husband. But Brando willingly granted her a settlement and child support. They have remained good friends. "What doesn't work out as a marriage sometimes shapes up all right as a relationship between a man and a woman," Brando once said in reference to his peculiar alliance with Movita. Many of the actor's friends feel that the stabilizer in this continuing friendship is Marlon's desire to be near their son, Mika. And that may also explain his long-term liaison with Tarita.

During his 1963 vacation on Tahiti, Marlon bought Tetiaroa, an atoll of thirteen islands about forty miles north of Papeete. Most of the islands were uninhabited and the biggest (on which Brando was to live) measures about five square miles.

From then on, Brando was to spend every free moment in Tahiti, and some people claimed he was escaping from acting.

Marlon denied it, but freely admitted that acting was not the justification of his being. His extracurricular activities now assumed the major portion of his energies. He had become an important figure in the battle for civil rights, and frequently demonstrated on the Southern front lines. In Gadsden, Alabama, he was quoted as saying, "It's like walking into an underground world . . . it's so hard to express it [his reaction] without being emotional."

For the next decade, he was to march, sit-in, speak, and protest for equal rights throughout the country, and often it was a shock to see that brooding face, feigning anonymity, among a throng of placard-carrying citizens. He was also among the first stars to include a clause in his contract banning the exhibition of his films in segregated theaters.

He met with Republican senator Everett Dirkson and tried to persuade him to modify his intransigent opposition to any "public accommodation" provision in the Constitution. He remained concerned about the plight of the American Indian, talked to Washington leaders, even petitioned the United Nations' U Thant about the problem, but got nowhere.

So he took matters into his own hands. He went to Washington State to protest a law against drift-net fishing on the rivers leading to Puget Sound. "Some of the forty-seven Indian tribes in this state derive their income from commercial fishing," Brando told reporters, as he and a minister from Tacoma canoed away on a drift-net fishing expedition. Before their nets hit the water, they were pulled off the river and hauled into court, where they were fined $500 each.

Some believed that Marlon's crusading was a prelude to political candidacy. Was he the Democrats' answer to Ronald Reagan? Definitely not, Brando exclaimed; running for public office was just another form of show business. "I think the best actors of our time are the politicians," he said. "It's the same racket."

When Marlon resumed his acting career, he checked in at Twentieth Century-Fox for *Saboteur: Code Name—Morituri.* It was produced by Aaron Rosenberg, the man behind Marlon's *Mutiny,* and co-starred Yul Brynner, Trevor Howard, and Janet Margolin. Also in the cast were Marlon's old friends William Redfield and Wally Cox.

Throughout the mid-sixties, the cast lists of Marlon's films were filled with the names of old buddies, many of whom were down on their luck, and among them was Cox. Once he abandoned his hugely successful "Mr. Peepers" characterization, the comedian lost his public following. His humor was too special.

"What a beautiful day!" someone said. "Thank you," Cox answered. Not enough people saw the joke to keep him on prime time.

He laid an enormous egg on the night-club circuit, tried movies without success, and eventually wound up as a guest panelist on TV quiz shows. Occasionally he was asked a question about Brando, and Cox deliberately gave a wrong answer, as though Marlon might disapprove if he told the truth. But if anyone knew the real Brando, it was Cox; they were best friends until the comedian's death in February 1973.

On paper, *Morituri* probably looked like a promising project. The time is 1942, the scene a German blockade runner en route from Yokohama to Bordeaux with a cargo of seventy thousand tons of crude rubber. The Nazis desperately need this rubber, as do the Allies. To intercept it, the English smuggle aboard Robert Crain (Brando), a Nazi deserter, threatened with return to Germany and certain death if he doesn't aid the British.

There's the possibility of a good political thriller in this material, but it's overburdened with a tangle of subplots and a heavy-handed German director, Bernhard Wicki. And there is another problem: Brando played this role once before. Robert Crain is *The Young Lions'* Christian Diestl hashed into very small potatoes.

While *Morituri* was filming on a greasy freighter off the Catalina coast, Brando sat down and mused over his career. "It may seem peculiar, but I've spent most of my career wondering what I'd really like to do," he said. "Acting has never been the dominant factor in my life. In six or seven years, who knows, I'll have to do something, but I don't know if it will be acting."

His retirement was not imminent; he had a few projects waiting in the wings. "After *Morituri*, I plan to do Jean Genet's *Forbidden Dreams* with Tony Richardson, probably in Europe, and then *The Deputy* for Anatole Litvak. I don't care if *The Deputy* doesn't make a penny; I'd do it for free."

Forbidden Dreams was later made as *Mademoiselle* with Jeanne Moreau and an all-French cast. *The Deputy*, Rolf Hochhuth's play about the Vatican's policy of indifference toward Nazi genocide, has never reached the screen.

Lowering his standards to half-mast, Brando next accepted a role in *The Chase*, Lillian Hellman's seamy drama about sex, violence, and hard drinking in a small Texas town. It's *Peyton Place* dramaturgy, Southern-style; each of the local citizens gets to do a juicy star turn, and since the cast includes Jane Fonda, Angie Dickinson, Martha Hyer, Miriam Hopkins, Robert Redford, and James Fox, the emoting ranges the spectrum from light mauve to deepest purple.

There's only one drab performance in the bunch and that's Marlon as the town sheriff. With fires banked, he shuffles through the film, looking like a baby Orson Welles. It's his dullest performance to date.

"We failed Brando because we didn't dramatize [the character] nearly well enough, and that to me is the conspicuous failure of the film," said director Arthur Penn.

"Marlon tried," claims producer Sam Spiegel, "but at times I thought he was sleepwalking. He gave an adequate performance, but the soul wasn't there." Spiegel theorized that Brando is good on screen only when unhappy in his personal life; that's why, he adds, Marlon was so great in his production of *On the Waterfront*.

The theory doesn't hold water. At the time of *The Chase*, Marlon had headaches galore in his personal life. He was involved in one of the nastier court battles with Anna Kashfi, and every time he walked off the set, he was accosted by a process server.

From *The Chase*, Marlon went directly into Universal's *The Appaloosa*, an arty Western about a prairie bum (Brando) whose horse is stolen. The slender plot, a paraphase of *One-Eyed Jacks*, details his efforts to reclaim his horse and make out with the thief's girlfriend.

In charge of the production was Sidney J. Furie, a British director with a fatal weakness for photographing actors through tequila bottles or grillwork or campfire. Once you cut through the arty camera work, there's real directorial talent at work in Furie's films. He's particularly good at handling actors—such as his staging of Diana Ross's spectacular film debut in *Lady Sings the Blues*—but he couldn't manage Brando. Marlon said that during production he considered the director "a phony, a liar, a dirty double-crosser." (He later admitted he had misjudged the director.) And Furie once told a reporter that "making the picture was like waging war." But he liked a good battle. "I knew Brando would be tough to direct," he said. "Maybe that's why I wanted to make the picture."

The first skirmish occurred when Marlon decided to use a Mexican makeup for his character. Furie took one look at his Zapata-like disguise and rejected it. He told Brando he looked like Genghis Khan.

After a few weeks of interior filming in Hollywood, *The Appaloosa* company went on location in Utah. And that's when the real trouble began. Brando started to haggle over the interpretation of every scene—or so Furie claimed. "Marlon questioned everything, even if the full cast was there and we had only five minutes left to finish the scene."

According to the director, Brando never knew his lines, he refused to discuss the script seriously, he moaned and groaned about imaginary aches and pains. Because of his constant flubbing, one three-minute scene took ten days to complete. "They'll never get the picture made," one crew member predicted. "The only question is whether Brando or Furie will land the first punch."

At one point, Furie packed his bags and threatened to return to England. But somehow things were patched up and the film was completed. It was in production four months, about six weeks longer than its original schedule.

When it opened, *The Appaloosa* was roasted by the reviewers; it even made several of the year's ten-worst lists. Most critics had written Brando off as yesterday's hero, but a few die-hard fans stubbornly maintained that all he needed was the right director and role.

Late in 1965, some thought he had found both in Charles Chaplin and *A Countess from Hong Kong.* They couldn't have been more wrong.

·18·
THE COUNTESS AND THE MAJOR

Marlon Makes a Boo-Boo:
A One-Reel Chaplin Comedy

(N.B. This little farce is to be photographed entirely in long shot. It is in color, but very washed-out, Universal-style color. Whenever possible, the same set should be used in every scene—a different location can be indicated by an additional vase of flowers, a new chair, a rearrangement of the paintings. The background music should be simple, heart-rending, and hummable—maybe a strain from The Mikado orchestrated by Mantovani. Most important of all, the actors must look as if they loathed each other, the director, and the film. Also, the tempo should not be farce-fast, but slow, almost stately.)

Title: Hollywood—The Early 1940s

Scene One: Chaplin's Hollywood mansion. Everywhere you look there are photographs of Chaplin posing with his famous friends. The little tramp is swinging his cane and dictating to Kono, his Japanese secretary. (We don't hear the words.) Kono writes with a long quill pen. Lying on a chaise longue in the background is Paulette Goddard, a smudge on her cheek and diamonds casually strewn through her hair. She is painting her toenails.

Cut to

Title #2: Many Years Pass

Scene Two: The exterior of a small movie theater in *Switzerland.* The marquee reads: *Yesterday, Today and Tomorrow.* Entering from frame left is the elderly Chaplin and wife Oona; following behind them in single file are their eight children. Chaplin buys tickets and enters the theater.

Cut to

Scene Three: A movie screen showing Sophia Loren, dressed in a black, merry widow corset, peeling off a black nylon stocking.

Cut to

Scene Four: Chaplin, Oona, and the children sitting in the darkened theater.

CHAPLIN: She reminds me of Duse . . . the great Eleanora Duse . . .

Cut to

Scene Five: This is a split-screen shot: on the left, we see voluptuous Sophia Loren, still peeling; on the right, a still photograph of the wraithlike Eleanora Duse, her face a tortured, exquisite mask.

Cut to

Scene Six: Chaplin's mansion in Switzerland. He's opening a Vuitton trunk, tossing aside old manuscripts. Finally he finds the one he wants.

Quick fade to

Scene Seven: A close-up of the manuscript: the title page reads A COUNTESS FROM HONG KONG.

Cut to

Scene Eight: A split-screen shot: in the middle of the screen we see Jay Kanter, sitting in the London offices of Universal Pictures. He's on the phone. Now the left side of the screen is filled by a shot of Chaplin in his Swiss mansion. He picks up the phone and begins to talk animatedly. Then the right side of the screen is filled by Sophia Loren, lying in bed in her Roman villa. Husband Carlo Ponti is snuggling next to her. Sophia picks up phone and listens. Suddenly both Chaplin and Loren vanish and Kanter is on the screen alone.

KANTER: He thinks you'll be the next Eleonora Duse. He wants you in his new film. Will you do it?

Cut to
Scene Nine: Sophia sitting up in bed, pushing Ponti aside.

SOPHIA: (at a loss for words) Yes, please!

Cut to
Scene Ten: Marlon sitting beside his Beverly Hills pool. He's idly banging on a Japanese gong. The outdoor phone rings. Brando picks up the telephone and talks in a little girl's voice.

BRANDO: (à la Shirley Temple) Hello, nobody at home!
KANTER: (at the other end of the line) Marlon, it's Jay. Chaplin wants you for his new movie, *A Countess from Hong Kong.* Are you interested?
BRANDO: Chaplin!?! I'd act the telephone book, with him directing.

Cut to
Scene Eleven: Scowling at each other, Brando and Loren sit on high stools and read the London telephone directory. Chaplin, roaring with laughter, waves a baton. In the background, Oona, surrounded by her children, nods encouragement to her husband.

A Countess from Hong Kong started shooting in London's Pinewood Studios in early 1966. Brando arrived a few weeks early, rented a fashionable apartment, and ran a nightly Charles Chaplin film festival for his friends. He studied every one of the director's films he could find, even looked at some of them three or four times. He was genuinely excited about working with the maestro of silent-screen comedy.

Before arriving in London, Marlon shed some of his excess tonnage, but there was still too much meat on his bones. "When I open a refrigerator, nothing is safe, not even the pipes," he said, and he wasn't exaggerating. He alternated between stuffing and starving himself. He tried reducing pills and all sorts of diets—some legitimate, some just fads. Once he heard that you could gorge as much as you wanted as long as you finished your meal with half a grapefruit, the theory being that the acid citrus juices would dissolve the previous caloric intake. It's a nice dream, but it would have taken a crate of grapefruit to counteract Marlon's dinners. He also tried self-hypnosis, and that worked spasmodically. As a last resort, he checked in at the exclusive Buxted Park reducing establishment in Sussex, England.

During his London period, Marlon was frequently seen with Esther Anderson, a young mulatto girl from Jamaica who played minor roles in a few forgettable pictures. "Esther is a pretty, rather silly creature, with a kookie ingenuousness that could have been a put-on, but was probably real," says a casual acquaintance, screenwriter Marilyn Goldin. "Anyway, she is quite appealing, and for a time she was a fringe celebrity of the London scene. If she had ended up in New York, she might well have become a member of the Andy Warhol entourage. She was that type. I spent a day with Esther and her Jamaican girlfriends, and they chattered continuously about Marlon and Christian and voodoo. I couldn't decide whether they really believed in voodoo, but I think they probably did. No one knew how seriously to take Esther's romance with Marlon, although it certainly got a lot of whispers. Later, I heard he took her back to California, but I don't think she stayed for very long."

The "Christian" whom Miss Anderson chattered about was not Brando's son, but Christian Marquand, a popular French actor. Tall and craggy-handsome, Marquand is perhaps best known to international audiences as one of Brigitte Bardot's several bedmates in *And God Created Woman*, and he has also appeared in several American films, including *Behold a Pale Horse* and *Lord Jim*. He and Brando were to form a close friendship that was subject to much international innuendo for several years.

During his London stay, Brando hobnobbed with the upper crust of British society. Once he had dinner with Princess Margaret and Lord Snowdon, and was reported to be so intimidated by Princess Margaret's rank that he could only talk to her through a third person.

But his active social life didn't keep his mind off his work. As the first day's shooting of *Countess* approached, Marlon was attacked by a bad case of the butterflies. "I started to think I had gone raving mad, Charlie had gone raving mad, and it was impossible," he said. "I can't do fades and triple takes and things like that, and I was longing to go to Charlie and say, 'I'm afraid we've both made a horrible mistake.'" He made a horrible mistake by not acting on his intuition.

Instead, on that first morning he showed up promptly at nine A.M. Sophia Loren had already arrived from her Grosvenor Square apartment, and was relaxing in her dressing-room trailer. Then, in marched the seventy-six-year-old Chaplin, looking pink-cheeked, dapper, and terrifically fit; he was obviously itching to get his hands on the camera. Behind him was his lovely forty-year-old wife, Oona, and most of their eight children. Several of the brood appear fleetingly in the film, as does Sydney Chaplin, Charlie's son by a previous marriage.

Countess was Chaplin's first movie since *The King in New York*, made ten years previously, and never shown in the United States because the comedian was then in a pique over scurrilous attacks in the American press. Hundreds of New York film buffs flew to Montreal when *The King* opened there, and they returned with very long faces.

Still, there was enormous excitement about Chaplin's return to the professional arena, and in the midst of all the puffery, several important questions went unasked. No one ever questioned Brando's abilities as a farceur, his compatibility with Chaplin, the relevancy of a thirty-year-old script to a world in chronic quest of new artistic sensations.

Chaplin was rather vague about when he wrote *Countess*. Sometimes he said thirty years ago, sometimes forty. Judging from its contents, one would place the date of authorship at about 1890.

Chaplin outlined his film as the story of "a multi-millionaire who gives up his lovely wife to marry a whore." That's not quite exact. It's about a White Russian countess (Loren) who's had so many tough breaks she's working as a Hong Kong dance hall hostess. It doesn't look like a hard life—in fact, it looks as pretty as an MGM musical. But she hates it, and to make a new life for herself, she sneaks aboard a liner headed for the States. Somehow she winds up in Brando's stateroom and pajamas. He's a diplomat, but he doesn't have much esprit de corps until, after a series of leadenly unfunny complications, Sophia lights his fire. They arrive in San Francisco where Brando discharges his beautiful wife, played by Tippi Hedren.

"A frayed lace valentine," a Chaplin fan later enthused about the film. Very frayed indeed.

At first, the filming was smooth sailing. Chaplin finished his first shot, and turned to Oona. She nodded her approval. After every take, the routine was the same: Charlie glanced over his shoulder, Oona smiled.

Marlon was apprehensive, but cooperative. "In the beginning, Brando was frightened of a funny part," Chaplin said. "He was terrified of 'business,' but I told him not to worry, as the character was meant to be humorless." Perhaps Chaplin didn't mean it as such, but that statement qualifies as one of the most impertinent pieces of directorial condescension ever handed out to an actor.

Chaplin had worked successfully with any number of first-class comics, but only rarely had he directed "straight" actors, and when he did, he got poor results. (Usually he chose third-rate actors.) And it appears as if he had no inkling of how to direct a modern actor like Brando.

"My style of acting has always been sort of, well, *roomy*,"

Marlon said. "This is different. It's a mosaic. Mosaic acting, with each tiny piece honed and polished and put into place."

On another occasion, he said, "If the picture is funny, it's Charlie being funny. I'm a glorified marionette, and damned glad to be one. It's comforting to work for a man who has a fixed notion of what he wants and the theatrical taste to back it up. . . . You have to get used to his special lexicon of communication. He doesn't direct as much as he orchestrates or conducts."

And he summed up, "With Charlie, it's chess; chess at ninety miles per hour."

Chaplin was an old-fashioned director who demonstrated for his players exactly how a scene should be executed; who emphasized intonation, tempo, and precision movement. There was little latitude for self-discovery for the actor.

"Marlon," he'd say, "when you pick up the glass and move to the door, don't pause. We must keep up the choreography."

Or: "No, no, Marlon, that's too broad. Timing, timing, keep up the tension. There's a sag in the middle of that word. Get it out!"

Often, there were an insane number of retakes as Chaplin struggled to achieve just the right zing from an exploding champagne cork or a properly pitched belch from Marlon. The belching scene became a real nightmare. In it, Marlon drinks a glass of Alka-Seltzer and then lets out a bellowing burp. Chaplin made Brando repeat it again and again, and was never satisfied with the results. "Marlon thought the point was the belch," the director said, "but actually the point was the man's dignified behavior."

Chaplin roared with laughter as he watched his daily rushes in the Pinewood screening room. No one else even giggled. Marlon quickly realized the mediocrity of the film, and his enthusiasm for Chaplin curdled into disillusionment. He still said nice things to the press, but behind Charlie's back he ridiculed his director, and Chaplin returned the disfavor in private by burlesquing the Brando mannerisms. And though there was never open warfare, the set was in a constant siege of subdued animosity.

The production was also cursed by bad health. Chaplin waged a two-week bout with the Asian flu, and no sooner had he returned to work than Marlon suffered an appendicitis attack. Cast and crew took up a collection to send him a get-well bouquet, and everyone signed the attached greeting card except Sophia Loren.

She wasn't a Brando fan. Miss Loren is a pro who has no time for on-set clowning. She arrives on time, knows her lines, does her stuff, goes home, eats dinner, pats husband Carlo on the head, kisses her bambinos, and is in bed by nine P.M. Off-screen, this gorgeous *ragazza* is a thoroughbred workhorse. And possibly Marlon found her a bit of a goody- two-shoes. She was bright and fresh each morning, while Marlon arrived bleary and tired like the true night owl. He spent lunch hours sleeping in his dressing room, rarely knew his lines, and frequently delayed her check-out time. While Marlon or Chaplin flubbed about, she was off-set, tapping her foot.

One day, during a fit of script passion, Marlon looked at Sophia and said, "You have black hairs in your nostrils." And that was the end of a barely civil co-starring relationship.

"I kept reminding them it was a love story," Chaplin said when asked if there were hard feelings between his stars. The question had been rhetorical, anyway. On-screen, Loren and Brando look as if they're playing their love scenes from the opposite sides of an iron curtain.

Their lack of rapport may have been intensified by a simultaneous awareness of the infernal mousetrap closing about them. It's misdirected animosity, but how can you help loathing your co-star when he's spouting lines like, "You won't believe me when I tell you this is the first real happiness I've known," or, "Common harlot! Are you trying to ruin my career?"

When it was over and done, Miss Loren insisted that she loved *Countess*, loved Charlie, hoped to work with him again. (Chaplin was talking about reviving another ancient project for "the new Duse.") But she didn't mention Marlon. And she

sent regrets, rather than appearing at the gala London première in January 1967.

After the opening, everyone staggered back to Jay Kanter's
home (he was then Universal's chief of London production)
where their spirits were revived by a champagne-and-caviar
supper. The soirée was a huge success. "It's too bad we can't
release the party instead of the film," quipped one Universal
executive—a bit of black humor that momentarily dampened
the happy atmosphere. Only Chaplin failed to realize the première had been a disaster; he had been given a polite ovation
that evening and was cheerfully confident that *Countess* was
a smash. He really loved the film.

He was enraged when he read the reviews the next morning. The English critics wrote that the film was hopelessly
old-fashioned, "a severe disappointment from the old master
filmmaker." Chaplin dismissed the reviewers as idiots and
defended his film as being a landmark. "This picture is ten
years ahead of its time," he said. "I think it's the first time
it's ever happened—a realistic treatment of an incredible situation." No one was impolite enough to argue with him, but
the entire history of the American cinema might be described
as incredible situations treated realistically.

Two months later, *Countess* opened in Paris and New
York. The reviews were even worse than in London. The film
cost upward of $4,000,000. It did not return a profit.

In July 1966 Montgomery Clift died at age forty-five. Two
months later, he had been scheduled to begin filming John
Huston's adaptation of Carson McCullers's *Reflections in a
Golden Eye* with his close friend Elizabeth Taylor. After
Clift's death, Brando was asked to fill in for his one-time
rival, and since the film fit his schedule, he did so happily.
Reflections was to be shot in Rome, a bizarre decision since
the film took place in Georgia with many crucial exterior
scenes. But Elizabeth Taylor Burton liked to be near her husband and family, then living in Europe. And whatever Mrs.
Burton wanted, Mrs. Burton got. Brando was probably pleased

by the Roman locale. The late sixties were his European years. He was in Paris and London as often as in California or Tahiti. New York was now a forgotten romance of his youth.

But he couldn't have been happy about his billing. In the credits, he is listed below Miss Taylor, the first time since *Streetcar* and Vivien Leigh that he had not led off the roster of leading actors.

Prior to the Italian filming, Huston assembled his cast—everyone, that is, except Miss Taylor—at Mitchell Air Field on Long Island for a week of authentically American location shots. At this time, Brando was unusually cooperative about granting interviews. Why was he doing the film? a reporter asked. "For seven hundred and fifty thousand dollars plus seven and a half percent of the gross receipts if we break even," Brando answered. "That's the main reason. Then there's the attraction of a book by Carson McCullers." And finally he admitted that he was glad to have a part for which both Richard Burton and Lee Marvin had been considered.

The *Reflections* company moved to Rome's elaborately equipped Dino di Laurentiis studios in November 1966. The Italian artisans' replica of a Georgian military post is convincing, and yet there's a curiously displaced ambience to the film—both time and place seem to be slightly out of joint. The story is supposed to be taking place in the early forties, but there's no sense of period. And it's badly needed, since the basic material stems from a faded literary fashion of the recent past.

Reflections in a Golden Eye is a Southern Gothic study of sexual aberration. On a small-town military post, Major Penderton (Brando), a repressed homosexual, lives unhappily with his overblown harridan of a wife (Elizabeth Taylor), who occasionally gives her husband a flogging with a horsewhip. ("That should clear the air!" she says after one lashing.) She's having an affair with another officer (Brian Keith)—every afternoon they bed down in the berry patch. His wife (Julie Harris) is deranged; she's cut off her nipples with gardening shears and dreams of setting up on a shrimp boat with her

Filipino houseboy (Zorro David), an Oriental flower child who makes Peter Pan look like Burt Reynolds.

Major Penderton has a crush on Private Williams (Robert Forster), a fetishist, an exhibitionist, and a zoolater who goes horseback riding every afternoon in his birthday suit. He also lusts after Mrs. Penderton, and occasionally creeps into her bedroom to finger her lingerie. One night, the Major discovers him fondling his wife's panties, and, in a jealous rage, shoots him dead.

Carson McCullers wrote her novella in 1941, but it wasn't until the permissive sixties that it was deemed suitable for film adaptation. By then it was too late: Mrs. McCullers's horror chamber of perversities had lost its old shock appeal. To punch it up, the screenwriters (Chapman Mortimer and Gladys Hill) spell out much that the novelist left covert, and dream up a few new perversities, like Brando's horsewhipping. Their overripe inventions only serve to make the film look more dated.

Though it is awash in unwanted titters, *Reflections* is always absorbing and frequently quite affecting. It's well directed and, considering the excesses of incident and dialogue, well acted. And for the first time in many years, Brando really commits himself to playing a character.

By the late 1960s, film audiences were accustomed to seeing homosexuals on the screen: there were queens to scream at; sweet, sexually insecure boys to be mothered; super-straight career men who were blackmailed because of a locker-room indiscretion in their past; and the halfway boys who were offered tea and a little sexual sympathy.

However, there had never been an on-screen homosexual like Brando's Major Penderton. As he stands before his mirror, dabbing his face with cold cream, artfully grooming his thinning hair, and smiling with pleasure at his own reflection, he becomes a true grotesque. There's a terrible fetid intimacy about this scene—we're being shown sick secrets we really don't care to know. At times, Brando is so painfully and uncomfortably *real* we want to look away from the screen, but he won't allow it. He's so far submerged in the part that he's hypnotic.

Many people were deeply embarrassed by the performance, and to protect themselves they said Brando was embarrassingly bad. They wanted some safety valve, wanted Brando to peek out from behind the role and reassure them that it's just Marlon camping up a storm as a closet queen. He refuses to pander.

His good work went for nothing. When the film opened in October 1967, press and public reacted with open hostility, not all of it aimed at Brando. Liz Taylor, then suffering from a surfeit of overpublicity, got her share of the derision, though she's great fun, as she always is when she lets all her harpy vulgarity hang out. And the striking visual look director John Huston designed for the film—he used a desaturated Technicolor process that gave a golden tone to all colors except scarlet, which photographed as rose—was dismissed as arty.

Reflections made Judith Crist's ten-worst list, and died a speedy death at the box office. Recently, the film has collected a small core of enthusiastic supporters, and Brando's performance is finally being recognized as one of his finest.

·19·
TO ACT OR NOT TO ACT

Despite the TNT packaging of Brando, Taylor, and Huston—all of them potentially explosive personalities—the filming of *Reflections in a Golden Eye* went without a hitch. Like Marlon, Liz Taylor can be very difficult when she's unhappy, and she was rarely happy when Richard Burton was out of her sight. Also, neither of the Burtons were noted for their hospitality. Though polite, they kept their distance, and some of their co-stars accused them of condescension.

Alan Webb, a venerable British character actor, remembered with amusement his first meeting with the Burtons, with whom he worked in the Zeffirelli *Taming of the Shrew.* "Invited" to meet Miss Taylor in her dressing room before the first day's filming, he was escorted to her suite, where he walked through three antechambers before reaching the star's boudoir. There was Liz, in partial dishabille, sipping a Black Velvet, surrounded by hairdressers, secretaries, children, husband, production assistants, and unidentified toadies.

Miss Taylor looked fleetingly at her visitor. "Margaret Leighton asked me to look after you," she said pleasantly. "But you look to me as if you're old enough to take care of yourself." And that was not only the end of the audience, but virtually the last words she said to the actor during the production.

The Roman *paparazzi* tried to foment Brando-Taylor warfare, but the stars never bit at the bait. "Liz Taylor is a great lady," Marlon said. "She's great people." And on another occasion, he remarked, "I owe Liz a lot. She was the one who insisted I get the role in *Reflections*. The studio didn't want me."

When Miss Taylor received the New York Critics Circle Award as best actress for *Who's Afraid of Virginia Woolf?*, Brando flew to New York to accept it in her place. At the time, he was staying in the Taylor-Burton Swiss chalet; Liz had told Marlon to use it any time he wanted to introduce Tehotu, his Tahitian-born son, to the pleasures of a winter wonderland. Much to everyone's surprise, Marlon actually showed up at the awards presentation, with a beautiful Chinese girl on his arm. He joked with some old Broadway buddies—actor Kevin McCarthy among them—accepted Liz's award graciously, and then quickly returned to Europe and work.

During the production of *Reflections*, Marlon became friendly with Richard Burton and convinced him to co-star in his next film, *Candy*. This porn parody, derived from a piece of comic erotica Terry Southern wrote for the Olympia Press in the fifties, was directed by Christian Marquand, Marlon's close friend. And that explains how he became involved in this ill-fated project.

Southern's novel was a mildly entertaining jape in its time; once there had been a liberating force behind his sick, bad-taste jokes, but by 1968 its surprise value had evaporated through overexposure and cheap imitation. The film is a disaster, though Brando (as a lecherous guru) and Burton (a Dylan Thomas–type poet) manage to make a few comic points.

Before *Candy*, Brando finished out his Universal contract with *The Night of the Following Day*, a kidnap thriller that maybe (benefit of the doubt) looked promising on paper. It belongs to the *Last Year at Marienbad* school of screenwriting, in which the characters have no names.

A girl (Pamela Franklin) arrives at a European airport and is picked up by (she thinks) her father's Rolls-Royce-driving chauffeur (Brando). A while later, the car stops and collects two hoods (Richard Boone, Jess Hahn), who sidle in beside the girl with B-movie kidnapper menace. Chauffeur, girl, and hoods abandon the Rolls, and, snuggled into a tiny foreign car driven by Rita Moreno, a stewardess on the girl's flight, they drive to a deserted town on the Brittany seacoast. There the kidnappers have a falling out, and the intricate ransom machinations grind to a bloody halt after ninety-three minutes. There's a double twist at the end: at first, it seems that the whole story is nothing but the girl's bad dream, but then it's hinted that her nightmare is about to come true.

Along the way, there's lots of violence and perversion. One of the hoods is a moron, another a sadist, and Miss Moreno sniffs heroin through rolled dollar bills. The design of the film is a handsome medley of gold, brown, black, and blue, and director Hubert Cornfield is so enamored of his fashion magazine color scheme that Brando and Moreno make love-hate in matching black turtlenecks and bobbed blond wigs. They look smashing (Brando's slimmer than he's been in years), and Miss Moreno is good as the tripped-out stewardess. But Marlon can't decide whether to play the role straight or to send it up, and his indecision results in a flat cipher of a performance.

The Night of the Following Day was ready for release in January 1968, but Universal shelved it for over a year. Then in March 1969, it opened with a minimum of advance publicity in second-run theaters, and quickly disappeared after only a few days' run. The reviews were poor, but there was a surprising amount of praise or sympathy for Brando. Some critics said Brando turned in his best performance in years, while others expressed the hope that he would soon find a role worthy of him.

The pendulum was beginning to swing back to Brando's favor. It's difficult to pinpoint when and how the shift started, but probably it began with an anti-Brando piece published by the New York *Times* in January 1967. It was an excerpt from a book, *Letters from an Actor*, by William Redfield, Marlon's old friend, and it trotted out all the old arguments against Brando. He had ruined his talent by acting in trashy movies, Redfield maintained; he belonged on the stage; he could have been America's finest Hamlet. The *Hamlet* reference was pointed—Redfield had played Guildenstern in Richard Burton's recent revival of the Shakespearean tragedy, directed by John Gielgud, the English actor who had once urged Marlon to play *Hamlet*. Redfield was tacitly comparing Brando to Burton, who had the fortitude to abandon a successful film career to return to the stage.

It was a below-the-belt attack. Richard Burton made a serious attempt at playing Hamlet, but the audiences turned the production into a freak show. No one came to see Burton as Hamlet; they came to see Burton, Liz Taylor's husband. And the performance of the play was only a bothersome prelude to the real attraction of the evening: Burton and Taylor's exit from the stage door. It was a three-ring circus of screaming crowds, gestapo police protection, and Liz and Dick, smiling valiantly while people scratched at their faces and diamonds.

The New York *Times* readers jumped to Marlon's defense. "If Marlon Brando has William Redfield as a friend," one letter writer said, "he need look no further for an Iago." Why should Brando return to the stage? asked another reader. What is being done on Broadway that is worthy of him? Another correspondent agreed that Marlon might have been our greatest Hamlet, but who would direct him and who was going to play with him?

Redfield answered rather haughtily that Brando's Hamlet could have been directed by Gielgud and cast with the same actors who supported Richard Burton—a strategic mistake, since the Burton *Hamlet* was an artistic wasteland except for the star actor.

Redfield went on to say that Brando's true talent was as a stage actor: those who knew his Stanley Kowalski only from the screen *Streetcar* knew only half the performance.

It's a debatable point. Because of the emotional impact of his performances, we tend to think of Brando as a heroic actor, and it's true that he takes the kind of chances and achieves the kind of effects we connect with only the boldest stage actors.

In fact, he's a very delicate actor. He attains towering ends with the smallest means—so small, in fact, that often we're not sure what he's done to move us to such depths of emotional response. While not incompatible with the demands of stage acting, it's a style which is allowed greater latitude and refinement by the screen. Maybe he might have become a great stage actor. As it stands, he's one of the greatest American film actors of all time.

"The only thing an actor owes his public," Brando once said, "is not to bore them." By that criterion he's failed several times. In *Teahouse* and *The Chase*, in *A Countess from Hong Kong* and *The Night of the Following Day*, he's boring. But the statement begs a bigger question—what does an actor owe himself? The conventional answer is this: to stretch one's God-given talent to the limit and beyond, to play Hamlet, Lear, Othello, and the other benchmark roles. But if you hold your talent lightly, if you consider it a frivolous pursuit in a troubled world, as Brando did, then the question is irrelevant. And one's God-given talent becomes an albatross.

Late in 1967 Brando agreed to appear in *The Arrangement*, Elia Kazan's film version of his best-selling, semi-autobiographical novel. Everyone hoped that the Kazan-Brando reunion would boost both of their sagging careers, but their appointment for *The Arrangement* was canceled. Marlon backed out, saying he was abandoning acting to concentrate all his time and energy on the civil rights battle. No one believed him; there were rumors that Brando backed out because he feared his talent had dried up, that he would fail his former mentor. When Kazan was asked why Marlon quit *The Arrangement*, he mentioned "personal problems," but wouldn't expand on the nature of Brando's inner turmoil.

Here's a wild guess at an analysis: Brando is haunted by the feeling that he has wasted his life, haunted by his own talent. "I don't think anybody *knows* Brando," an actor friend said recently, "but I have the feeling that he believes somewhere along the line he missed something he could have done, something he could have *been*. This sounds strange, but it's as if somebody had put an angel inside of him, and he's aware of it, and it's more than he can *contain*."

A writer, H. A. L. Craig, speaks about Marlon's inborn propensity for acting. He recalls that he and Marlon were discussing a famous Hollywood producer, and suddenly the actor began to finger the air. "What are you doing, Marlon?" his friend asked.

"He [the producer] wears knit suits," Brando answered. "I'm touching his suit."

Both stories are spooky, sad, and strangely touching. And of all the millions of words ever written about him, these two accounts come as close as any to piercing the public shell of Marlon Brando, movie star.

At the time of his withdrawal from *The Arrangement*, Brando was involved in a serious civil rights controversy that arose when an Oakland, California, policeman shot a young black boy, Bobby James Hutton, as he emerged unarmed from behind a police barricade.

Hutton was a member of the Black Panther Party for Self-Defense, a terrorist organization that lived up to its Mao Tse-tung motto: "Political power grows out of the barrel of a gun." His funeral drew large crowds—Hutton was awarded martyrdom by Panther supporters—and Brando appeared as guest eulogizer. "You've been listening to white people for four hundred years," he proclaimed to the predominantly black crowd. "They have done nothing as far as I am concerned. I am going to do something now to inform white people what it's about. Time is running out for everybody!"

Later, he discussed the Hutton case on TV, and was promptly slapped with a $2,500,000 defamation suit filed by the Oakland Police Officers Association. (The suit was thrown out of court.) On another TV show Marlon promised to donate ten percent of his salary to Dr. Martin Luther King's Southern Christian Leadership Conference. Some said Marlon didn't know what he was doing—that it was impossible to support both the Black Panthers and King's nonviolence policies. While that may be true, there is no doubt that Brando was deeply concerned about black issues.

At this time, he announced that he was considering dyeing

his skin and living as a Negro in an attempt to understand the black dilemma from the inside. This extraordinarily naïve scheme shows that no matter how hard he tried Marlon couldn't get away from acting: his solution to the black problems adds up to nothing more than role-playing. And it wasn't long before he was once again in front of the cameras.

In spring 1968, Brando signed for another film, then called *Quemada*. It was a Franco-Italian coproduction, directed by Gillo Pontecorvo, a young Italian director who made a big splash with *The Battle of Algiers*, a reconstructed documentary about the French-Algerian war.

Since the early 1950s, Brando had flirted with the possibility of appearing in a European film—he was on record as saying that all the most interesting movies came from abroad. But, until *Quemada*, he had never found a project or a director that really appealed to him. Pontecorvo was a socially committed director—he was, in fact, a Marxist—and his new film meshed with Brando's civil rights interests. It was a swashbuckling, but serious, Fanonian account of Spain's colonization of the Caribbean.

As Pontecorvo originally planned it, the film told the history of Quemada, a Caribbean island burned by the Spaniards (Quemada means "burned" in Spanish) in the sixteenth century to suppress an Indian rebellion. Later, the island is repopulated with African slaves. The picture begins in 1840 when Quemada is the most important of Spain's sugar colonies. In order to further their own interests, the British send Sir William Walker (Brando), a drunken and amoral *agent provocateur*, to Quemada. His assignment is to preach independence (and avarice) to the Spanish plantation owners and to teach revolution to the slaves.

With the help of José Dolores, a dock porter who grows into a black Bolivar, Sir William is triumphantly successful. The Spaniards flee the island and the independent nation of Quemada is established with the support of the British Antilles Sugar Company. Once independence is achieved, Sir William convinces Dolores, now the leader of the government, to disband his black army and leave the running of the country to British commercial interests.

Ten years pass, and then Sir William returns to the island to put down a new black rebellion led by Dolores, who now is an inconvenience to British interests. Sir William succeeds—Dolores is killed—but as he embarks for his return voyage to England, he is stabbed by a black porter, the inheritor of the Dolores legacy.

That's the way it was written, but not the way it reached the screen. *Quemada* (or *Burn!* as it was called in America) turned out to be a mini-*Mutiny on the Bounty*, and, though there were many contributing factors, Brando was once again used as a scapegoat for a production overrun with bad luck and misunderstandings.

The trouble began as Brando boarded a jet that would take him to Miami and from there to Colombia, the site chosen for the filming of *Burn!* Sporting a stubbly beard and long hair pulled back into a mini-ponytail, Marlon jokingly asked a stewardess, "Is this the plane for Cuba?"

The stewardess mistook the actor for a hijacker and reported him to the captain, who notified the airport police. Ten minutes later Brando was escorted off the plane. He passed an airline representative who did a double take. "Oh, my God, it's Marlon Brando!" he moaned.

Marlon was invited to rejoin the flight, but he called his lawyer instead. There were threats of suits and countersuits, all of which came to nothing. Later that night Brando flew to Jamaica, and there chartered a plane to Colombia.

Brando and Pontecorvo were not a well-matched team. The Italian director was accustomed to working with nonprofessionals or with nonstar actors who deferred to him without comment. He fancies himself as an *auteur*, that is, a director who believes a film must be the expression of one man's genius, not a collaborative effort. He wanted compliance, not suggestion or invention from Brando, and that's where the trouble began.

Brando said, "If Pontecorvo wants a purple smile from me and I give him a mauve smile, he continues ordering me to smile until he gets exactly what he wants, even if I get a dislocated jaw in the meantime."

Pontecorvo made Marlon film one scene forty times and couldn't understand the actor's hostility. "Brando is a little— how you say—paranoiac," the director commented. "He thinks when I make forty takes it is because I want to break him. Why? Why should I want to break him?"

"He has no fucking feeling for people," Brando said about Pontecorvo. Marlon was enraged when he learned that the white actors were making almost double the salaries of the black members of the *Burn!* cast. And he never really forgave the director for dismissing the inequality as being outside his jurisdiction.

Brando also had co-star problems. Originally, the producer of the film (Alberto Grimaldi) wanted another star for the role of José Dolores, and Sidney Poitier was seriously considered. Brando approved Poitier as his co-star, but Pontecorvo thought the black actor's face was "too civilized." He took a look at every well-known black actor in the United States and England and none of them pleased him. Then he spotted Evaristo Marques, a native of Colombia, and decided his was the only face for the role. He screen-tested Marques, a nonprofessional, with disastrous results. Marlon studied the test and, though agreeing that Evaristo had a fantastic face, he doubted that the Colombian would be effective as an actor.

Against everyone's advice, Pontecorvo signed Evaristo for Dolores. The actor spoke no French, Italian, or English, only Lengua, the native language of Colombia, and so communication was limited to sign language. Marques flubbed every scene but Pontecorvo refused to fire his protégé. He stayed up all night working with Evaristo and eventually thought the Colombian understood what he wanted. "It dawned on him what it meant to play José Dolores," said Pontecorvo. "From that moment onward he gave a sensitive performance and he often prompted applause from the crew, too."

Evaristo does have a great face, but there was no applause for his performance as it unreeled in the released version of the film.

With the exception of Brando and Italian actor Renato Salvatori, the cast of *Burn!* is nonprofessional, and though Pontecorvo denies it, Marlon must have had difficulties in adapting to the very special problems of working with raw acting talent. Tempers grew very short as the Colombian temperature rose as high as 120 degrees, a lot of heat to bear when you're carrying around Marlon's excess weight.

Brando is very heavy in this film, but it works for the character. His Sir William is a spin-off from Fletcher Christian—he's a licentious dandy with morals as flabby as his body. And yet, his performance doesn't really work to the film's advantage. Brando stands out among the nonprofessionals like a cat among pigeons. Without him, *Burn!* might be didactically dull—it needs a touch of theatricality to maintain audience attention; with him, there's a patchouli aroma to the film which muddies its clearheaded intentions.

During the Colombian filming of *Burn!*, Marlon stopped up his ears with wax plugs, just as he had done while shooting *Mutiny.* Unlike Lewis Milestone, Pontecorvo didn't take Brando's self-imposed deafness as a personal snub; he reasoned that an actor bred in the quiet of studio facilities couldn't concentrate in the hullabaloo of on-the-spot production.

The din, the heat, insects, jungle living quarters, and palm-leaf toilet facilities eventually became too much for Brando. He told producer Alberto Grimaldi that unless the film was relocated in a civilized climate, he was going to quit. Brando backed up his threat with a letter from his physician, saying the Colombian weather was detrimental to the actor's health.

A few weeks later (spring 1969), the production moved to an area near Marrakesh in Morocco, which approximated the Caribbean locale and also met Brando's specifications. Of course, the relocation sent the film way over its modest budget, but it was cheaper than starting from scratch with a new Sir William.

Marlon stayed at Marrakesh's elegant Hotel Mamounia. He was often seen sitting in the hotel bar, drinking rum out of a brandy snifter, and appraising the local beauties. He was very direct in his attack. He went up to one girl and asked point-blank if she'd like to share his bed that evening. The girl was offended at first, but Marlon wheedled her into taking his phone number. The next day she sheepishly admitted to a friend that she had called Marlon and, much to her disappointment, he wasn't in his room.

After the move to Morocco, relations between Brando and Pontecorvo improved, but there was still some wrangling. "It may seem strange, but Brando, because of his sensibility, after years and years of sets, after years and years of success, is very often afraid of difficult scenes, extremely afraid," the director explained. "And in such a situation, he is tense and nervous; he is not able to function."

Pontecorvo insisted he was a Brando fan. "I think he's the greatest actor of the contemporary cinema," he said. "With one expression, he conveys more than ten pages of dialogue. And he is the only one who can do it. His eyes simultaneously express sadness, irony, skepticism, and the fact that he is tired. . . ."

Just as director and star were heading toward a cease-fire, the production crashed against an unexpected obstacle. Producer Grimaldi's petition to photograph a few *Burn!* scenes in Spain was answered with a resounding rejection. Spain's Minister of Information, Fraga Iribane, told Grimaldi and United Artists (the American distributor of *Burn!*) that they would be barred from any further commercial or production activity in that country if they insisted upon presenting Spain as the villain in their Caribbean drama.

Iribane wasn't bluffing. Five years before, Columbia Pictures produced *Behold a Pale Horse*, a Spanish Civil War drama which met with the disapproval of the Franco government. Afterward, Spain refused to import Columbia films, a boycott that cost the company several million dollars—Spain boasts a large movie-going population.

United Artists wasn't about to risk a similar blockade. *Quemada* quickly became *Queimada*, the Portuguese spelling of "burned," and the Spanish conquistadors of the drama were transformed into Portuguese opportunists. Historically,

Portugal played only a small role in the conquest of the Antilles, but it was also a very small contributor to modern-day film grosses; UA could risk offending the Portuguese.

With a little redubbing and reshooting, the island of Quemada was easily transformed into Queimada. The cowardly change wasn't enough to ruin the film; the irrevocable damage occurred when UA, which had little faith in the film, turned over Pontecorvo's final cut to a New York editor, best known for his jazzy molding of coming attractions. He took more than ten minutes out of the footage; it doesn't sound like a lot, but it was enough to throw the film into a chaos of confused meaning and continuity.

How extensive other changes were we may never know. When Marlon saw the film, he elbowed a friend and complained, "I never said those things!" He insisted that dubbed words had been put in his mouth. He should know best, though Sir William sounds like Marlon throughout.

But it's such a discombobulated film that anything's possible: anyone could be dubbed, any scene might be a misinterpretation of Pontecorvo's concept.

To recover from his *Burn!* ordeal, Marlon vacationed in Tahiti. As the years passed, he spent more and more time there, surrounded by his children in what one friend describes as "a Swiss Family Robinson idyll."

"Being in Tahiti gives me a sense of the one-to-one ratio of things," Brando says. "You have the coconut in the tree, the fish in the water, and if you want something to eat, you somehow have to get it."

Brando turned his attention from civil rights to "the problems that concern us all": in other words, "aggression, pollution, overpopulation." And Tetiaroa would be, if it worked out to his blueprint, an ecological paradise. "I want to develop the island as an example of how you can use less power to live, and to show that you don't have to use our conventional resources to stay alive. We will make do without oil or gas or steel or auto companies—we want to avoid feeding these parasites fostered by our technocratic existence."

Tetiaroa's main power sources, Brando says, will be methane gas (derived from compost heaps), the sun, and the wind. There will be lots of chickens and other animals. Vegetables will be grown by solar energies. The island will be open to "anybody who is qualified to make a contribution."

Many of Marlon's ideas were drawn from *The Last Whole Earth Catalog*, a fashionable book on ecology. Among other helpful hints, the book tells how a car can be run on chicken manure. And that probably explains why Brando specifies chickens as a major part of the island livestock.

Brando's life-style in Tahiti is very simple. An unexpected visitor once found him stirring a pot of soup in the kitchen of his unpretentious home; across the room, a native woman was folding a pile of laundry; outside, a blond-haired, brown-skinned toddler played in a soft rainfall.

"Marlon's asked me to visit him several times," Edith Van Cleve said, "but it sounded too primitive. I told him I was too old to ride in a dugout or canoe or whatever native conveyance he used to get to his island. He laughed and said for me he'd hire a motorboat, but I never took him up on it."

Though Brando's Tahitian existence didn't eat up too many dollars, his ecological research cost plenty—or would once it got under way. He planned to explore a theory that bacteria can be used to supply power. As he explained it, you put two different types of bacteria in two metal containers, connect them with an electrical conduit, and soon there's enough power to light a Westinghouse bulb. Marlon also planned to establish a research center devoted to discovering new sources of food from ocean plankton.

Brando finagled financing for these projects from some of his rich movie acquaintances—and his tales of how he hoodwinked them into opening their wall safes are as uproarious as those he told about scrounging quarters in the old pre-*Streetcar* days. But the money he collected was just a drop in the bucket. And so, he went back to acting.

Burn! revived all the old *Mutiny on the Bounty* stories, and once again Marlon was on every producer's list of troublemakers. To make matters worse, few (if any) of his films since *The Young Lions* had shown a profit—he wasn't even a good calculated risk.

But for some the Brando name retained its allure. Sam Spiegel wanted him for either Rasputin or Lenin in his film version of *Nicholas and Alexandra,* and director David Lean sought him as the lead in *Ryan's Daughter.* Neither film was very good, but they had more prestige than Brando's next assignment, *The Nightcomers,* a small, not very promising British production. Perhaps Marlon agreed to appear in it as a favor to Jay Kanter, who had left Universal and was now working for an independent English company, Winkast Films.

The Nightcomers was a spin-off from *The Turn of the Screw,* Henry James's classic mystery story about a governess who believes her two charges are haunted by the ghosts of a former governess and their father's valet. The film fills in the strange, lurid history of James's ghosts. According to screenwriter Michael Hastings, the children's governess was having a wild, sadomasochistic affair with Quint (Brando), the valet. He's a real brute—he tweaks his lady's waxy nipple whenever he's in the mood. The children spy on their lovemaking and try to copy the intricate choreography of their coupling. It's no easy job. At one point, Quint ties up the governess as though he were trussing a chicken; what he does afterward is blessedly left off-screen. For reasons that don't make much sense, the children unintentionally bring about the death of Quint and the governess, and the sordid experience corrupts their impressionable minds.

Well, it's not boring—you watch it with titters and mouth agape—but the picture adds up to nothing more than quirky, very soft-core pornography. It violates the ambiguous spirit and decorous style of James's story, but on its own terms it's smoothly directed and acted. Stephanie Beacham as the governess is straight out of *My Secret Life,* or some other piece of Victorian erotica: a snooty priss who becomes a flaming harlot between the sheets. Brando plays Quint as a depraved, filthy lout with a load of sexual mischief and menace. It's a striking performance, truly threatening, and much too big for the small framework of the film.

Brando's Quint makes *The Nightcomers* worth seeing, but it was generally overlooked when it was released in February 1972. It was swamped by the preopening hullabaloo over Marlon's next film, *The Godfather*, which opened three weeks later.

·20·
THE MULTIMILLION-DOLLAR
COMEBACK

At the end of 1971, *Variety* reported that in the last three years the combined losses of the major studios totaled a whopping $600,000,000. Only four out of ten American movies were returning a profit—and that was a generous estimate. With those kinds of odds, it seemed a wonder that producers kept grinding out films. But they were all betting on the outside chance that someday they were bound to hit upon a *Godfather*. And, once in a blue moon, it really happened.

One of the great success stories in the history of the movies begins in the late sixties. Mario Puzo is having trouble paying the rent with his meager earnings as a serious writer. His agent advises him to write a big, trashy novel, one of those fast, sexy "reads" that keep Jacqueline Susann at the top of the best-seller list. Someone else suggests that Puzo draw on his Italian heritage to fashion a story about the Mafia. The author takes the idea to a publisher, who offers a $5,000 advance. With dollar signs dancing in his head and the bill collector knocking at the door, Mario sits down and starts punishing the keys.

One hundred pages later, he turns in a partial manuscript to agent and publisher. Everyone is pleased. The novel is developing nicely; it promises to be a trash masterpiece. The agent begins thinking about subsidiary rights, and sends the

210

first portion of the novel to the major film companies. Paramount nibbles. It offers Puzo a $12,500 option payment against $50,000, with "escalators" if the option is exercised. (These are Puzo's figures; other sources say he sold the rights for a total of $35,000.) The agent advises Puzo against signing; he can get more, much more, if the book becomes a best-seller. But a bird in the hand is more than Puzo can resist; he accepts Paramount's meager offer.

The book is published and makes the best-seller list for sixty-seven consecutive weeks. Paramount exercises its option and signs Puzo to write the screenplay. For his work, Puzo says Paramount gave him $500 a week expenses plus 2½ percent of the net; other sources say he received $100,000 plus a small percentage.

The book ads for *The Godfather* carried the slogan "Soon to Be a Major Motion Picture," but Paramount wasn't thinking big. It was on the brink of bankruptcy because it had financed several expensive losers, including the $15,000,000 *Paint Your Wagon* and a previous Mafia story, *The Brotherhood*. The company was playing very safe—no more multimillion-dollar follies. *The Godfather* was assigned to Al Ruddy, a thirty-seven-year-old producer whose only major credit was the creation of TV's "Hogan's Heroes." He ordered Puzo to rework his novel into a "quickie" that could be photographed in modern dress against a St. Louis background on a $2,500,000 budget.

In the spring of 1970 Puzo moved into the Beverly Hills Hotel, where his suite cost more than his $500 a week expense money. He was very impressed by his office on the Paramount lot—it came equipped with a water cooler and a real live secretary. He wasn't so impressed by the conferences about who was to direct and star in the film; nobody liked his ideas.

For director, Paramount was considering Peter Yates (*Bullitt*), Costa-Gavras (*Z*), and Richard Brooks of *Elmer Gantry* fame. They all turned thumbs down, for unspecified reasons, though rumor said they all thought the novel was a glorification of the Mafia.

This charge was to be leveled against novel and film. Puzo dismissed it with a wave of his hand. The book, he said, was never intended as serious sociology. "Of course, it's a romantic story. The Mafia is certainly romanticized. There are much worse guys than that."

Nearly every actor of the proper vintage was considered for the role of Don Corleone, the Godfather. Paramount discussed Laurence Olivier, George C. Scott, John Marley, and Richard Conte as key contenders. Someone suggested Carlo Ponti, Sophia Loren's producer husband. Flamboyant San Francisco attorney Melvin Belli hinted that he might be persuaded to play the role, but nobody twisted his arm.

Puzo suggested Marlon Brando. The Paramount executives gave him a glassy stare and the author realized his "stock had dropped fifty points." Brando was strictly taboo, explained a studio exective. Look at what he did to *Mutiny!* Look at what happened on *Burn!*

In the midst of the great casting debate, Francis Ford Coppola signed on as director and co-screenwriter. Still in his thirties, Coppola was one of the first graduates of an American film school to make an impact on the industry. He had directed several films, none of them successes, all of them the handiwork of an up-and-coming talent. He had set up an independent studio in San Francisco and lost a small fortune running it. Later he said that he agreed to direct *The Godfather* only because it promised to bail him out of debt.

Coppola won the assignment, claimed Paramount production chief Robert Evans, because he was of Italian descent: "He knew the way these men in *The Godfather* ate their food, kissed each other, talked. He knew the grit."

Coppola wasn't happy with Puzo's script. "I saw important ideas in the book that had to do with dynasty and power," he said. "Puzo had turned in a slick, contemporary gangster picture of no importance. It wasn't his fault. He just did what they told him to do." The two men began a massive overhaul:

Coppola rewrote one half of the script, while Puzo rewrote the second half; then they switched sections and rewrote each other.

The director nagged at Paramount to raise his budget to $6,200,000. He insisted that the film be played in period (the mid-1940s to the late fifties) and shot on location in New York, Las Vegas, Los Angeles, and Sicily. Paramount finally agreed. *The Godfather* was now too important a literary property to sneak into theaters as a poverty-row production. Also, the company was once again flush, thanks to its $50,000,000 profit on *Love Story*.

Puzo convinced Coppola that Brando was the ideal choice for Don Corleone, but no one at Paramount would hear of it. Then producer Al Ruddy sided with Coppola on the Brando debate, and eventually Robert Evans agreed to look at a screen test, apparently in the conviction that Marlon would never submit to such a humiliation.

When first approached about playing Don Corleone, Brando hadn't read the book. He dipped into it for three days and then said, yes, he was definitely interested in impersonating the Don—so interested, in fact, that he immediately agreed to a screen test, his first since his days as a Broadway juvenile.

The test took place in the privacy of Brando's home. Ruddy and Coppola lugged in and set up a videotape machine, while Marlon applied an elaborate, if crude, makeup. He streaked his hair with white, slicked it back, put shoe polish under his eyes, and stuffed his cheeks with wads of tissue paper. Then he sat down, sipped a cup of espresso, puffed an Italian cigar, and silently scowled at the camera. He kept alternating between scowls, puffs, and sips, with an occasional smile or grunt for variation, until Coppola and Ruddy felt they had enough footage to convince Paramount that here was the one and only Don.

Robert Evans looked at the test and said, "He looks Italian, fine. But who is he?" When he learned the unknown actor's identity, Evans gave Brando his vote.

Paramount board chairman Charles Bluhdorn immediately

recognized Brando and jumped from his screening-room seat. "Oh, no! No!" he groaned as he strode up the aisle, but just as he reached the door, he glanced over his shoulder in time to see Marlon totally disappear into the role of sixty-five-year-old Don Corleone. "That's terrific!" he exclaimed. The part was Brando's.

For his services, Brando says Paramount paid him $250,000 plus a percentage, but other sources place his wages at a much lower figure—anywhere from a flat $50,000 to a straight percentage of the gross. Whatever his base salary may have been, it now seems definite that he did receive a small percentage of the film's take, which was to bring his earnings from the film to over a million dollars.

To prepare for *The Godfather*, Marlon went on a strenuous diet and succeeded in losing a substantial amount of weight. When Robert Evans saw the comparatively sylphlike Brando, he said, "My God! You're too thin to play the part." Marlon stepped up his calorie intake and by the time he walked in front of the cameras, there was a sizable paunch beneath the Don's starched shirtfront.

A few weeks before filming began in New York in March 1971, *The Godfather* zoomed into the headlines with some very unsavory publicity. Al Ruddy told a hostile New York press that the film version of *The Godfather* would carry no mention of either the Mafia or the Cosa Nostra, a piece of diplomacy argued out in a series of conferences with the Italian-American Civil Rights League.

What was Ruddy getting in exchange for this favor? a reporter asked. The producer answered that Coppola wanted to shoot in Staten Island's fashionable Todt Hill area—a section mainly populated by wealthy Italians—but the local inhabitants had been reluctant to cooperate. Since the *entente cordiale*, the League had been going to individual homes on Staten Island, urging people to be hospitable to cast and crew when they began production.

As his concluding remark, Ruddy casually mentioned that the opening of *The Godfather* would be a benefit for the

League's hospital fund. The announcement exploded like a stink bomb in Paramount's executive offices. One of the company's top troubleshooters hastily recalled the press and canceled Ruddy's première plans, which had been arranged, he said, without the studio's consent or approval.

Ruddy's concession did not materially damage the film—no one could fail to identify the spaghetti-eating killers on the screen as anything but Mafioso henchmen—and it freed him from threatened labor intervention. But it lent credibility to all sorts of lurid tall tales.

One New York actor claims he came out of an audition with the plum role of Michael, the Don's favorite son and successor, in his pocket. As he walked through the door, he was surreptitiously accosted by two sinister George Raft types who "suggested" he donate ten percent of his salary to "a certain organization." In outrage and fear, the actor doubled back to the audition hall and tossed his script on the table. Maybe his story is true, but it carries the faint aroma of sour grapes.

The competition for the supporting roles was grueling. At first Paramount considered Peter Fonda and Robert Redford for the Don's sons, but later decided to lower the budget by using unknowns. New York stage actor Al Pacino won the role of Michael by default—his tests were poor, and though he gives a tense and intelligent performance in the finished film, in the auditions he was the best of a bad lot. James Caan, a former Universal contract player, was cast as Sonny, the Don's aggressive and sexually oversized son. And Robert Duvall was selected for Tom Hagen, the Corleones' Irish-German *consigliere*.

With the exception of Duvall, who had worked with Brando in *The Chase*, few of his fellow players had met their illustrious co-star prior to the party Al Ruddy threw at a Manhattan restaurant on the eve of filming. The mixer got off to a bad start, but Marlon quickly broke the ice by playing the Don. He grabbed a bottle of wine, uncorked it, and passed around filled glasses. As soon as the *vino* warmed the veins, the troupe staged a euphoric Sicilian celebration.

The morning after lasted for three weeks. For reasons that have never been spelled out, a goodly portion of cast and crew took an immediate dislike to Coppola and tried to push him around, perhaps because he looked young and maneuverable. He says he did nothing to deserve such insubordination, and several eyewitnesses back him up. Paramount threatened to fire him three times, a trial of indecision that brought the director to the edge of a nervous breakdown. He persevered with the staunch support of Robert Evans and Brando, who announced he'd quit if Coppola was replaced. That quelled the rebellion. Coppola expelled the worst troublemakers from the set and coaxed the others into obedience.

There's another version of this incident which casts Marlon as the villain. He supposedly told Coppola he wouldn't need any directorial editing of his interpretation. It doesn't sound like Marlon's style and Coppola vehemently denies the story.

"Everyone advised me to assert myself and say, 'Now, Marlon, I'm the director, you just act,'" Coppola remembers. "But that would have been suicidal. Brando wants to do what you want, but he wants people to be honest and not try to manipulate him."

Coppola listened to Marlon's suggestions, and allowed him to execute them, even when they seemed entirely inappropriate. "His ideas were so bizarre, so crazy," the director said, "and yet, without exception, every one of his crazy ideas that I used turned out to be a terrific moment."

Brando's most inspired contribution to the film appears at the beginning of the Don's death scene. To amuse his grandson, Corleone takes a lemon peel, slices it into a zigzag pattern, and places it in his mouth; then he turns to the child who screams in terror at the sight of the yellow-fanged bogey.

Some say the lemon-peel masquerade is a game Brando invented to amuse his children, but one writer, H. A. L. Craig, suggests that it draws on Marlon's own childhood memories; that it's Brando Senior scaring little Bud with some well-intentioned but alienating piece of parent play. Wherever it came from, it's a master stroke.

Marlon kept spirits aloft on *The Godfather* set. He joked, pranked, and reassured the young members of the cast who were playing their first important roles in a major Hollywood production. "I felt that Brando really cared for me personally," said Al Pacino, "and that acceptance was a great thing for me."

Pop singer Al Martino was cast as Johnny Fontaine, Mario Puzo's roman-à-clef comment on Frank Sinatra. A last-minute replacement for Vic Damone (who withdrew because he was "advised" that the movie "was not in the best interests of Italian-Americans"), Martino had little acting experience, and had trouble meeting the emotional requirements of his scenes. Marlon occasionally slapped him about, says an admiring Coppola, "to get the right reactions, to make Martino look good."

During the production, Marlon's assistant jester was James Caan, an actor with a reputation as "an exuberant put-on artist and stand-up comic." Caan was passionately fond of a game called "mooning," in which the object is to drop your trousers and expose your bare buttocks at the most surprising moment.

"My best 'moon,'" Caan boasts, "was on Second Avenue. I was in one car and Brando was in another. As my car drove up beside his, I pulled my pants down and stuck my ass out the window. Brando fell down in the car with laughter."

Marlon had his usual trouble with the Don's lines, and the set was littered with "idiot cards." Once or twice he was late for an early Monday morning call; otherwise he was, says Coppola, an exemplary actor: cooperative, helpful, never temperamental. He even agreed to work an additional week without pay.

Brando saw *The Godfather* as an allegory of American capitalism. "I don't think the film is about the Mafia at all," he said. "I think it is about the corporate mind." He went on to compare the Don's tactics to those used by General Motors against Ralph Nader.

Whether by coincidence or star influence, Coppola arrived at an identical interpretation. "It is not about the Mafia," he stated. "The Mafia is nothing more than the ultimate capitalistic phenomenon. The Mafia came out of Sicily to the United States because the United States is where there's that system. I mean, I never thought of the book as anything but fiction. I don't think those people were or are like that—romantic figures. I think they're awful people . . . it just struck me that this sense of honor—taking care of your own—is what the country doesn't have. What if the United States took care of its people the way Don Corleone took care of his own? So to me *The Godfather* is total fiction and metaphor."

But Coppola's fiction bears little resemblance to Puzo's. The director turns the fast-reading novel into an elegiac, almost epic, film, and translates the novelist's American-gangster pulpisms into a European director's loose and exploratory language. Puzo zaps his audience; Coppola does too, in his stylized bloodbaths, but elsewhere he allows his audience its intelligence. He permits them to explore his rich images, to discover (and accept or reject) his metaphor of Mafia murder as capitalist monopoly.

He subtly altered Puzo's ending. The novelist implies that within ten years the Corleones will become law-abiding American citizens. (His ending is sociologically valid; according to university-sponsored reports, many Mafia families have attained respectability by the second or third generation.) The film goes along with Puzo until the closing sequence, which shows the Italian grandees kissing the hand of Michael, their new Don. Coppola seems to be saying that the violence will go on until the whole rotten system is decimated. And by then it's clear that the system the director is referring to is much bigger than the Mafia.

The world première of *The Godfather* was held in New York on March 11, 1972, with many of the picture's players present for the gala event. Well aware of Marlon's publicity shyness, Paramount had slipped a clause into his contract requiring him to appear at the opening—a benefit for the Boys Club of New York. Brando sent invitations to his old New York friends, including Edith Van Cleve and Stella Adler, but he never showed. He had been unavoidably detained in Los Angeles, where he was trying to solve the mystery of Christian's disappearance from the Ojai School.

On the Sunday before the opening, the New York *Times* ran a rave review of the film, and most of the other daily and weekly critics followed suit. But then there was the inevitable, fashionable backlash. It became smart to denounce the picture for selling death, or for "promoting the new pornography of violence" (a phrase culled from a New York *Times* editorial about the film). And Brando's Don Corleone was denounced by some as all makeup and no fury.

While Brando's role is too small for him to dominate the film as we might expect, his performance is a tower of sinister strength and dignity, much more than surface mimicry and Max Factor. It's a complete characterization, filled with rich detail, dark secrets, and a chilling inner isolation. There's none of the old Kowalski electricity in Brando's Don Corleone—the part doesn't permit it—but there is the redolence of a former, formidable sexual potency. It's not surprising to learn that when *The Godfather* opened in Palermo all the local Dons envied and imitated Brando's Mafioso allure.

Neither critical slaps nor editorial outrage nor heavy rain stopped people from queuing up for *The Godfather*. In New York it opened in five theaters, and five more were needed to handle the crowds. One theater stayed open twenty-four hours a day. Sharkies sold their places in line for as much as $20. Two weeks after the New York opening, *The Godfather* was playing in 305 cities and had raked in over $26,000,000. Nine months later it had replaced *Gone with the Wind* as the all-time box-office champion, with a record gross of $81,500,000.

Brando was back in fashion. He made the covers of *Time* and *Life,* and the TV imitators were brushing up the old Marlon mumble. How did he react to his new lease on life? Well, everyone had good years and bad years, he said. And what was success anyway, except being packaged and sold as if you were a Mickey Mouse wristwatch?

·21·
LAST TANGO IN PARIS

One night, several months before the opening of *The Godfather*, Brando attended a screening of *The Conformist*, a highly praised Italian film by Bernardo Bertolucci, Europe's latest wonder-boy director. The movie, a lush and glamorously stylized reconstruction of the pre–World War II Italian Fascist period, greatly impressed Marlon, who idly commented to a friend that someday he'd like to work with the thirty-year-old Bertolucci.

Meanwhile, across the sea, the Italian director was having trouble casting his new film, *Last Tango in Paris*. He had offered it to Dominique Sanda and Jean-Louis Trintignant, the stars of *The Conformist*. Miss Sanda said yes, but Trintignant, a modest man, was embarrassed by the script's explicit sex scenes and begged off.

While mulling over a second choice, Bertolucci went to an exhibition of English painter Francis Bacon. One picture of an anguished man—his emotional despair expressionistically contorting his face—struck Bertolucci as capturing the emotion he wanted to evoke in *Tango*. (The painting appears in the film's credits.) It also reminded him of Brando.

A few days later, he had dinner with his producer, Alberto (*Burn!*) Grimaldi. Almost as a joke, Bertolucci mentioned Brando as Trintignant's replacement. Grimaldi immediately contacted Marlon, who left for Paris three days later.

Brando went to the Bacon exhibition. It moved him. He

met Bertolucci. For fifteen minutes he said nothing, just stared at the director. Bertolucci bravely talked on about the film and its leading male character. Marlon listened carefully, and then said he'd do it.

Bertolucci and Grimaldi had unexpected problems in financing the film. Paramount agreed to back it—as long as Brando didn't play the lead. The company had backed Bertolucci's *The Conformist,* and won glory but little cash in the deal. Probably the Paramount money-men thought Brando was too big a risk; he might take an on-set dislike to Bertolucci, as he had done to Pontecorvo, and thereby turn the modestly priced ($1,000,000-plus) *Tango* into an overbudget nightmare like *Burn!*

Eventually, United Artists gave Bertolucci partial financing in exchange for the distribution rights. Brando was paid $250,000 plus a percentage of the gross.

After the Paris visit, Brando returned to California where he was later joined by Bertolucci for a two-week marathon of interpersonal exploration. At their first meeting, Bertolucci said to Brando, "Let's talk about ourselves, about our lives, our loves, about sex. That's what the film is going to be about."

Only the fly on the wall knows the intimate details of their discussions, but here are some biographical facts Brando may have learned about Bertolucci. He was born in Parma, Italy, in 1942, the son of a well-known poet and occasional film critic. He was blessed with a comfortable, bourgeois childhood, filled with sunshine, servants, and literary pursuits. He often went to movie screenings with his father, and became a Brando fan at age eleven when he saw *Viva Zapata!*

Four years later, he made his first film, a ten-minute documentary, *Cable Car,* shown only to family and friends. By his twentieth birthday, he was the author of an award-winning book of poetry, but a year later he abandoned literature for filmmaking. He snared a small international audience with his second professional picture, *Before the Revolution* (1964), a semi-autobiographical account of a young man torn between Communist ideology and an inborn taste for the sweet life.

He is a big, puffy man—not fat, really, but soft-looking—with an attractive babyface. He wears good clothes, usually well-crumpled, always carefully thrown together with casual chic. He speaks good French and verbless English, as well as his native Italian.

He was a member of the Communist Party and, like Brando, a devotee of "Saint Sigmund" Freud. Their mutual psychoanalytic orientation proved to be a great synchronizer. For two weeks, they took turns playing analyst and patient.

Then, early in 1972, Brando flew to Paris and settled into a rented Left Bank apartment. On his time off from preproduction conferences, Marlon renewed old friendships and saw a lot of Christian Marquand, who was having a liaison with Dominique Sanda, the original leading lady for *Tango*. (Miss Sanda had been forced to withdraw because she was carrying Marquand's baby.)

Bertolucci wasn't unduly concerned about unexpected cast changes. He never wrote his scripts with specific actors in mind—in fact, he regards a scenario as nothing more than a very flexible outline. Once on the set, he improvises entire scenes and refashions characters to his players' measure. "Directing is really a matter of discovering and bringing out of the actors what they really are. Characters must be built on that—on what the actors are in themselves."

As conceived for Jean-Louis Trintignant, Paul, the hero of *Tango*, was a youngish French widower. Brando speaks good French, but not good enough to pass as a native-born Frenchman, and he no longer qualifies as young. Therefore, in the finished film, Paul becomes a forty-five-year-old expatriate American with a checkered past: he's been an actor, a boxer, a journalist in Tahiti, and for the last seven years, the parasitic husband of the *patronne* of a Parisian flophouse. Brando's never been a reporter and he's never lived off any of his wives, but otherwise there's an obvious and playful biographical similarity between actor and character.

As the film begins, Paul's wife has just committed suicide for unspecified reasons. Her seemingly irrational, possibly vengeful act floods him with a raging guilt and despair. We are introduced to Paul as he stands under a trestle bridge. He's unshaven, disheveled, and emotionally unstrung—a sharp contrast to the golden autumnal picture-postcard scenery. The camera moves swiftly into a close-up. "Fucking God!" Paul cries, a lacerating yowl of torment that goes unheard in this mysteriously unpopulated landscape.

"Brando is an angel as a man, a monster as an actor," Bertolucci once said. And angel and monster seem to have joined hands to create this overwhelming moment. It was the first scene Bertolucci shot and he was staggered by the power of Brando's performance. "My camera isn't worthy of his acting," he told a friend.

Despite their friendly preproduction rapport, the director was now intimidated by Brando, and for the next week he shot around him, delaying the moment when he would have to tackle the actor's important scenes. Finally he went to Brando's apartment and openly confessed his fears. Marlon listened sympathetically, and then admitted that he was afraid of Bertolucci and had doubts about the whole project. They spent the whole day bolstering each other's morale.

"There's always a deep doubt lurking inside Marlon," Bertolucci said. "He's always asking himself, 'Is it really worth it?' And that doubt becomes very stimulating for the director. You have to answer Marlon's question. You have to keep asking yourself, 'Is it really worth it?'"

Brando's *Tango* co-star was Maria Schneider, a twenty-year-old unknown. Bertolucci chose her after interviewing over fifty girls. "It was always like seeing the same one," he commented, "because they were all exactly alike. All absolutely the same—same makeup, same hairdress." Miss Schneider is a true original. Bertolucci described her as "a Lolita—only more perverse." She also looked a little like a kewpie Jane Fonda decked out in a cascading corkscrew wig.

The illegitimate daughter of actor Daniel Gelin, Miss

Schneider was raised by her mother, the owner of a Paris bookshop, who was too square for Maria's tastes. At fifteen, she ran away from home and school in search of "kicks," and found plenty of them in Montparnasse, Marrakesh, and wherever else her vagabond soul led her. An untrammeled sprite, her true-life confessions later scandalized New York *Times* readers. "I've had more men lovers than women," she told a reporter, and then proceeded to tally them up as she puffed a joint of marijuana.

Bertolucci asked her to screen-test, and, once the cameras were rolling, told her to remove her clothes. She stripped without a moment's hesitation. "Undressed," Bertolucci said, "she became much more natural." Her carefree nudity won her the role.

Asking a relatively inexperienced actress to play opposite Brando is a hellish request, but Miss Schneider wasn't the impressionable sort. She took Brando in stride. To test their compatibility, Marlon took Miss Schneider to lunch a few days before shooting started. He insisted that they stare at each other in total silence for thirty minutes. Miss Schneider passed the test with flying colors. The next day she received a big bouquet of flowers from her co-star.

In *Tango*, Schneider plays a twenty-year-old *petite bourgeois* named Jeanne. She lives with her mother in a cozy flat decorated with military mementos of her dead father, an army captain. As the film begins, she is looking for an apartment to share with her fiancé, an undersexed and terribly precious filmmaker who's making a cinema-verité documentary on Jeanne's life. She meets Brando while apartment-hunting, and in a matter of minutes they are in the throes of fully dressed, vertical passion.

For the next three days, the couple meet in the apartment to act out their deepest sexual fantasies, most of them of a sadomasochistic variety. At Paul's insistence, they reveal nothing of their outside lives to each other, not even their names. In reaction to the death of his wife (whom he had suspected of flagrant infidelity), Paul has decided that the only honest relationship between two people is sex stripped of romance and personality.

As the affair progresses, Jeanne becomes Paul's sexual slave: she promises to eat vomit for him, even to allow a pig to fart in her face as she reaches orgasm. In an attempt to free herself, she tells Paul that she is soon to marry her filmmaker fiancé and, in anger, he ends their relationship. Then, in an abrupt about-face, he insists that he needs her, loves her, wants her to live with him. Outside their sex-nest she sees him for what he really is—an aging bum—and when he won't leave her alone, she extricates herself with an act of deadly, unpremeditated logic: she shoots Paul with her father's revolver. "I never knew his name," she mutters over and over. "He followed me home . . . he tried to rape me . . ."

While writing the script, Bertolucci wondered whether the sex scenes should be shown on screen; he decided that not to show them would be "morbid." But in the finished film, the sexual aggression is simulated, and it's neither prurient nor erotic. Bertolucci was after the hard-core psychology of sex, not its physicality.

Everyone was quite nervous about the filming of the sex scenes except Miss Schneider, who prances through scene after scene in full frontal nudity. "I'm much more free sexually than Bernardo or Brando," she said. Marlon was self-conscious about exposing his body, but agreed to disrobe entirely if Bertolucci wanted it that way. And the director did photograph one scene which showed Brando's genitals, and then later excised it from the finished film "for structural reasons, to shorten the film."

Later, the women's liberationists attacked *Tango* for cloaking Brando while exposing Schneider. Everyone else breathed a sigh of relief. Was the world really ready for the sight of Brando, age forty-seven, totally stripped? The sex scenes don't require it—they are violent, spur-of-the-moment acts of libido—and they seem more aggressive because Brando never entirely sheds his clothes.

Paris buzzed with rumors that Schneider and Brando were

having an off-screen romance, but Maria denies it. Marlon was just a "daddy" to her. "I never felt any sexual attraction for him, though all my friends told me I should," she said. "But he's almost fifty, and he's only beautiful to his waist."

As an actress, however, she admitted she was "full of his vibrations," and so was everyone else on the set. "At first, I was absolutely terrified of him," said screenwriter Marilyn Goldin, a frequent visitor to the set, "and gave him a wide berth. But he was very polite, and often very friendly—though sometimes in the most peculiar ways. Every time I took out a cigarette, he ran over to light it. Once when I was sitting on the floor talking to Maria Schneider, he suddenly yelled, 'Don't move!' I froze to the spot and the next thing I knew there was Brando somersaulting over my shoulder. God knows why he did it—probably for a laugh or from exuberance—but let me tell you, it's quite a shock to see Marlon Brando go cannonballing over your shoulder."

Brando was not always so carefree during the filming. In one scene, he had to cry, and just before he went before the camera, he told Bertolucci, "I don't know how to do it." The day before, he had told the director about a nightmare he'd had about his children. "Use your nightmare," Bertolucci suggested. Marlon stared at him with such hatred that Bertolucci decided to revise the scene to eliminate the tears. But then Brando said, "Okay, I'll do it." It's one of the most memorable scenes in the film.

Bertolucci asked Brando not to immerse himself in the character, but rather to superimpose his own personality and psychology on Paul. The director says Brando both loved and hated this method of working: "He loved it because it was the first time he had done it, but he hated it because it seemed to him a violation of his privacy." And much of the power and fascination of *Tango* stems from our uncertainty as to where Marlon leaves off and Paul begins.

"Forty years of Brando's life experiences went into the film," says Christian Marquand. "It is Brando talking about himself, being himself. His relations with his mother, father, children, lovers, friends—all come out in his performance as Paul."

Bertolucci's script was originally written in Italian, then translated into French, then into literal English, and finally into idiomatic English by two American writers (one of them Chris Mankiewicz, son of Joseph L.). Brando had his usual difficulties in remembering lines. The set was papered with cue cards—once Marlon asked Bertolucci if he could scribble his lines on Maria Schneider's naked derrière. Bertolucci refused this farcical request, but he did allow Marlon to re-phrase any lines he found unspeakable.

Much of the dialogue is pure and prime Brando. Asked by Jeanne to define their relationship, he answers, "Let's just say we're taking a flying fuck on a rolling doughnut."

When she inquires about his education, he says, "I went to Melbourne U. and studied whale-fucking."

After she mocks his flabby body, he retorts, "In twenty years, you'll be playing football with your tits."

In a moment of candid self-appraisal, Paul says, "What the hell, I'm no prize. I picked up a nail in Cuba in 1948, and I got a prostate like an Idaho, but I'm still a good stick man. I don't have any friends. I suppose if I hadn't met you, I'd probably settle for a hard chair and a hemorrhoid."

The lines often sound like Norman Mailer, one of Bertolucci's culture heroes, but then Marlon often talks the way Mailer writes. It's rich, pungent dialogue, bursting with crude wit and vitality, and it's often very shocking, very titillating. Brando throws off the locker room one-liners with such force and at such surprising moments that they catch us off guard like a series of unexpected slaps in the face. He doesn't allow us the protection of being blasé.

When Marlon got into the swing of Bertolucci's free-wheeling method of work, he asked the director if he could try an improvisation. Bertolucci loaded the camera with the largest spool of film it could hold, and told him to go ahead.

In the scene, Jeanne asks Paul why he hasn't returned to America. He says he has bad memories. "My father was a drunk . . . a super-masculine type . . . a screwed-up bar fighter . . ." Brando/Paul says. "My mother was also a drunk. My memories as a kid are of her being arrested. . . . We lived in a small town, a farming community. I used to milk a cow every morning and I liked that. . . . But I remember one time I was all dressed up to take this girl to a basketball game. My father said, 'You have to milk the cow,' and I said, 'Would you please milk it for me?' And he said 'No, get your ass out there.' I was in a hurry, and I didn't have time to change my shoes, and I had cow shit all over them. Later on it smelled in the car. . . . I can't remember many good things."

Jeanne says, "I've tricked you. I thought we weren't going to talk about our pasts."

Paul/Brando smiles at her sweetly. "What makes you think I've told you the truth?" And so, we're back where we began. Here's Brando once again making a public confession, and maybe no more than forty percent of it is truth.

It is dangerous and probably erroneous to make a blanket identification between Paul and Brando. Certainly, some of Bertolucci's own psyche has been superimposed on the character. It's no secret that during the production of the film Bertolucci's romance of five years' standing ended, and apparently for reasons directly related to the making of the film.

Bertolucci was living with Maria Paola Maino, an antique dealer, whom he always introduced as his wife, though in fact she was married to another man; the Italian divorce laws prevented her from dissolving her previous union to marry Bertolucci. The director's friends speculate that *Tango* expresses the conflicts in this relationship, and evidently Miss Maino, who worked on the production, also believed this to be true. She left Bertolucci halfway through the filming.

In private conversation, Bertolucci told a friend, "I am both Paul and Jeanne," but in interviews he wouldn't be drawn into personal revelation. "It's hypothetical," he said. "I don't choose my movies, they choose me. I don't know how, but they do." Whether he chose *Last Tango* or *Last Tango* chose him, it must have cost a large emotional toil to create. You can't look so deeply into yourself, pull out such emotion, and remain unscathed or unchanged.

Last Tango premièred at the New York Film Festival in October 1972. During the screening, the auditorium was charged with excitement, but at a champagne reception afterward, the guests were subdued and faintly hostile. Some said the film left them "speechless," others admitted they had been "terrified" by it, but the majority had a bad case of the sophisticated blahs. A well-known critic who's also a celebrated lecher (the girls in his office cross themselves whenever he enters the room) dismissed the movie as naïve, and several confreres were heard making similar snorts.

Two weeks later Pauline Kael wrote about the film in the pages of *The New Yorker*. The film festival opening of *Tango*, she said, was a date "that should become a landmark in movie history—comparable to May 29, 1913—the night *Le Sacre du Printemps* was first performed—in music history. There was no riot, and no one threw things at the screen, but I think it's fair to say that the audience was in a state of shock. . . . This must be the most powerfully erotic movie ever made and it may turn out to be the most liberating movie ever made. . . . Bertolucci and Brando have altered the face of an art form."

And that was just the start. Miss Kael went on to say, "It is a movie you can't get out of your system, and I think it will make some people very angry and disgust others. I don't believe that there's anyone whose feelings can be totally resolved about the sex scenes and the social attitudes in this film . . . it's like seeing pieces of your life, and so, of course, you can't resolve your feelings about it—our feelings about life are never resolved."

Twenty-four hours later, the review and the film were tops on the list of what New Yorkers were talking about. Four months before its scheduled American release, *Tango* was already a cause célèbre.

At the end of 1972 it opened in Paris, receiving excellent reviews and attracting record crowds. Then in January 1973, after an initial snafu with the Italian censors (cuts were demanded and made), *Tango* opened in Bertolucci's native land. After a brief run, prints of the film were confiscated by officials, who charged the director and his co-stars with "crude, repulsive, naturalistic and even unnatural representation of carnal union, with continued and complacent scenes . . . accompanied off-screen by sounds, sighs and shrieks of climax pleasure." The case was eventually thrown out of court.

On February 1, 1973, the film finally opened in New York, unwinding in a small East Side theater on a reserved-seat basis. It cost five dollars to get in, the same price porno fans shelled out to see Casey Donovan in *Boys in the Sand* or Linda Lovelace in *Deep Throat*. (At the time the regular admission price was three dollars.)

United Artists was accused of selling *Tango* as a porno flick, but the company didn't care. It was very high-handed in its promotion of the film. Getting invited to an advance screening, even for those with legitimate credentials, was like wangling an invitation to an Onassis yachting party. Some critics were barred unconditionally. Others were given a very hard time—there are only two or three screenings, they were told, but we'll try to sneak *you* in. They'd arrive to find the screening room filled with UA employees or hangers-on.

Seeing *Tango* in advance of its release became a status symbol, and UA scheduled most of its screenings for TV talk show celebrities. Peggy Cass discussed it on the Jack Paar show with a "Wow! Gee! Did you ever imagine you'd see . . ." enthusiasm that should have had UA blanching, but apparently it was the kind of cheap, exploitative publicity the company wanted.

Three days after *Tango* opened there was a fist fight in the theater. A group of rowdies came expecting hard-core titillation and, disappointed by what they saw, worked off their frustration by beating up ushers and the theater manager.

Tango was a film people used to work off their hostilities.

The critics who resented Pauline Kael used it to throttle her. ("*The Rite of Spring* or *Nude Descending a Staircase*, it is not," declared one archrival.) The critics who had been manhandled by UA used it as an excuse to attack the company. The critics who felt it behooved them to support "clean" films used it to put down pornography. The critics who approved of pornography ridiculed it because it didn't have the courage of its convictions (i.e., its sex scenes are faked). The women's liberationists campaigned against it because Maria Schneider was presented as a piece of "meat." And many men loathed it because it showed them as male chauvinist pigs.

The film itself has got lost in all the ballyhoo. Very few people were able to judge it with any detachment, and it was some time before they could.

But even in the heat of first controversy, it was apparent that *Tango* had serious flaws. Today those failings look even more serious. The subplot of Jeanne's filmmaker fiancé doesn't work, possibly because Jean-Pierre Léaud is so quirky and precious in a part that calls for simplicity and charm. And then there are a large number of oddball excessive scenes, all of them typically Bertolucci, which add little to Paul and Jeanne's story, and actually prevent it from achieving the classic purity of French tragedy to which Bertolucci seems to have been aspiring.

The purple emotions of the big set pieces continue to devastate or offend, with no possible middle ground or compromise. Paul's funeral oration over his wife's bier is an opera aria of profane grief and anger. It's too much, and either it sweeps you away or it has you looking at the floor in embarrassment. (At one of the first New York screenings, Dustin Hoffman sprang from his seat and hid behind a pillar during this scene.) Later, when Jeanne says she doesn't want to be alone, Paul excoriates her in a blistering diatribe that ends as he proclaims that we are all alone until we "look into the asshole of death." Then he devises the final sexual humiliation of Jeanne (and of himself): he orders her to sodomize him with her hand, forcing her to declare her sexual subservience as she does so. It's like nothing that's ever been shown on screen before—in fact, it has few equivalents in any modern art form. Redolent of Baudelaire, Huysmans, and Jean Genet, these scenes pull the spectator into a world where preconceived standards of good and bad taste are not applicable.

As Pauline Kael wrote, *Last Tango in Paris* is a film that you can't get out of your system. And it's not a movie you want to revisit in the near future. It leaves you scarred and depleted and staggered.

After seeing it, you understand Brando's parting words to Bertolucci. "We will never do something like this again. This is the last time I use up my energies."

·22·
NO HOME FOR OSCAR

On the day of *Last Tango*'s screening at the New York Film Festival, Brando called Lincoln Center and asked for a ticket to the performance. The lady who received the call almost dropped the receiver in excitement. Was he coming? she asked. No, Brando answered; he wanted the ticket for a friend. "I'm sorry," he said, "but I've got an appointment in Tahiti."

When the film was theatrically released, Maria Schneider and Bertolucci flew to Manhattan and were welcomed as instant celebrities. Bertolucci was lionized by *Women's Wear Daily* as one of its "juicy" people; he met Norman Mailer; he gave a lot of foolish interviews. "I fall in love with all the actors in my films," he said. "Actresses *and* actors. I fall in love with them all; they are the prolongations of my penis. Yes, my *penis*. Like Pinocchio's nose, my penis grows!"

Marlon stayed well out of the *Tango* fray. No one is sure whether he saw the movie. He called UA's Los Angeles office and requested a screening; forty friends showed up, but no Marlon. The next day he called, apologized, and requested a second screening; forty more friends showed, but Brando never appeared. He was in Tahiti. If he wanted to see it, said UA, he could pay at the box office, just like Richard Nixon, who was refused the privilege of a special White House screening.

In February 1973, Brando received his sixth Academy Award nomination for his performance in *The Godfather*. For months everyone had been predicting he would win the Oscar, but once he was nominated, there was a backlash of public protest. Many people believed the role of Don Corleone was too small to merit a citation in the best actor category and argued that the nomination should have gone to Al Pacino for his portrayal of Michael, the Don's son, a role twice as long as Brando's. (Pacino was nominated in the supporting actor category, along with co-players James Caan and Robert Duvall.)

Some forecasters predicted that Brando's chances of winning the Oscar for *The Godfather* had been weakened by his *Tango* cavorting. The American film industry was staunchly behind the production of "clean films"—X-rated pictures couldn't be shown on TV, a major source of income for the major studios—and the vast majority of the Hollywood establishment took a dim view of the sexual calisthenics Marlon had executed for Bertolucci.

When the film opened in Los Angeles, the superstar first-nighters were nervous and reserved. "Sex is just not a good spectator sport," said one studio executive. Mae West was more enthusiastic. "It's *good* and dirty," she said, and then drawled, "but, of course, I'm easily shocked."

A more typical reaction was voiced by Debbie Reynolds. When *Tango* was mentioned, she pursed her lips and said, "I'm a great admirer of Marlon's, but from what I hear about the film, I don't think I'd care to see it."

Still, on the day of the Oscar presentations, March 27, 1973, Marlon was the odds-on favorite as winner of the best actor award. No one knew whether he would show up to pocket his statuette. There were reports that though he was in California, he didn't plan to attend the awards ceremony at Los Angeles's Dorothy Chandler Music Center. And late in the afternoon of the 27th, a TV news show broadcast a rumor that Brando intended to refuse the award. No explanation was offered, but it was conjectured that Marlon intended to walk in George C. Scott's footsteps and reject the Oscar as an artistically invalid award.

Howard Koch, the producer of the forty-fifth annual

Academy Awards presentation, was backstage getting into his tux when a network page told him that an Indian was expected to represent Brando at the evening's festivities. "I got a little nervous," Koch said. "What if he sent a whole tribe?" A few minutes later, the producer was informed that Marlon's advocate was demanding a conference in the theater lobby. Koch rushed to the front of the theater where he encountered Sacheen Littlefeather, an Apache princess handsomely robed in white buckskin and turquoise beads. She showed Koch a three-page speech Marlon had written to explain his declination of the Oscar. At first, the producer refused Miss Littlefeather TV time, but she argued until she was granted a forty-five-second close-up. (According to one reporter, she threatened to stage a demonstration on the floor of the auditorium if she were not permitted to talk from the dais.) With severe misgivings, Koch ushered Sacheen to the seat reserved for Brando.

Shortly thereafter, the presentation began with Angela Lansbury singing "Make a Little Magic," an ironic opening for an evening filled with snafus, snide humor, plastic glamour, poor sportsmanship, and unexpected victors. Rarely has an Academy Awards ceremony been overrun by so many upsets. *The Godfather* had been nominated in nine categories and was expected to win most of them with ease. Somewhere along the line, the industry prognosticators had made a major miscalculation. Envelope after envelope was opened to disclose *Cabaret* and not *The Godfather* as winner. In most categories the two movies were, qualitatively speaking, neck-and-neck contenders, but still there seemed to be a conspiracy against Puzo's Mafia drama. In hindsight rehashes of the event, it was widely hypothesized that *The Godfather* lost many awards because of a delayed reaction to its gratuitous violence.

After two hours of misread cue cards and sartorial lunacy—ranging from Julie Andrews's prissy, G-rated Mother Hubbard through Diana Ross's sleazy Supreme tuxedo to Raquel Welch's masterfully engineered red strapless—the ceremony finally arrived at its crucial moment: the citation for best ac-

tor. Swedish actress Liv Ullmann and English TV star Roger
Moore marched out to the podium, struggled to unglue the
Price, Waterhouse envelope, and then announced Brando the
Winner.

NBC's TV cameras caught Sacheen Littlefeather as she
sprang from her seat and walked to the stage. Across the
country there were a lot of knowing titters—Princess
Hiawatha looked like the latest installment in Marlon's en-
during romance with exotic vamps—but as Miss Littlefeather
waved away the Oscar statuette Roger Moore offered her,
laughter was quelled by gasps of surprise.

Turning to the microphone, Miss Littlefeather announced,
"Marlon Brando very regretfully cannot accept the award because of the treatment of the American Indians in this country today on television, on reruns, and recent happenings at
Wounded Knee." Before the words were out of her mouth,
there was a raft of jeers followed by a token outburst of ap-
proving applause. Miss Littlefeather stood her ground with
dignity. When the commotion ended, she told the audience
Marlon had prepared a lengthy apologia which she would read
to the press after the ceremony. Then she left the stage, leaving a very bemused Roger Moore holding the unclaimed Oscar. (Later he tried to return it to Academy officials, but they
also refused it. At last report, Moore still has Brando's Oscar
and is talking about auctioning it off for charity.)

Brando's eloquent and very moving statement read in part:

> For two hundred years we have said to the Indian
> people who are fighting for their land, their life, their
> families and their right to be free: "Lay down your
> arms, my friends, and then we will remain to-
> gether. . . ." When they laid down their arms, we
> murdered them. We lied to them. We cheated them
> out of their lands. We starved them into signing
> fraudulent agreements that we called treaties which
> we never kept. We turned them into beggars on a
> continent that gave life for as long as life can re-

member. And by any interpretation of history, however twisted, we did not do right. . . .

Perhaps at this moment you are saying to yourself, "What the hell has all this got to do with the Academy Awards?" . . . I think the answer to this question is that the motion picture community has been as responsible as any for degrading the Indian and making a mockery of his character and describing him as savage, hostile and evil . . . I, as a member in this profession, do not feel that I can as a citizen of the United States accept an award here tonight. I think awards in this country at this time are inappropriate to be received or given until the condition of the American Indian is drastically altered. . . .

I would have been here tonight to speak to you directly, but I felt that perhaps I could be of better use if I went to Wounded Knee to help forestall in whatever way I can the establishment of a peace which would be dishonorable as long as the rivers shall run and the grass shall grow.

The speech implied that Brando was on his way to Wounded Knee, South Dakota, the site of the last great massacre of the nineteenth-century Indian wars. A few weeks before the Oscar ceremony, Wounded Knee was seized by a group of militant Oglala Sioux who waged a combination siege and guerilla war against Federal forces in the hope of pressuring the U.S. government to open new Senate hearings on Indian treaty rights and to recognize an Oglala tribal government.

Brando's speech focused nationwide attention on Wounded Knee, and during the next two weeks everyone waited for his arrival at the battlefront. He failed to appear, though there was a rumor that his request to enter Wounded Knee had been vetoed by government officials.

On April 5, 1973, the Oglala Indians signed an agreement to end hostilities at Wounded Knee. As the treaty was signed, an eagle flew overhead, a good omen according to the Indians.

But many Americans feared that the peace treaty was, as Brando had predicted, a dishonorable peace which guaranteed the Sioux none of the demands they had requested.

In the hullabaloo over the incident, Brando was charged with both grandstanding and insincerity. Few remembered that he had been criticizing the government's Indian policy since the early 1950s, that he had been arrested while protesting the inhumane treatment of Washington's Puyallup Indians, that he had once commissioned a screenplay in which he was to play an Indian dying of an incurable disease on a wretchedly maintained reservation. The film was never produced, but according to a New York director-writer who has read the script, it was an extremely powerful and excoriating statement on the problem of Indian civil rights.

Many people who approved of Marlon's gesture criticized him for not appearing at the Oscar ceremony. And certainly it is true that there would have been more dramatic impact had Brando pleaded his cause himself. But, as the pro-Brando faction was quick to point out, it is not etiquette to reject an award—whether it be the Oscar or the Nobel prize—in person.

Brando was also criticized in choosing Sacheen Littlefeather as his surrogate. Journalists soon unearthed some supposedly discreditable facts about Marlon's stand-in: she was a would-be starlet who sometimes went by the name of Maria Cruz, and in 1971 she had won a studio publicity contest as Miss American Vampire. One columnist hinted that she had used Brando and the Oglala Sioux to further her career and would soon be guesting on the TV talk show circuit. This did not happen.

The Hollywood establishment was alternately enraged and confused by Brando's condemnation of the industry. Raquel Welch followed Sacheen Littlefeather, and in presenting the best actress award to Liza Minnelli, she quipped, "I hope she doesn't have a cause!" The lame joke collected few laughs. After Miss Welch's departure, Clint Eastwood appeared to present the best picture award to *The Godfather*, and he, too, strove for a humorous touch, saying he didn't think he should present the award "in honor of all those cowboys shot in John Ford westerns through the years." Then, almost on cue, in walked a very glum and seemingly belligerent John Wayne, and for an angry second he looked, said one wag, as if he were going to insist everyone join in a prayer for General Custer. Instead, he led award winners and presenters in a rousing chorus of "You Oughta Be in Pictures," which, considering the events of the evening, was as satiric a finale as could be imagined.

In the extensive postmortems of the event, the anti-Brando faction found a loose and acid-tongued spokeswoman in Rona Barrett, the TV generation's answer to Louella Parsons. In a blistering syndicated editorial, Miss Barrett told Marlon to put his money where his mouth was. Why, she asked, was he squandering his *Godfather* and *Last Tango* profits on his Tahitian paradise when he might be building hospitals and schools for the American Indian?

Less censoriously, *Newsweek* magazine wondered what would happen at the 1974 awards ceremony "when Brando's sensational performance in *Last Tango in Paris* is almost certain to get him another Oscar nomination." When that eventuality did occur, the Academy voters acted in predictable fashion. As best actor, they chose Jack Lemmon for *Save the Tiger* over Brando. Even if Marlon had not rejected the Oscar the previous year, it is doubtful that he would have won for *Tango*, as the Academy membership was too conservative to give any kind of sanction to a film as sexually explicit as Bertolucci's.

For several months Marlon remained outside the fray, making no comment except that if he did win a third Oscar, he would definitely refuse it—he now regretted picking up his first for *Waterfront*. Then he made an announcement that seemed to answer Rona Barrett's challenge. He was donating forty acres of shrub-covered California ranchland to the Survival of the American Indian Association (SAIA) to use in whatever way it deemed fit. The acreage, which he had only recently purchased, had once been home to the Chumash tribe, and Marlon hoped his gift would inspire others to give up land that rightfully belonged to the Indians.

The original idea was to use the land as an Indian-operated movie production site or as an amphitheater for Indian theatricals and tribal dances. But eventually SAIA voted to give a local real estate developer the option to buy the land for $500,000 and build forty single-family homes that would sell for $100,000 each. As this hardly seemed the proper way to preserve Indian culture, SAIA was soundly rebuked by the press, but Marlon defended the sale because "the insurance and taxes on the property [were] posing a real economic hardship" on the organization.

Shortly before he made this gift of property, in early 1974, Marlon told the press he was going to produce a film based on the incident at Wounded Knee in 1973, and might also take on one of the major roles. About the latter, however, he hedged. "I think my days as an actor are coming to an end," he said.

Never to be realized, *Bury My Heart at Wounded Knee* was to take up nearly eighteen months of Brando's life, and was as handicapped by indecision and an ever-changing shift of personnel as had been *One-Eyed Jacks* twenty years earlier. Abby Mann, best known for his Oscar-winning screenplay for *Judgment at Nuremberg*, was hired to write a script. Things went well at first—at least Mann thought so. "Marlon makes wonderful contributions," he exclaimed. "He can sit down and improvise a story better than I can write it." Brando eventually came to the same conclusion. Mann, he said, turned in "three really bad scripts" before he was dismissed.

Directors came and went. First was Martin Scorsese—like Coppola, a young Italian-American who had managed the giant step from film school to professional filmmaking with ease: his first great critical success, *Mean Streets*, released in 1973, convinced Brando he was ready for the job. But Scorsese departed after only a few weeks, later saying privately that he felt Marlon had no clear idea of what he wanted to express in the film.

Forgetting the disagreements that had occurred while

making *Burn!*, Marlon next turned to Gillo Pontecorvo, whose documentary orientation made him an ideal choice. Pontecorvo was enthusiastic—until he met some of Brando's Indian friends. "I thought they were going to scalp me," he said. "They scared him shitless," Marlon confirmed. "Indians are strange folks till you get to know them."

Once Pontecorvo disappeared, there were no further progress bulletins on *Bury My Heart at Wounded Knee*, and the press and industry correctly assumed that the project had been abandoned. This was a signal to producers that Brando might now be interested in an acting assignment, and immediately the offers started coming in.

For several years there had been plans for a European film version of Marcel Proust's *Remembrance of Things Past*, and many directors and screenwriters had tried to hone a script out of this vast, multivolume meditation on the metamorphoses caused by time and sexual desire. In 1974, it looked as though everything was about to fall into place. Director Joseph Losey, an American who worked primarily abroad, had a screenplay by Harold Pinter and a dream list of the actors he wanted for the leading roles. As the depraved, homosexual Baron de Charlus, Losey had two top choices—Marlon Brando or Sir Laurence Olivier.

Losey flew to Tahiti to talk in person with Brando, who expressed mild interest. When there was a firm shooting schedule, he would give a definite answer. But he was never asked to commit himself since Losey lost his financing. When finally, in 1983, Proust's novel—more exactly the *Swann in Love* segment of the novel—was finally produced, Baron de Charlus was played with leering panache by Alain Delon. Still, it's a shame Brando never got a chance at Charlus, a potentially fine character role which might have called on the full range of his imaginative powers.

Around the same time Robert Evans invited Marlon to play the title role in the third screen remake of F. Scott Fitzgerald's *The Great Gatsby*. The Paramount production chief recalls that Brando refused because he was unhappy about his income from *The Godfather*. "He asked for the moon and stars," Evans says. "He was angry about not having a larger percentage of *The Godfather.*" Evans insisted Paramount couldn't afford what he was asking. "Then take a slice off *The Godfather*," Marlon replied. Other sources say Marlon didn't much care for Fitzgerald's novel and felt he would be miscast as the titular hero. At fifty, he was too old for Gatsby, though certainly he would have provided the allure of sexual danger so essential to the part and so missing from the performance of the actor who replaced him, Robert Redford.

For a while Brando made a lot of noise about turning down the big parts that came his way. "I want to make films that concern all of us," he said. "Films about pollution, aggression, and overpopulation. Not movies with stories, but things like documentaries." One possibility was an adaptation of Jane Goodall's *In the Shadow of Man*, an account of life in a colony of chimpanzees. It was a fine book, without a trace of a traditional plot.

But the aborted *Wounded Knee* film and his ecological experiments had burned up a lot of cash, and eventually Brando had to set aside his idealism and retreat to the arena of high-paying practicality. He accepted the first offer that came his way. Late in 1975, he signed a $1,500,000 contract to star in a top-budget Western, *The Missouri Breaks*. It was to be one of the worst films of his career.

·23·

MISSOURI MUD

The Missouri Breaks is a perfect example of how a film shouldn't be made. It all started with producer Elliott Kastner who had a group of tax shelter investors and a rough outline for a screenplay by novelist Thomas McGuane. The original idea was to take two top male stars and have them romp their way through a *Butch Cassidy and the Sundance Kid* rip-off. As Kastner was responsible for *The Night of the Following Day* and *The Nightcomers*, he immediately thought of Brando and, as his co-star, Jack Nicholson, who had just won an Oscar for *One Flew Over the Cuckoo's Nest*. An acting duel between the old grizzly bear and the sly young fox—what more could audiences ask? It was a long shot that either actor would return his calls, but Kastner decided to start at the top and then work his way down.

Much to his surprise, Brando and Nicholson were interested, though both warned that the film would have to go into production almost immediately if it were to fit into their schedules. And each made it clear that their interest was contingent on the participation of the other. If Brando backed out, Nicholson would have to reconsider and vice versa. Also, both wanted a director they respected. This proved to be no problem. Promised Brando and Nicholson as his leading actors, Arthur Penn (who had gone on to direct *Bonnie and Clyde* and *Alice's Restaurant* after working with Marlon on *The Chase*) signed on with alacrity, though he was told that he had only two months to prepare his production if *The*

Missouri Breaks was to meet the Memorial Day 1976 release date set by United Artists, Kastner's distribution affiliate.

Penn's chore was made the more difficult by the geographical distance separating the key participants in the film: he was in New York, Brando was in Tahiti, Nicholson in Beverly Hills, McGuane in London editing *90 in the Shade,* an adaptation of one of his own novels which he himself had directed. Penn got out to California to talk to Nicholson, then hopped across the Atlantic to confer with McGuane, but there was no time for Brando and Teiteroa. This meant, he realized, that work on the set was going to be one long improvisatory exploration, particularly since Marlon was reportedly making a fuss about getting some Indian propaganda into the picture.

Before the starting date, McGuane found time to amplify his outline into a barely coherent screenplay. Set in the 1880s, it is the story of a rich and cultivated rancher, Braxton (John McLiam), who is constantly harassed by a rustler named Logan (Nicholson). It is, however, the landowner who is the villain of the piece—he's a mean-spirited tyrant who deserves what he gets from the horse bandit.

The transformation of the outlaw into avenging hero was a convention of the modern Western, but McGuane had a few other novelties up his sleeve. The heroine, Braxton's daughter (Kathleen Lloyd), is a hot-blooded minx who keeps sneaking out of her papa's home to bed down with Logan. Young ladies in John Ford films didn't carry on this way, and they certainly didn't speak as lewdly as Miss Braxton. Critics were later to describe her as an "anachronism," which is one way of saying she seems a fugitive from *Looking for Mr. Goodbar.*

Brando does not appear until the film is well under way. He plays Robert E. Lee Clayton, a mercenary hired to do away with Logan and his gang of thieves. Clayton was designed as a smallish role, as Marlon had stipulated that he could spend only twenty-five days on the set. Nicholson had by far the larger part, but as his co-star was to prove, it's not the amount of time you're on screen that matters; what counts is what you do with the time you're allotted.

The Missouri Breaks is the name of the headwaters of the

Missouri River in Montana, and most of the film was shot in that area, about fifteen miles from Billings. The cast and crew had been working for five weeks before Marlon arrived, looking very scruffy and at least thirty pounds overweight. But as he was playing what was essentially a character role, the excessive poundage was no liability—except to Marlon's vanity. He dieted throughout the production, eating mainly cereal and vegetables, and drinking juices. But his weight never seemed to diminish.

He was billeted in a mobile home close to the set where he was constantly pestered by local young ladies who knocked on his door in search of (they said) nothing more than "a handshake." Still he remained extremely affable and cooperative, though one of his after-hours amusements terrified Elliott Kastner. Nearly every evening, he would hop on his Honda trail bike and ride for hours over the nearby mountain paths.

"Where's he going?" someone asked.

"Just pray he comes back alive," Kastner murmured.

No sooner had he arrived than Marlon began worrying Penn about the Indian propaganda he wanted to add to the script. The director tried to accommodate Brando in any way possible, but finally he had to tell him that he was asking the impossible: the picture didn't have anything to do with the American Indians. Marlon accepted this decision without animosity. He simply shifted his attention to his role and how it could be built up in importance.

In the script Clayton is described as being "as weird as weird can be," which Brando took as an invitation to do practically anything he wanted. He worked up so many elaborations on his character that McGuane later complained that he had destroyed the contours of the original script. Several people came forward in Marlon's defense. "I'm not sure I ever had the feeling there was a 'finished' screenplay," Arthur Penn said. "There was, essentially, a kind of meandering tale of the character played by Nicholson . . ." And Nicholson facetiously remarked, "The contracts took longer to write than the script."

During the shooting, Brando was interviewed by *Rolling Stone* magazine, and, as was to be expected, he made his favorite comment: "I'm only doing it for the money." Penn later insisted this should be taken with a grain of salt. "I wish there was a way of telling you how both publicly frivolous and privately serious Brando is," the director commented. "He'll say things like that . . . but when the reporter walks out of the room, he'll say, 'Now, how do we do this scene?' And he goes to work then, and works alone for three or four hours in the most intensely personal, improvisatory way—searching for some kind of resonance inside himself."

Judging from what turned up on the screen, Penn was an all too admiring audience for Brando's improvisations. He seems never to have edited or squelched any of the actor's ideas, and as a result, Brando's performance is so perversely wrongheaded that it makes no sense within the context of the film. The sense of dislocation starts with Clayton's first appearance. He arrives hanging so low over the far side of his horse that the beast seems to be riderless. What does this mean? the viewer wonders. Is Marlon telling us he'd prefer to be out of the picture?

Things go steadily downhill. Brando's performance seems to be a series of "transformations," an exercise used by actors to stretch imagination by shifting characterization at will and without psychological motivation. At first Clayton speaks with a very thick, menacing Irish brogue, though with certain people he switches to a Midwestern twang. Occasionally he assumes—for no apparent reason—the disguise of a preacher or a pioneer woman. And throughout there is a suggestion of the epicene about him. Braxton's henchmen give him a wide berth because he smells of lilac cologne.

Penelope Gilliatt, one of the few critics who genuinely admired Brando's work in *Breaks*, later wrote in *The New Yorker*, "Brando's performance has a lot to do with his opulently witty sense of Restoration comedy, which had never been more evident than in this film—not even in *Mutiny on the Bounty*." This may be true, but then shouldn't Marlon be playing Sheridan or Congreve instead of mincing his way through a horse opera? His foppery made sense in *Bounty*, but here it's totally out of place.

Furthermore, the intimations of homosexuality don't make much sense, since Clayton seems to be attracted mainly to his horse. In one scene he busses the animal and in another he appears to be trying to seduce him by placing a carrot in his mouth and letting the horse nibble away. This is a kind of witty send-up of deep throat pornography, but the Lord only knows what it has to do with Clayton and his relationship with the other characters.

Jack Nicholson had to stand by and watch Brando go through these picture-stealing machinations, and reports were leaked to the press that all was not well between the two co-stars. Penn dismissed this as a fabrication of the publicists— for the most part, anyway. "Nicholson's relationship to Brando—every actor's relationship to Brando—is very complicated. It's like an act of *hommage* just to work with Brando. Every once in a while Jack would get frustrated by some of the stuff that Marlon was doing. He was also responsive to the frustration, and as a good actor could use it. Every once in a while, it would catch him unawares, that's all."

Nicholson knows how to pull out all the stops—sometimes he's been known to pull out one too many—but he had the wisdom to realize that it would be folly to try to outplay Brando. The only way the young fox could outwit the old bear was by underplaying, and by doing so, he was just about the only major participant of *The Missouri Breaks* who would be treated kindly by the critics. The picture opened on schedule at the beginning of the Memorial Day weekend in 1976. The initial newspaper and magazine reviews were scathing, but then a handful of critics came forward with the argument that the film had been judged by standards that were not applicable. Penn was a master filmmaker whose philosophy (in the words of one high-flying analyst) "is opposed to what would normally be termed organic artistic unity." In other words the anachronisms and the drastic shifts in tone and performing style were part of a personal credo of how films should be made.

United Artists, which had been promoting the film as the acting duel of the decade (Brando vs. Nicholson) now started to play up this critical controversy in the hope that it would pull people into the theaters. That ploy had worked with *Bonnie and Clyde,* an earlier Penn film, but history was not to repeat itself with *Missouri Breaks.* Audiences hated it, and warned their friends to stay away. Hordes of people walked out on the film, the exodus often starting soon after Brando's first appearance on the screen.

Most critics tried to be generous toward Marlon, but only two or three could work up real enthusiasm. The majority opinion was expressed succinctly by Stanley Kauffmann, who wrote in *The New Republic,* "By showing yet again that he has a talent so large that it cannot be completely smothered, [Brando] only makes us more impatient with the fact that he's making a complete ass of himself."

If anything, Kauffmann is too kind. He suggests there's some juice in Brando's performance, and there isn't. He's all dead weight. Before, when he'd camp his way through a picture, there was some joy for the audience—he let us in on the joke. But this time, he seems to be serious, and we feel left out because we can't take what he's doing seriously. This time the joke is at the audience's expense, so it's no wonder people left the theater in a sullen, resentful mood.

Though he doesn't quite admit it, Stanley Kauffmann must have felt the same way. He had written a play for children that Marlon had appeared in back in the days when he was still studying at the New School. Kauffmann had always been a Brando supporter, but at the end of his review of *Missouri Breaks* he asked, "If Brando doesn't like acting, why doesn't he quit?" At the time, the question seemed not at all impertinent. If this was the kind of performance Marlon was to give from now on, perhaps his swan song should have been *Last Tango.* It would take some time before the bad taste left by *Missouri Breaks* could be rinsed away.

Much ado was made over the whiff of homosexuality running through *Missouri Breaks.* Several publications printed a photograph of Brando in his gingham and sunbonnet drag, one film magazine using it as a front cover. Marlon initially laughed at the uproar. "If there is someone who is convinced that Jack Nicholson and I are lovers in this film, may they continue to do so," he commented. "I find it amusing." No one had any suspicions about Nicholson or his character, but about Brando's Clayton, it did not seem such an illogical conclusion.

Later when the subject came up during an interview with a French journalist, Brando said the same thing, but then went on to make a personal revelation. "Like a large number of men, I too have had homosexual experiences and I am not ashamed," he said. "I've never paid much attention to what people said about me. Deep down I feel a bit ambiguous and I'm not saying that to spite the seven out of ten women who consider me—wrongly perhaps—a sex symbol. According to me, sex is something that lacks precision. Let's say sex is sexless. . . . Homosexuality is so much in fashion, it no longer makes news."

Well, Marlon's homosexuality made news—for a week or two. Of course, his admission came as no great surprise: rumors that he was bisexual dated back to his Broadway days. His statement got the reception he probably hoped for: people sniffed or tittered for a while, and then shrugged it aside. It added nothing unexpected or particularly enlightening to the Brando dossier.

As soon as Marlon finished his stint on *Missouri Breaks*, he returned to his home on Mulholland Drive in Beverly Hills. Around the house was a fence with a forbidding sign: TRESPASSERS WILL BE DESTROYED. Marlon wasn't fooling when he posted the notice. "Mulholland Drive is full of crazy people," he told a *Playboy* interviewer. "We have nuts coming up and down all the time . . . I didn't want someone coming in my house and committing mayhem. . . . Three or four times I've pulled a gun on someone."

The neighbors didn't object to a pistol-packing Brando; what disturbed them was the bivouac of teepees set up on his

Tarita as she appeared in *Mutiny on the Bounty* (1962)

The final sequence from *Mutiny on the Bounty*

Movita (the second Mrs. Marlon Brando) chats with Franchot Tone during the filming of the 1935 *Mutiny on the Bounty*

Brando just after he has been horsewhipped by Elizabeth Taylor in *Reflections in a Golden Eye* (1967)

With Sophia Loren in *A Countess from Hong Kong* (1967)

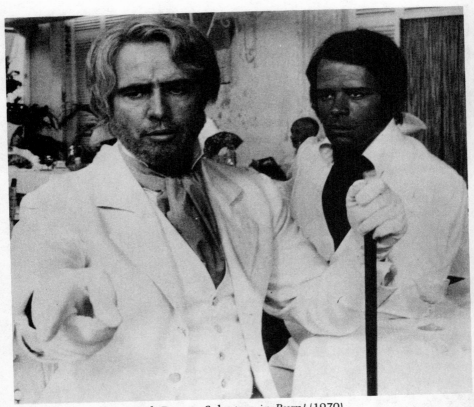

With Renato Salvatore in *Burn!* (1970)

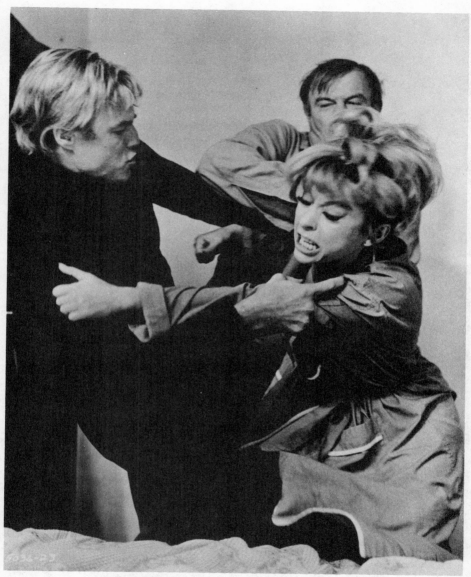

Brando, Rita Moreno, and Jess Hahn in *The Night of the Following Day* (1968)

The Godfather (1972)

With Maria Schneider in *Last Tango in Paris* (1973)

Brando donating land to the Survival of American Indian Association

With Jack Nicholson in *The Missouri Breaks* (1976)

Brando and Francis Ford Coppola during a break between takes of *Apocalypse Now* (1979)

With Terence Stamp, Jack O'Halloran, and Sarah Douglas in *Superman* (1978)

The Formula (1979)

front lawn. At Marlon's invitation, some migratory Indians had set up housekeeping in one of the wealthiest residential districts in America. Public officials also considered the Mulholland Drive wigwam community an eyesore, and swiftly hauled the Indians in on charges of disorderly conduct and possession of marijuana. Marlon immediately bailed them out.

Indian affairs continued to occupy a large share of his time, an involvement that occasionally led him into dangerous situations. Just before making *Missouri Breaks*, he had joined a group of Menominee Indians who were occupying, and demanding the deed to, a monastery in Gresham, Wisconsin. Shots were exchanged before the confrontation was resolved, though never to Marlon's satisfaction. The monks had promised to turn over the property to the Indians, but, Brando claimed, "those goddamn Alexian Brothers took it back once everything died down, after giving their word the Indians could have it."

At the end of 1975, when Indian activist Dennis Banks fled sentencing on a riot and assault conviction, he left South Dakota in a car owned by Marlon, who later sheltered him in Tahiti, praising him as an inspiration for other young Indians. There were rumors that Brando might be charged with aiding and abetting a fugitive, but no action was taken.

It was mainly his involvement with the Indians that kept Brando in the States. He would have preferred to be in Tahiti—more precisely in Teiteroa. Tahiti had become too corrupted by Western civilization to please him. "The Tahitians are being sold on an acquisitive society," he said. "They buy refrigerators and TV sets, not because they need them, but because such things give them status. . . . Within a few years Tahiti will be covered with gas stations and smog."

Teiteroa itself was not entirely unmarked by the inroads of Western civilization. Two years earlier Brando had been persuaded by a Tahitian businessman to build a hotel on his private atoll. Named the Teiteroa Hotel, but known locally as the Brando Grand, it consisted of twenty thatch-roofed bungalows, surrounding a similar but larger structure which served as restaurant, bar, boutique, and reception center. Adventuresome tourists started flocking to the hotel to catch a glimpse of Marlon playing beachcomber. The revenue the visitors brought in was welcome, but their gawking invasion was sometimes more than the proprietor could bear. Once when a boatload of guests was coming in, he ran to the dock, screaming, "Go back! All booked up!"

Sometimes when the hotel wasn't too crowded, Brando would take over one of the vacant cottages, but caveat emptor, he isn't often to be seen. Not long after the hotel opened, he built a home on one of the uninhabited coral reefs that make up the Teiteroa atoll. In princely solitude he lives and dresses as he pleases. "I love to walk the beach naked at night," he told *Playboy*, "with just the wind caressing my body. It's an awesome sense of freedom and very sensual. Sometimes I sleep all night on the beach."

Such pleasures were not always solitary. He had his companions, some old, some new. Around this time Marlon began speaking of Tarita as his wife (though when and where they married is not known), and they continued to be on close terms though occasionally Brando would reprimand her for permitting their children to ruin their teeth with bubble gum. She lived in Papeete, but frequently brought the kids to Teiteroa when it suited Marlon's plans. She had a laid-back, islands attitude toward affairs of the heart, apparently content to be number one consort among her husband's harem of favorites. Marlon was reported to have two other lady friends at this time—Eddy, a Polynesian, and Eriko, a Japanese. Only trusted friends were invited to Marlon's private hideaway, and they weren't going to say much about what went on there. Brando guarded his privacy there even more fiercely than he did in Beverly Hills. Once when a reporter waded ashore to see what was going on, he was greeted by Brando: "I'm going to give you to the count of three to start swimming back to your launch, and then I'm going to punch you in the face." Before the count of one, the reporter was waist-deep in water.

Producers and directors who tried to reach Brando about

film offers were also told to keep their distance, more politely perhaps, but in tones of unmistakable finality. Those persistent enough to keep on trying eventually realized there was a way of storming Marlon's no-trespassing no-acting barricade. In the past you offered him a role in which he was roughed up; now you offered him a mountain of money for an anthill of work.

·24·
WHITE MAN—HE DEVIL

Francis Ford Coppola was one of the people who wouldn't take Brando's no for an answer. Though Don Corleone had died in *The Godfather*, Coppola was ready to revive him, Brando willing, for *Godfather II*, and at first Marlon seemed enthusiastic. But then he suddenly pulled out of the project. "The problem with Marlon," Coppola said, "is that he just doesn't want to work." But there was more to it than that, as the director went on to admit. Still rankling over the little he had earned from the first film, Brando had requested much more from Paramount for the second, and Paramount refused to meet his terms. (In the sequel, Robert De Niro appears as Corleone. The part was revised for a younger man once Brando withdrew.)

The success of the two *Godfather* films raised Coppola to a position where he could write his own ticket, and when in 1975 he chose to adapt Joseph Conrad's *Heart of Darkness* as a comment on the Vietnam war, he had no trouble in raising financing, though most film investors were wary of Vietnam as a subject with mass audience appeal. And this was going to be a very expensive picture—about $14,000,000, according to initial estimates, taking five or six months to shoot on location in the Philippines. Still it seemed like a safe bet—Coppola had a track record of bringing in big productions almost on time and never more than a million or so over budget.

Apocalypse Now, as Coppola called his Conrad adaptation, is the story of a battle-fatigued Vietnam officer, Willard, who

254

is assigned to travel upriver and eliminate the renegade Colonel Kurtz, a brilliant officer who has taken the war into his own hands. Kurtz is "playing God" with his private army of deserters and natives, just across the border in Cambodia.

Willard and Kurtz were the major characters, though Kurtz would appear only in the concluding moments of the film. It was a brief role, but all-important, because Kurtz was that "heart of darkness" that Willard comes to realize exists within himself. From the start Coppola realized that his two leading characters were different sides of the same personality: one was what the other might become. This gave him some leeway in his casting—an actor who turned down the role of Willard could be offered the part of Kurtz.

Coppola started off with Steve McQueen, who rejected Willard as being too strenuous an assignment—Martin Sheen, who eventually played the part, suffered a heart attack during the shooting—but thought he could manage Kurtz if Coppola would pay him $3,000,000 for the three weeks he would be required to spend in the Philippines. Coppola put him on hold while he talked to Robert Redford, Jack Nicholson, and Al Pacino. Nicholson said no to both parts—he had other commitments—but the other two were interested in playing Kurtz if the script were reworked to suit their talents and personalities. Coppola started drafting revisions.

Early on Coppola had tried to reach Brando, only to be told by his agent that Marlon wasn't interested in any film role and didn't want to be bothered. But in the midst of his Pacino/Redford revisions, he was interrupted by a call from Marlon's agent saying Brando would like to see him. After several conferences, Marlon agreed to play Kurtz for $3,500,000—more than McQueen had requested, but he agreed to work a week longer than McQueen had stipulated. He was ready to spend a month with *Apocalypse* on location. A contract was drawn up and signed in February 1976, with a clause stating that Brando would not have to report for work until the end of summer, though *Apocalypse* was to start production in May. In making this stipulation, Brando explained that he wanted to spend the summer with his children on

Teiteroa. This presented no problem since the sets for his scenes—an immense temple modeled on Angkor Wat—wouldn't be ready much before then.

Coppola and his crew arrived in Manila early in May, and almost immediately started to run behind schedule. The whole terrible saga of how *Apocalypse Now* went from a $14,000,000, five-month production into a $40,000,000 nightmare that lasted over two years—the typhoons, the ruined sets, the insects, the heat, the malfunctioning latrines, the dysentery, a heart attack, major cast changes, unhappy romances, and strained marriages—has been told so many times that it hardly bears repeating here, especially since little of the story has much to do with Brando. This was one time when he could not be blamed for a picture coming in late and way over budget.

Only one of the many problems that plagued the production related to him, and it wasn't of his making. Artistically, however, it was the most important of the difficulties, the one which would keep the picture from achieving the scope and significance to which it aspires and which it occasionally achieves. Who is Kurtz? This is the question the film keeps asking, and Coppola unfortunately doesn't supply the answer. If Kurtz could be played by Steve McQueen or Al Pacino or Robert Redford or Jack Nicholson or Marlon Brando, then either he was one of those multidimensional characters (like Hamlet) who can be successfully interpreted by a wide variety of actors, or he is a cipher who has to be fleshed out by a star presence of any age or shape.

Before reporting to the Philippines, Brando checked in at Saint John's hospital in Los Angeles for a weight-loss program, and though he managed to shed twenty pounds in two weeks, he was still corpulent when he arrived in Manila. A crowd of fans was waiting at the airport to welcome him, but he dashed to the car that was to take him to Pagsanjan, a two-hour drive from the capital. Reaching the film location, Marlon expressed embarrassment about his girth and asked Coppola if there was not some way his weight could be disguised. Short of shooting him only from the neck up, there wasn't, but Coppola told him not to worry. His swollen figure would help establish Kurtz as "a man who was eating all the time and over-indulging."

Brando arrived in Pagsanjan on September 4, 1976, and left on October 8. Much of his time with Coppola was spent in trying to build up a characterization for Kurtz, Brando often improvising possible approaches which Coppola later mulled over, incorporating some of Brando's ideas in the screenplay, eliminating others. One thing was decided early on—Marlon would shave his head for the role, so that he would look like an enormous, malevolent Buddha. At one point actor and director decided Kurtz should be played bigger than life, as a "mythical figure" or "a theatrical personage." But then Coppola felt Kurtz should be realistic, closer to his vision of the character in Conrad's novel. Brando admitted sheepishly that he had never read the book, though months before he had promised to do so.

While the director and actor went on searching for the key to Kurtz's personality, the crew was kept waiting, and by the time there was something to put before the cameras, it was often too dark or rainy for work to continue. Coppola was responsible for the delays—often he was uncertain as to how he wanted Brando to play a scene. But by the time of Marlon's departure, he felt he had enough footage to edit the Kurtz sequence—designed to last about ten minutes in the finished film—into a shattering climax.

Apocalypse Now finally opened in August 1979 to respectful but decidedly mixed reviews. Most of the critics complained that the film ended with a whimper not a bang, a representative comment coming from Pauline Kael, who wrote in *The New Yorker*, "What the picture boils down to is: White man—he devil." Still *Apocalypse* managed to return a small profit and certainly it did Brando no harm. Though more through presence than performance, he leaves an indelible impression on the mind.

The release of *Apocalypse* was preceded by that of a picture Brando shot afterward, the multimillion-dollar *Superman*.

Once again Brando was paid $3,500,000 for a few weeks work, only this time all his footage appears at the beginning, not the climax of the film. He plays Jor-El, the embattled leader of the planet Krypton and the father of the titular hero.

Superman was shot at the Shepperton studios in London at the beginning of 1978. Marlon arrived in England a week or so early, trying to drum up financing for a semidocumentary series on the American Indian he wished to produce for TV. He described it as an Indian "Roots," but nowhere in America, not even at the public television stations, was he able to spark much interest. The English weren't intrigued, either. Perhaps this was the reason Brando was reportedly temperamental during the shooting of *Superman:* there were charges of "appalling vanity." Director Richard Donner, however, insists Marlon was not difficult, just very sick with influenza.

Jor-El is the kind of part Brando might be expected to camp his way through, but instead he plays it with the utmost dignity. He speaks his dialogue—a stream of ponderous, comic book aphorisms—in the straight-faced, sonorous manner of Ralph Richardson or Claude Rains in one of those old British adaptations of H. G. Wells. And he looks magnificent. With a halo of white hair and swathed in flowing dark robes that camouflage whatever excess weight he may be carrying, he's a stone-hewn monolithic figure. Later a critic would say (with admiration) that he seemed to be taking on the appearance of an Indian chief, but actually he looks like a Druid priest. If he could sing, he'd be perfectly cast as Oroveso in *Norma*.

Though short on energy and style—the special effects are particularly chintzy—*Superman* pleased audiences and most reviewers when it opened in late December 1978. There was some carping about Brando's performance, most of it centering on his being paid so much for doing so little. This, perhaps, was also the source of the "vanity" English newsmen had complained about.

Brando eventually got around to answering his critics. "I have a right to the money I get," he said. "First of all, because I'm not forcing anyone to give it to me. Secondly, I've gained a lot of experience over the years and I don't need the same kind of coaching a newcomer does—I use my rage, my entire catalog of human emotions." Then he paused—perhaps thinking of the lesson Jacob Adler had taught him years earlier—before adding, "Of course, I don't totally let loose, because that's not my style."

He offered another rationalization: The money he earned for *Apocalypse* and *Superman* was to be used to finance his Indian "Roots" TV series. Why then was he constantly searching for outside investors? Since no one asked Brando that question, the answer can only be surmised from a different, but related, comment he made. "It takes a lot of money to own your own atoll." Throughout this period, Marlon kept passing out pamphlets about Teiteroa and his plans for making it an unpolluted, non-Westernized paradise, but little progress had been made toward achieving that goal. Ecology was far in the future; the best he could boast was his hotel and a lobster farm, two enterprises employing ninety Polynesians who might otherwise be spearfishing or picking bananas and coconuts off the trees. Somehow a lot of money was being taken from the consumer society to create—exactly what? A brochure and an outline for a TV series.

But there can be no doubt that the television series was—and remains—one of Brando's abiding interests. His interest in TV had been minimal until he watched "Roots" in 1977. The kind of scope he had envisioned for *Bury My Heart at Wounded Knee* could best be accomplished in a similar kind of miniseries, consisting of eight or ten episodes, each segment an hour or two in duration. Pauline Kael announced (without enthusiasm) that "Roots" could make the American movie obsolete—it was no longer necessary to push and pull material into a brief evening's entertainment. Now author-filmmakers could be as expansive and dawdling as Dickens and the other Victorian novelists.

When Brando heard that there was to be a spin-off of "Roots"—"Roots II: The Next Generation"—he called Alex Haley and asked if he could be a part of it. Just a small role and—on this Marlon insisted—a villainous one. There seemed no danger of Brando being cast sympathetically, since nearly all the whites in "Roots" are either loutish, mean-spirited, or corrupt. Haley offered the part of George Norman Rockwell, the American Nazi leader whom Haley had once interviewed during his career as a journalist. (Marlon was to appear for about five minutes in the final episode of the sequel.) No one questioned Brando as to why he insisted on playing a villain, perhaps because the answer was obvious: "White man—he devil," whether he's brandishing a swastika or a Simon Legree whip, a green beret or Buffalo Bill buckskins. Marlon seemed intent on toting a really heavy load of national guilt.

Asked how much Brando was paid, producer David Wolper said, "Less than he deserved, and all of it he donated to charity." If "Roots II" was a labor of love, he more than made up for it on his next assignment, his last to date, *The Formula*. For this picture, he was paid $2,500,000 for ten days' work, and insisted that he receive the wages in daily installments—a check for $250,000 was delivered to him every afternoon.

Once again there was a great brouhaha about his presumption and vanity. Now all articles about Brando centered on two issues: his inflated salaries and his equally inflated waistline. His off-screen weight now hovered at about 240–250, almost a hundred pounds more than he carried in his *Streetcar* days. Photographers delighted in finding angles that would emphasize his great belly, though they were careful to use long-distance lenses, as Brando had been known to rough up cameramen in the past. Back in 1974, on a street in New York, he had a set-to with *paparazzo* Ron Galella, notorious for his harassment of Jacqueline Onassis. Once he got out of the hospital, Galella sued Brando for $500,000, though eventually an out of court settlement was reached which left Marlon only about $40,000 poorer.

Only once has Marlon discussed his weight problems in recent years. "One's not allowed to age in this country," he said. "Wrinkles, balding, and overweight are almost prohibited, particularly for someone in the public eye. For a woman it's akin to death." He then went on to express sympathy for his friend, Elizabeth Taylor.

Usually Marlon tried to lose weight before his picture assignments, and he did drop about twenty-five pounds for *The Formula*, which was shot in California at the beginning of 1979. (Many of Brando's scenes were shot in a Bel Air mansion once owned by Marion Davies and later rented by Louis B. Mayer.) Directed by John Avildsen *(Save the Tiger, Rocky)* and written by Stephan Shagan, the picture is a heavy-handed political thriller steeped in paranoia. The formula of the title is for a synthetic fuel developed by Nazi scientists at the end of World War II. It has been kept off the market since then by the collective efforts of oil companies in order to keep up the price of natural resources. When people thought to possess the secret of the formula start to disappear mysteriously, a Los Angeles detective begins an investigation that will lead him through a labyrinth of international intrigue.

Brando plays the head of one of the oil companies involved in the conspiracy; the LA detective, a far bigger role, was taken on by George C. Scott. There is a certain air of gimmickry about casting the only two actors ever to reject the Oscar in the same picture, though not much was made of it in the publicity about the film. And while there was no puffery about another acting duel, the only reason to watch *The Formula* is to observe the distinctive methods used by the two actors in attacking their roles. Scott is deadly earnest, and though his playing can't be faulted, he's dull. Marlon, on the other hand, keeps tongue in cheek, and almost vanishes beneath all his makeup.

Most of the effort he put into the film seems to have been expended on creating a disguise that would keep audiences whispering "Is it really him?" And for the first few moments Brando is nearly unrecognizable. Wearing granny glasses and a hearing aid, a halo of white hair curling around a shiny tonsure, his corpulence discreetly camouflaged by expensive tailoring, he looks strikingly like Orson Welles in the final moments of *Citizen Kane*. (Could it possibly have been the location work at the old Marion Davies estate that gave him this idea?) But when he speaks, he sounds more like Lester Maddox than Welles; he adopts a cornpone, down-home drawl. The performance is fun because it cuts against the grain of the creaky solemnity of what surrounds it—he uses wit, not a sledgehammer to make his points. Brando makes the cartel boss the most avuncular of villains, though there can be no mistake that this was another candidate for his rogues' gallery of societal satans. This time the white devil is a power-crazed corporate executive in a three-piece suit.

Nobody liked *The Formula* very much when it opened at the end of December 1979. On the whole critics were kinder than the public, who needed more than faint praise to lure them to line up for tickets. The film was a bust, and while Brando couldn't be held responsible for lack of cooperation or a foolish performance, he could be held accountable for adding millions of dollars to the picture's budget by his salary demands.

The Formula opened at the end of a decade, and one reviewer, in a summary of the dubious film achievements of the 1970s, led off with Brando. For his last four professional TV and movie appearances, Brando had received close to $10,000,000 for what added up to about thirty minutes of screen time. People who went to the lavatory or concession stand during the start or end of one of his movies could have missed him entirely. Worse yet, what they may have missed while standing in line for the popcorn wasn't essential viewing. Brando's occasional and brief appearances were beginning to look like footnotes to a career already crowded with marginalia.

·25·
THINGS TO COME—MAYBE

What has Marlon been up to during the 1980s? It's a question Brando himself has heard many times. "People keep asking me what I do on an island in the middle of nowhere," he once said. "I ask them what they do in Hollywood, a small-minded little town in the middle of nowhere."

Every so often, he leaves his Pacific retreat, usually to immerse himself in the tide of Indian and civil rights affairs. No one at this point doubts his sincerity, though many wish he was not quite so humorless or single-minded about his commitments. Frequently he has been lured before the TV talk show cameras, but discussion is limited strictly to humanitarian affairs, and for both interviewer and audience, Brando too often comes off as a bore. A little charm, some warmth, a bit of personal information would certainly serve to offset the solemnity of these network conversations.

In recent years, Marlon has carefully orchestrated his interviews, and can become quite high-handed if his beat is not followed. One reporter from the New York *Times*, impressed by Marlon's knowledge and seriousness of purpose, was astounded when the actor suddenly broke off their dialogue and stormed out of the room. Brando was miffed because the reporter didn't know what misfortune befell a certain Indian tribe in 1863. It was not, the newsman felt, the kind of information that anyone should be expected to have at his fingertips.

Marlon still maintains a home near that small-minded

community, Hollywood, and he frequently stays there. It is a convenient gathering place for his non-Polynesian children. (His son and daughter by Movita are in school in the Los Angeles area; Christian owns and works a ranch in Montana, but frequently visits his father.) And it allows Brando to keep up with old friends, those a bit too timid to rough it on Teiteroa.

Recently he attended a party given in his honor by a new lady friend, Yachio Tsubaki, at a posh Beverly Hills hotel. The occasion was a celebration of his sixtieth birthday. Marlon choked up when a cake was wheeled in, and undoubtedly so did many of his fans on reading about the event. It seemed hard to believe that so many years had passed since Stanley Kowalski and Terry Malloy and the Wild One . . .

Reaching sixty might not be as traumatic a milestone for an actor as for an actress, but it imposes definite limitations. Brando had wasted nearly ten years appearing in (*Apocalypse* excepted) trivia, and how many challenging roles lay in wait for him now that he was at an age when actors had to suck in their gut and depend on the kindness of cameramen?

It is not impossible that his career could be revitalized. There is the precedent of Burt Lancaster, eleven years older than Brando, who during the 1970s and 1980s received some of the best parts of his career in films like *Atlantic City, Local Hero*, and Bernardo Bertolucci's *1900*. Without taking anything away from Lancaster, these were all roles Brando could have played with equal success. And there is the case of Paul Newman, one year younger than Brando, who in 1982 scored a major success in *The Verdict*, playing a role to which Marlon was arguably better suited. Newman was too chic, wore too many Rodeo Drive suits to be entirely believable as a seedy, alcoholic lawyer.

There were major differences separating the three actors. Paul Newman has kept his figure and sexual glamour; Lancaster (also trim for his age) doesn't demand a multimillion-dollar pay check—if he did, he never would have been offered those roles which have added such luster to his reputation in recent years.

At times it does seem as though Marlon had deliberately

inflated his figure and his salary as a way of placing himself outside the market place. Too fat to tango and too greedy to be approachable by budget-minded producers, he seems willingly to have restricted himself to tiny roles in escapist entertainments. He has relegated himself to the kind of film he could sneer at, to the kind of roles that make acting seem like a self-indulgent profession.

Brando is by no means the only actor who claims he goes on acting only for the money, taking whatever comes along as long as the price is right. Sir Laurence Olivier owns up to doing the same, but with better reason. In his youth and middle age, Olivier never received the salaries Brando got, and with young children to support, he clearly needed whatever cash he was offered. And illness has made it impossible for him to take on anything more demanding than the occasional film or TV assignment.

But even in such trifles as *The Betsy* or *Marathon Man* or *The Boys from Brazil*, Olivier gives us more than we expect: there's always something new, some bravura touch that tells us that this lion in winter, while weather-beaten, is still rightfully proud. And in his most recent TV appearances—a much abbreviated *King Lear* and the sentimental *Voyage around My Father*—Olivier quite consciously pulls us toward him with thoughts of his own mortality, and the intimacy would be embarrassing except for his tact and consummate skill.

In equivalent assignments, Brando stays aloof. He comments on his roles, sends them up, occasionally suggests that he's having fun, but there's precious little commitment on his behalf as an actor. He relies heavily on the good will of his fans, and that good will is often repaid. He can be engaging, but over the long haul, one wonders why he's wasting our money and his time.

So the question Stanley Kauffmann asked in his review of *Missouri Breaks* remains pertinent—"If he doesn't want to act, why doesn't he quit?" There are several possible answers. First, with all his children and Teiteroa to look after, he can't afford to. Second, he must be aware that his opinions about the evils of the white man receive attention mainly because of his prominence as a screen actor. Third, no matter what he says, he may really want to go on acting.

At the time of *Missouri Breaks*, Arthur Penn insisted that between Marlon's much-repeated disdain for acting and his private feelings about his profession, there existed a wide gulf. Brando has occasionally echoed the same sentiment in a more down-home fashion. Acting couldn't be considered a serious or important occupation like farming, but nonetheless when he took a screen job he gave it as much loving, tender care as a farmer nurturing his crops. The analogy unfortunately worked to Brando's disadvantage. His harvest in the mid-seventies might have embarrassed a window-box gardener.

Every so often Brando talks of taking on a real acting job. Several times in the 1970s he mentioned that he would like to play Pablo Picasso if someone could come up with a suitable script. No one ever did, so the project has been tabled. In the spring of 1984, it was reported that Marlon was mulling over a $3,000,000 offer to play former FBI chief J. Edgar Hoover in the screen version of Noel Behn's book, *Seven Silent Men*. Only a few weeks later it was said that he and writer/producer Adrian Malone were putting the finishing touches on a TV miniseries tentatively titled "Vision Road," in which Marlon would play a leading role. The story of several North American Indian tribes, this final evolution of *Bury My Heart at Wounded Knee* could go into production in fall 1984 if approved by CBS.

It is not unlikely that both these projects could fall through—"Vision Road" seems especially casualty-prone as a similar Indian miniseries, "The Mystic Warrior," recently fared poorly in the network ratings. Still, it seems unlikely that some day a producer will not come along with an offer Marlon cannot refuse. One can only hope that it will also be an offer to which Brando will be able to give all of himself. It has been over ten years since his last fully committed performance, in *Last Tango*. By now his artistic batteries should be recharged.

Even if this is not to happen—if he continues to fight destiny and trifle with his talent—his reputation seems secure. It may be true, as a friend has said, that he wants to be remembered as someone who did some good in the world, and not as a film star. But even if he should succeed in turning Teiteroa into a model ecological paradise, and simultaneously correct the wrongs done to the Indians, he is fated to be remembered longest for his stage and screen work. Almost single-handedly he changed the look and emotional temperature of American acting, and he did it almost entirely through his screen performances, thereby raising the status of the performer who decides to work mainly in movies rather than in the theater. No one sneers at Robert De Niro for abandoning the stage as they once did when Brando made it clear he would not be returning to Broadway. No one thinks the less of Al Pacino or Dustin Hoffman because they haven't played Hamlet or Oedipus or Uncle Vanya on the stage.

Brando created a style, and he was—is—an original. The best of the actors who have grown up in his shadow—Pacino, De Niro (or, to choose among an up-and-coming group), William Hurt, Mickey Rourke, John Malkovich, and Sean Penn—have had the wisdom to know he can't be imitated, though they would be the first to admit that he has been a seminal influence. Probably it isn't a contest he would enter, probably it would be an honor he would refuse to accept, but in the sweepstakes for the title of the greatest American actor of our time, Marlon Brando is the only true contender.

A MARLON BRANDO
FILMOGRAPHY

The Men (1950). United Artists. Directed by Fred Zinnemann. With Teresa Wright, Everett Sloane, Jack Webb.

A Streetcar Named Desire (1951). Warner Brothers. Directed by Elia Kazan. With Vivien Leigh, Kim Hunter, Karl Malden.

Viva Zapata! (1952). 20th Century-Fox. Directed by Elia Kazan. With Jean Peters, Anthony Quinn, Joseph Wiseman, Mildred Dunnock, Margo.

Julius Caesar (1953). MGM. Directed by Joseph L. Mankiewicz. With James Mason, Sir John Gielgud, Louis Calhern, Edmond O'Brien, Greer Garson, Deborah Kerr.

The Wild One (1954). Columbia. Directed by Laslo Benedek. With Mary Murphy, Robert Keith, Lee Marvin, Jay C. Flippen.

On the Waterfront (1954). Columbia. Directed by Elia Kazan. With Eva Marie Saint, Karl Malden, Lee J. Cobb, Rod Steiger.

Desiree (1954). 20th Century-Fox. Directed by Henry Koster. With Jean Simmons, Merle Oberon, Michael Rennie, Cameron Mitchell, Cathleen Nesbitt.

Guys and Dolls (1955). MGM. Directed by Joseph L. Mankiewicz. With Frank Sinatra, Jean Simmons, Vivian Blaine.

The Teahouse of the August Moon (1956). MGM. Directed

by Daniel Mann. With Glenn Ford, Michiko Kyo, Paul Ford, Eddie Albert.

Sayonara (1957). Warner Brothers. Directed by Joshua Logan. With Miiko Taka, Red Buttons, Miyoshi Umeki, Ricardo Montalban, James Garner, Martha Scott.

The Young Lions (1958). 20th Century-Fox. Directed by Edward Dmytryk. With Montgomery Clift, Dean Martin, Barbara Rush, Maximilian Schell, Hope Lange, May Britt, Liliane Montevecchi.

The Fugitive Kind (1960). United Artists. Directed by Sidney Lumet. With Anna Magnani, Joanne Woodward, Maureen Stapleton, Victor Jory.

One-Eyed Jacks (1961). Paramount. Directed by Marlon Brando. With Karl Malden, Katy Jurado, Pina Pellicer, Ben Johnson, Slim Pickens.

Mutiny on the Bounty (1962). MGM. Directed by Lewis Milestone. With Trevor Howard, Richard Harris, Hugh Griffith, Tarita.

The Ugly American (1963). Universal. Directed by George Englund. With Eiji Okada, Sandra Church, Arthur Hill, Pat Hingle, Jocelyn Brando.

Bedtime Story (1964). Universal. Directed by Ralph Levy. With David Niven, Shirley Jones, Dodie Goodman, Marie Windsor.

Morituri (1965). 20th Century-Fox. Directed by Bernhard Wicki. With Yul Brynner, Trevor Howard, Janet Margolin, Wally Cox.

The Chase (1966). Columbia. Directed by Arthur Penn. With Jane Fonda, Robert Redford, E. G. Marshall, Angie Dickinson, Miriam Hopkins, James Fox, Robert Duvall, Janice Rule.

The Appaloosa (1966). Universal. Directed by Sidney J. Furie. With John Saxon, Anjanette Comer, Emilio Fernandez.

A Countess from Hong Kong (1967). Universal. Directed by Charles Chaplin. With Sophia Loren, Sydney Chaplin, Tippi Hedren, Margaret Rutherford.

Reflections in a Golden Eye (1967). Warner Brothers. Directed by John Huston. With Elizabeth Taylor, Julie Harris, Brian Keith, Robert Forster.

The Night of the Following Day (1968). Universal. Directed by Hubert Cornfield. With Richard Boone, Pamela Franklin, Rita Moreno, Jess Hahn.

Candy (1968). MGM. Directed by Christian Marquand. With Ewa Aulin, Richard Burton, James Coburn, Walter Matthau, John Huston, Charles Aznavour, Ringo Starr.

Burn! (1970). United Artists. Directed by Gillo Pontecorvo. With Evaristo Marquez, Renato Salvatori.

The Nightcomers (1972). Avco Embassy. Directed by Michael Winner. With Stephanie Beacham, Harry Andrews, Thora Hird, Verna Harvey, Christopher Ellis.

The Godfather (1973). Paramount. Directed by Francis Ford Coppola. With Al Pacino, James Caan, Robert Duvall, Diane Keaton, Richard Castellano, Richard Conte, Sterling Hayden, Talia Shire, John Marley, Al Martino.

Last Tango in Paris (1973). United Artists. Directed by Bernardo Bertolucci. With Maria Schneider, Jean-Pierre Léaud.

The Missouri Breaks (1976). United Artists. Directed by Arthur Penn. With Jack Nicholson, Kathleen Lloyd, Randy Quaid, Frederic Forrest, Harry Dean Stanton, John McLiam.

Superman (1978). Warner Brothers. Directed by Richard Donner. With Christopher Reeve, Margot Kidder, Gene Hackman, Valerie Perrine, Ned Beatty.

Apocalypse Now (1979). United Artists. Directed by Francis Ford Coppola. With Martin Sheen, Robert Duvall, Frederic Forrest, Albert Hall, Sam Bottoms, Dennis Hopper.

The Formula (1979). MGM. Directed by John Avildsen. With George C. Scott, Marthe Keller, Beatrice Straight, Sir John Gielgud.

Index

271